KU-320-685

Spon's Landscape Contract Manual

A guide to good practice and procedures
in the management of landscape contracts

'When you have to draw up a will or a
contract, you have to choose your words
well. You have to look into the future
– envisage all the contingencies that
may come to pass – and then use words to
provide for them. On the words you use,
your clients' future may depend.'

Lord Denning, *The Discipline of Law*,
Butterworths (1979), London

Spon's Landscape Contract Manual

A guide to good practice and procedures
in the management of landscape contracts

HUGH CLAMP
OBE, VRD, FCIArb, FRIBA, FILA

Senior Partner
Manning, Clamp and Partners
Chartered Architects and Landscape Consultants

LONDON
E. & F. N. SPON

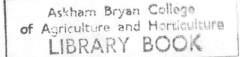
Askham Bryan College
of Agriculture and Horticulture
LIBRARY BOOK

First published in 1986 by
E. & F. N. Spon Ltd
11 New Fetter Lane, London EC4P 4EE
Published in the USA by
E. & F. N. Spon
29 West 35th Street, New York NY 10001

© *1986 Hugh Clamp*

Printed in Great Britain by J. W. Arrowsmith Ltd, Bristol

ISBN 0 419 13480 8

All rights reserved. No part of this book may be reprinted,
or reproduced or utilized in any form or by any electronic,
mechanical or other means, now known or hereafter
invented, including photocopying and recording, or in any
information storage and retrieval system, without
permission in writing from the publisher.

British Library Cataloguing in Publication Data

Clamp, Hugh
  Spon's landscape contract manual : a guide to
  good practice and procedures in the management
  of landscape contracts.
  1. Landscape architecture——Great Britain——
  contracts and specifications
  I. Title
  712'.3   SB472.56

  ISBN 419-13480—8

Library of Congress Cataloging in Publication Data

Clamp, Hugh.
  Spon's landscape contract manual.

  Bibliography: p.
  Includes index.
    1. Landscape contracting——Handbooks, manuals, etc.
  2. Landscape contracting——Great Britain——Handbooks,
  manuals, etc. I. Title. II. Title: Landscape
  contract manual.
  SB472.55.C54 1986   636.9'61   85–26194
  ISBN 0–419–13480—8

Contents

Contents

Contents

Appendices 139

Preface

This manual is intended for all who are involved in the landscape industry: landscape architects, local and county authority parks directors and managers, landscape contractors, and the nurserymen who supply them. Most will know in detail their own duties and responsibilities but few will know in equal detail the duties and responsibilities of those with whom they come in daily contact.

It is hoped that by explaining the best practice and procedures of all the parties concerned in the satisfactory completion of landscape contracts – large and small, in public and in private sectors – each will be enabled to play his or her own part as effectively as possible.

This manual is particularly intended to ensure that plants which are tended with loving care over several years in the nursery are handled with equal care in transit to their new location, and are then planted and looked after in such a way that they thrive and grow unhindered in the years to come. It requires only one careless slip by any one of the many people responsible in the chain for the plants to become irreparably damaged or even killed as they are passed from one to the other.

The Joint Council for the Landscape Industry (JCLI) – comprising senior representatives of the Landscape Institute (LI), the British Association of Landscape Industries (BALI), the National Farmers Union Horticulture Division (NFU), Arboricultural Association (AA), the Institute of Leisure and Amenity Management (ILAM) and the Horticultural Trades Association (HTA) – was set up in 1974 under the chairmanship of J. Berhnard. It meets regularly throughout the year to ensure that best practices are achieved, as does its sister committee: the Joint Liason Committee for Plants Supplies and Establishment (CPSE). It has to be admitted that in spite of much effort their recommendations do not always reach those for whom they are intended; it is hoped that by publishing them in the form of this book they will reach a wider audience.

Preface

The success of any landscape project depends on many things but few are more important than the successful relationship between the grower, the contractor and the manager or designer, and it is hoped, in the following pages, to attempt to build bridges between them.

Although primarily intended for the practicioners the needs of the educationalist must not be overlooked and if the advice given is of assistance to the staff and students in the many schools of landscape architecture and horticultural colleges throughout the country then this might alone justify its production.

Acknowledgements

This book would not have been written but for the encouragement of the JCLI.

In acknowledging their help I must emphasize that all opinions are my own, written as a practising landscape architect and not a legal expert; they do not necessarily represent the views of any of the professional institutes to which I belong, nor of any of the committees in which I am involved.

Extracts from British Standards are reproduced with permission of the British Standards Institution. Complete copies can be obtained from BSI at Linford Wood, Milton Keynes, MK14 6LE

The JCT Standard Form of Tender by Nominated Supplier is reproduced in Appendix F with permission of RIBA Publications Ltd, Finsbury Mission, Moreland St, London EC1V 8UB. The NJCC Code of Procedure for Single-stage Selective Tendering is reproduced in Appendix G with permission of the National Joint Consultative Committee for Building, 18 Mansfield Street, London W1M 9FG.

1

Introduction

A landscape architect designs a scheme and arranges for a landscape contractor to contract to carry it out. The work to be executed under the contract is that stated in the contract documents. If it is in the contract documents it will be carried out; if it is not included it will not be carried out unless the contractor is paid extra for it. If it is not clear what is in the contract, interminable arguments will ensue. More important, the goodwill and trust between the parties (with the consequent loss of quality) may vanish overnight.

On the other hand if the contract documents are crystal clear the project has every chance of success and will proceed as smoothly as on well-oiled wheels.

The contract documents comprise:

1. A **specification** giving specific details as to the exact quality of workmanship and materials to be provided – *what*.
    Schedules of Quantity listing in similar detail the quantity of material to be provided – *how much*.
2. **Drawings** showing precisely the location of the materials (*where*). These are brought together by:
3. The **Articles of Agreement** and **Conditions of Contract,** setting out the obligations of the parties, when it is to be carried out, how it is to be controlled, paid for, insured against accidents during its execution and what happens in the event of a dispute between the parties.

1.1 THE CONTRACT DRAWINGS

It should not be forgotten that working or production drawings indicate to the contractor the exact location of the materials included in the specification; they are not the drawings prepared to show the client what it will look like when it is finished (or, as so often happens, five years after it is finished).

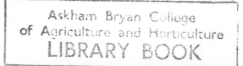

Askham Bryan College
of Agriculture and Horticulture
LIBRARY BOOK

It must also be remembered that if there is written information on the drawing it must be clear, legible and intelligible. The chances are that it may be referred to, on site in the depth of winter – just before dusk and if it can not stand up to this test it is not worth the dyeline paper it is to be printed on. Either it will not be referred to at all or it will be referred to and then misread – there is no other alternative, and both are equally disastrous.

If instructions are not to be written but drawn, it is essential to use the same shorthand of graphic symbols as BS 1192: Part 4 (Recommendations for landscape drawings) otherwise there is as little chance of communicating one's intentions as if the foreman were being addressed in Esperanto. Novel coding systems should be resisted also, there is a very good one already: it is called the alphabet, whose symbols are combined to form things called words.

Always use figured setting-out dimensions and centres – the foreman has no adjustable set-square or compass on site!

1.2 THE FORM OF CONTRACT

There has been since 1978 a new (and hopefully more concise and more comprehensible) Standard Form of Contract for Landscape Works. It is called the **Standard Form** – let us all keep it that way. This is a contract agreed between the landscape architect and the contracting side of the industry, the clauses of which are a compromise attempting to strike a fair balance between both parties. It attempts to include only clauses which are universally applicable and acceptable on all contracts and any alterations therefore will almost certainly mean increased tenders.

This is not to say that experience of its application and changing circumstances, practices, procedures and economic forces on the industry will not involve amendments, e.g. vandalism (if it continues to increase at its present rate). These amendments must and should happen. They are, except in the most extreme cases, made on a 12-monthly basis (and only then after discussion and agreement between all sides of the industry).

It must also be realized that there may be some instances where a particular aspect of a contract justifies an alteration to the standard clauses; but before doing so, careful consideration must be given to the implications: the almost certainly increased cost and possibility of rejection either by one or all of the contractors, or by a local authority or government department on the part of the clients.

2
Landscape contract drawings

Of the four components of a set of contract documents: the illustrative, the qualitative, the quantitative and the conditions (or as they are more comprehensibly known: the drawings, the specification, the Bills of Quantity, and the Form of Contract), the drawings are the one aspect on which the landscape architect considers he needs little or no guidance, even if this view is not so universally held by landscape contractors.

Neither will however deny the statement in the foreword to BS 1192 : Part 4 : 1984 – even if they are unaware of its existence – that the recommendations regarding the production of graphical information are needed:

'. . . to provide communication with accuracy, clarity, economy and consistency of presentation between all concerned with the construction industry, including architects, civil engineers, contractors, landscape architects, services engineers, site operatives and structural engineers . . . It is hoped that this Part of BS 1192 will encourage the standardisation of drawings and schedules. Familiarity with commonly accepted forms of presentation is likely to result in greater efficiency with the preparation and interpretation of landscape drawings and minimise the risk of confusion on site'.

The translation of a landscape architect's design into reality by the landscape contractor is like painting a portrait by numbers with the contractor holding the brush, and the designer trying to tell him in words what colours to use and where to put them. This is similar to instructing an orchestra on the sounds they are to make when playing a symphony through the accepted convention of a musical score – no more than a range of dots of various shapes and sizes arranged in accordance with a universally accepted convention across a series of parallel lines on a piece of paper. It is a matter of some regret that the same effect is not devoted to learning an equally universal set of conventions acceptable to the landscape industry, since without them the successful creation of a landscape design is doomed to failure.

2.1 GRAPHIC SYMBOLS

A commonly accepted set of conventions to indicate on landscape drawings, by means of symbols and abbreviations, the most commonly used elements of landscape work (both hard and soft) is essential to the landscape industry. Their universal adoption on production drawings will convey the maximum information in the minimum time and effort, clearly and with the minimum risk of misunderstanding and error. BS 1192 Table 2 sets out the 50 symbols most commonly found to be needed (Figs 2.1 and 2.2). Irrespective of personal preference the temptation to improve certain of the more obscure must be strenuously resisted if all landscape contractors throughout the British Isles are to recognise instantly the work they are required to do on all projects, irrespective of the different offices from which they have originated.

For new planting, the choice of symbols is dependent on the range and complexity of the work and the scale at which it has been drawn. Currently the reproduction of drawings still has to be in one colour and identification has therefore to be by symbol, hatching or by abbreviation. Colouring the multiple copies that are required on a landscape contract is costly, time-consuming and the risk of error rises in direct ratio to the number of copies required. Rarely should colour therefore be used on any landscape drawings other than those which are required for presentation purposes.

At whatever scale the drawing has been prepared (and one must not overlook the ability to photo-reduce or enlarge drawings on many commercial photocopiers) the lines, symbols, dimensions, figures and text must always be capable of reproduction clearly and legibly.

(Note detailed guidance is also given in BS 1192 : Part 4 on schedules (see p.32–33), reference grids, interpolation of contours, intervisibility and drawing contours in perspective. The Standard, PD 6479 : 1976, – Recommendations for symbols and other graphic conventions for building production drawings – is now presumably superseded and will be withdrawn.)

2.2 SCOPE

In contrast to BS 1102, which covers all aspects of landscape drawings, it is only intended in this chapter to cover those drawings which are used for the landscape contract itself although the same principles will of course apply to those used by the architect and landscape architect for his discussions with his client and with local and other authorities in the exercise of their statutory obligations.

2.3 SIZE

Production drawings for landscape contracts should be prepared on a standardized sheet chosen, irrespective of the size of the site or project, for ease of handling on site compatible with the need to present as much information on as few

4

Existing trees (to be retained)

(to be removed)

New trees (BS 1192 lists additional symbols to differential nursery stock, advanced nursery stock and semi-mature trees in the various sizes currently available from BS 3936)

Transplants and whips

Shrubs (similar species linked)

Climbers

Grass   grass seed
               grass turf

Existing levels/contours   (25.5)   (25.5)

Proposed levels/contours   25.5   25.5

Top soil

Hardcore

Fig. 2.1   Basic graphic symbols listed in BS 1192 : Part 4. (Note that BS 1192 provides for both the conventions of trees being indicated by the basic symbols indicated here, symbols to differentiate between transplants, nursery stock and semi-mature trees, and even the information required on their sizes within each group. It remains to be seen whether, in view of their complexity and the possibility of error, the latter two categories will be widely adopted.)

Symbols for proposed trees			
Basic symbol	General symbol for transplants, nursery stock, advance stock and semi-mature trees	Detailed symbol when tree sizes are to be shown	
	+	+	**Transplants & whips**
Outline to be thicker than symbol for existing trees			**Nursery stock** Short standard: ss
			Half standard: hs
			Light standard: ls
			Standard: s
			Tall standard: ts
			Selected standard: sel s
	Add abbreviations to indicate sizes if required		**Advanced nursery stock** Heavy standard: hs
			Extra heavy standard: ehs
			Selected heavy standard: shs or sel. hs
			Semi-mature trees May be divided into: small: ssm medium: msm large: lsm

(a)

(b)

Fig. 2.2 Detailed graphic symbols for trees. (a) Part of Table 2 on recommended tree symbols, reproduced from BS 1192 : Part 4. (b) Despite the roughness of this typical sketch, the details of the tree symbols used are quite clear.

sheets as possible. For most projects A1 and A2 sizes for location, site, setting-out and layout plans, with A3 and A4 for assembly component drawings and planting plans, will be appropriate at scales from 1:50 000 down to 1:200 for the former, and between 1:200 and 1:5 for the latter.

Production drawings must be concise and have been prepared so that they remain legible at all times of the day (and night) and at all seasons of the year, both in the contractors' hut and out on site, for that is where they are intended to be used. They must contain sufficient information for the design to be implemented and for accurate quantities to be taken off and measured by the quantity surveyor and/or the estimator.

2.4 CONTENT OF DRAWINGS

No rules exist at present regarding the content of drawings, although work has started under the aegis of the Coordinating Committee for Project Information (CCPI) which has attempted to synthesize the rules for drawings, specification and method of measurement under a Common Arrangement. BS 1194: Part 4 however includes check lists (see Table 2.1) which attempt to itemize the minimum information that should appear on the various types of drawings.

Drawings should only in exceptional circumstances duplicate information already indicated elsewhere on other drawings and in the specification or schedules – in view of the risk of error in the event of subsequent changes being made on one document and not on the other (irrespective of the duplication of effort needed to make the same change twice). Even the temptation to repeat the same information to more detail on a subsequent drawing to a larger scale – with the requirement in the Bill or specification: 'Always work to the largest scale drawings' – is to be avoided in view of the contractors' undeniable pre-ference (irresistable temptation?) to use the most comprehensive drawing with the maximum information on one sheet (i.e. the one to the smaller scale).

Layout drawings must always be crystal clear and in some instances it may be helpful if successive elements of the work are shown in separate sheets, e.g. site clearance, setting out, hard landscape, planting, etc. (Figs 2.3 and 2.4 show examples.) The use of copy negatives, and overlay draughting techniques, with one basic drawing from which copies are made before adding the additional note is particularly useful in this connection.

Discrepancies on drawings indicating the extent of cut-and-fill frequently give rise to problems on landscape contracts and it is essential that this is accurately indicated both on plan and section with the utmost clarity if such disputes are to be avoided. (See Fig 2.5.) In addition the location of the surface finishes should be indicated, with, more importantly, the location of the details for which additional component and assembly details have had to be prepared.

Most landscape projects will involve the treatment of both the horizontal sur-faces and the vertical enclosing elements of walls and fencing. The latter will

Table 2.1 Checklists of information required on various types of drawings

Type of drawing	Information required	Preferred scale
Location plans:	Site location, access and site surroundings	—
Site plans:	Existing and proposed building, fencing and hedges within and adjoining the site, paths, roads, trees, shrubs, grass and water features	1:500
Site work plans:	Contractors' working area, existing trees other features to be maintained and protected. Site restrictions as to location of temporary accommodation, surplus excavated material and top soil	1:200
Setting-out plans:	Reference points levels and setting-out dimensions for hard and soft landscape	1:200
Layout plans		
I Hard landscape:	Hard surfaces, walls, fencing, gates, curbs and edging, location of details	—
II Soft landscape	New and existing levels and contours depths of topsoil, irrigation and land drains, tree, shrub, herbaceous, grass areas and water features	—
III Services:	New and existing soil and surface water drainage, gas, water, electricity and telephone services	1:100/1:50
Assembly and construction details:	Plans, sections and elevations enlarged as necessary to show details of construction and assembly	1:20/1:5
Planting plans and component details:	Location, number, size and species of trees hedges, shrubs and herbaceous plants, grass seeded and turfed areas	1:20/1:5

inevitably involve the preparation of the larger scale component details which are best prepared in the form of separate sheets of component details (see Fig. 2.6). Their existence should be noted on the relevant locations on the layout drawings by a section line in conjunction with the detail reference number enclosed in a circle. It is of course essential to indicate on the layout drawings the exact extent of the surface finishes both hard and soft, and the precise length of all enclosing walls and fences.

Key

▨ Brick paving

▦ Precast concrete slab paving

⊠ Tree pits in hard areas

◉ Existing trees retained

—ı—ı— Timber fence

———— Brick mowing margin

◯—• Reference to details

▨ Plant bed: 400 mm depth of top soil

▨ Grass areas: 150 mm depth of top soil

NOTE. On more complex drawings sizes can be shown on separate setting-out drawings

Fig. 2.3 Example of hard-landscape plan. (After BS 1192 : Part 4 : 1984.)

5 Robinia pseudoacacia

1 Fraxinus excelsior

9 Rhus typhina   P2

Grass-seeded
3 Jasminum officinalis
and climbing wires to detail
20 Vinca minor

162 Vinca minor at 9 per m²

Grass-seeded   P3

486 Vinca minor alba at 9 per m²

P1

4 Prunus laurocerasus zabeliana

1 Parthenocissus tricuspidata

Existing Quercus robur No. 1

1 Parthenocissus tricuspidata

House

10 Amelanchier laevis

Grass-turfed

Grass-turfed

Existing Fraxinus ornus No 2

5 Cornus alba

3 Betula papyrifera

NORTH

1 Quercus cerris   3 Fraxinus excelsior

Key

	Nursery stock Short standard		Advanced nursery stock Heavy standard
	Standard		Semi-mature trees 6·m to 6.5 m
	Tall standard	P1	Plant bed numbers

Fig. 2.4 Example of planting plan. (After BS 1192 : Part 4 : 1984.)

2.5 COMPONENT AND ASSEMBLY DETAILS

While these often may be a set of photocopies of relevant standard details with or without the name of the particular project inserted in the job title panel, they may also be issued having been traced onto a larger sheet for inclusion in the contract documents. In either case there is no doubt of their relevance to any particular contract, whereas their inclusion by reference to a standard library of details, both relevant and inapplicable, available for inspection on demand

Plan

Section AA

Key

(21.75)   Existing grade
21.75   Proposed grade

••••••••   'No cut, no fill' line

||||||| Area of cut (section)

▨▨▨   Area of fill (section)

Fig. 2.5   Example of grading, showing extent of cut-and-fill. (After BS 1192 : Part 4 : 1984.)

will always cause problems particularly if they are amended subsequent to the date of the contract.

It is essential that the contractor has all the drawings at the time of tender preparation for any omission can lead to serious delays in progress and a claim situation. All drawings must be carefully numbered or referenced and these identifications noted in the specification and Bill of Quantities.

11

Lead core DPC under coping

Brick on edge coping

215 mm brickwork laid in 1:1:6 mortar, flush joints

Topsoil backfill mixture

300min.

225

Class B bricks in 1:3 mortar, below ground

1:6 concrete foundation, 525 x 225 stepped as shown in cut B-B

A→

30.90

31.35

Fairfaced

Gate

249

900 x 600 x 50 mm thick precast concrete slabs (butt joints)
25 mm sand bedding
150 mm hardcore base

Cut A-A

Cut B-B

Path 1

Back garden

Path 2

113 /1

215

equal

equal

215 thick brick wall

A→

Plant bed P4

900

215

Plant bed P1

Gate

317

0.860

House

Slabs cut to fit

29.00

A→

Ramp

29.60

29.60

Path 3

B↗

28.94

Plant bed P2

29.54

B↗

Plan

NORTH

521

Fig. 2.6 Example of component detail for hard landscape. (After BS 1192 : Part 4 : 1984.)

2.6 CURVES

Curves that are drawn roughly freehand on preliminary drawings are never satisfactory when the time comes for them to be translated on site if accurate dimensions for their setting out are not provided by the designer. 'French curves', which are so easy to use on the drawing board, do not exist on the ground. All curves, whether derived from circles with compasses or templates (circular curves) or irregular (non-circular) curves that must rely on dimensioned offsets, therefore must always have their origins clearly indicated on the

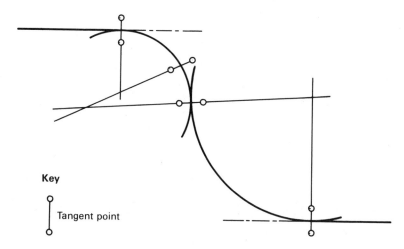

Fig. 2.7 Drawing of circular curves, showing tangent point. (After BS 1192 : Part 4 : 1984.)

drawings with radii, tangent points for circular curves and closely spaced offsets for irregular curves clearly dimensioned. (See Fig. 2.7.)

In practice on most landscape projects, carefully selected circular curves will be found to suffice in the majority of instances, irregular curves set out by offsets (Fig. 2.8) or coordinates of points along the curve being required only for the larger projects involving major recontouring or major road layouts.

Irrespective of whatever type of curve is used the sizes and locations should be clearly indicated and dimensioned, without the need to scale off the drawings – a method which is never sufficiently accurate and inevitably results in much 'trial and error' on site, expensively wasting the time of all concerned.

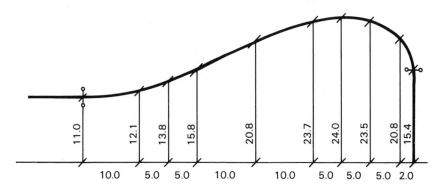

Fig. 2.8 Location of an irregular curve by offsets. (After BS 1192 : Part 4 : 1984.)

13

2.7 SETTING OUT

Accurate setting out is crucial to the success of every project and a clearly dimensioned drawing must always be the first priority. Where existing features on site are involved, or setting out relies on certain aspects being set out or aligned by eye this must also be clearly indicated (Fig. 2.9) so that those responsible for setting out clearly understand the intentions of the designer.

Fig. 2.9 Location of setting-out lines from existing features. (After BS 1192 : Part 4 : 1984.)

2.8 LEVELS

The indication of new and existing levels must be a key feature of any landscape project. Whereas the addition of contours to a plan gives a clear indication of the designer's intentions, spot levels at precisely dimensional locations are usually equally essential for those responsible for the execution of the work on site. The conventions that new levels should be shown unenclosed – 32.1, existing levels being enclosed in brackets or boxes – (32.1), new contours being shown by a solid line, and existing contours dotted. Arrows pointing 'up' the slope must always be followed if mistakes are to be avoided. (See Fig. 2.6 for examples.)

3

Landscape contract specification

The word **specification** is defined in the Concise Oxford Dictionary* as:

'specification – . . .specified detail, esp. (in *pl.*) detailed description of construction, workmanship, materials, etc., of work (to be) undertaken, prepared by architect . . .' .

Clearly, therefore, when used as a contract document, it must describe precisely and unambiguously the quality of materials, workmanship and in some cases the performance of a particular element or component required to be provided. A specification must always be clearly identifiable so that the purpose and the needs of the specifier are immediately recognized; the contents must be set out in an organized and orderly way so that the requirements of the specification are immediately understood and priced accordingly by the estimator.

The description of the quality of the workmanship and materials required is as essential a part of the contract documents as the drawings and Schedules of Quantity in conveying the designer's intentions to the contract, and to ensure that he has allowed in his tender for the proper execution of each element of the work.

It must be obvious therefore that the only member of the team able to undertake the proper preparation of the specification element of the contract is the designer and only rarely can he delegate this aspect of his work to another, such as the quantity surveyor.

It is unfortunate that in some earlier Forms of Contract where Bills of Quantities were included in the contract documents the 'specification' was expressly excluded, the reason being that in those instances the specification

*Concise Oxford Dictionary, 5th edn (1971) Oxford University Press, Oxford.

of the quality of the work had been included elsewhere, i.e. in the trade preambles to the measured items prepared by the quantity surveyors. Fortunately this anomaly has now been removed and all Standard Forms of Contract now provide for the specification of workmanship and materials to be included either as trade preambles or as a separately identified contract document whether Bills of Quantities are prepared by the employer or not. In either case it is important to ensure that all elements of qualitative description are kept clearly separate from the measured items, even if this seems illogical – as in the instance of the measurement of facing brickwork where the tenderer is referred to the specification clauses for the type or make of brick to be included. Unless this rule is strictly observed, however, as soon as some aspects of quality appear in the measured items, the temptation becomes irresistible on the part of the contractor to overlook, forget or ignore the specification in the day-to-day pursuance of his work.

3.1 THE SPECIFICATION AND SCHEDULES OF QUANTITY

The essence of a good specification is achieving the right balance as regards both quantity and quality and the right size for the job.

The preparation of a good specification requires great skill and judgement on the part of the draughtsman. From a vast library of clauses he has to select those applicable to that particular project (nothing shows up lack of experience and lack of confidence more quickly than a specification incorporating clauses which are inapplicable or incapable of achievement). He has to be cautious of clauses specifying in too much detail some comparatively unimportant item, e.g. four pages on tree surgery when only one limb of one tree is involved. Secondly it is essential only to specify what one is competent to check one is getting resisting the temptation to pad out the specifications with clauses included as insurances to hide one's own ignorance; contractors will spot them a mile off and turn it to their own advantage!

If the contractor is to give a job the attention it deserves – give an equal amount of attention to the specification. Running off a few standard sheets in the hope that they will do, because one is too lazy or too inexperienced or too busy to have typed out a specification omitting the inapplicable clauses and (more importantly) adding those clauses which were not necessary on the last job but are for this. Always go back to the full library, not an abridged version of a specification of a previous project.

Equally, the Schedules must be practicable (do not schedule a 2.0-metre E.L.N.S. Ginko, Ilex or Taxus!) and accurate so that the tenders when submitted are comparable.

Finally you will note that reference has been made to Schedules of Quantity – the words adopted from the GLC for the JCLI Landscape Contract – and not Bills of Quantity (which are something quite different, prepared in accordance with the 6th SMM for Building Work, and are quite inadequate for soft landscape works).

3.2 STRUCTURE AND WORDING OF SPECIFICATIONS

It is now a generally accepted convention that specifications are divided into two. The first part comprises the 'preliminary' clauses covering the Form of Contract to be used, the responsibilities of the parties to the contract, the definition of the procedures to be followed as a consequence, and a simple description of the scope of the work, the site and any particular restrictions as to access, sequence of the work, hours or working rules. The second part of the specification describes the quality and performance of the materials, workmanship and 'prefabricated' components to be used. These are best set out by describing the materials and components for any particular element followed by the workmanship required in the preparation of adjacent surfaces, the location, assembly, planting and subsequent protection of the element itself. Other aspects which may have to be described are those affecting appearance, performance and any requirements for off-site or on-site testing, tolerances, and the provision and retention of samples.

The clauses themselves must also be written in clear and concise phrases, and words chosen to indicate the designers' intentions simply and unambiguously. They should, wherever possible, start with a 'Keyword' indicating the scope of the clause, e.g. 'TOPSOIL', 'WEEDS', 'HERBICIDES', followed by a verb in the imperative, e.g. 'to be', 'provide', 'lay', 'fix', 'plant', etc. (Table 3.1).

Vague phrases such as 'in all respects', 'the best of their respective kind', 'free from all faults' should be avoided at all costs, lest they exceed the bounds of practicability or involve exhorbitant cost far beyond that intended by the specifier. Specification clauses should never require anything not capable of being checked by the specifier ('policed') nor should you use meaningless phrases such as 'and the like'.

Words should always be used consistently, the same word being used for the same thing throughout the specification, and the same word or term used where it occurs elsewhere in the other contract documents and standard clauses.

Clauses should always be concise using the minimum number of words to convey their intended meaning without ambiguity, i.e. 'Arrange ...' and not 'The contractor shall make all arrangements as are necessary to ensure...'. Describing operations in great detail or to an accuracy or tolerance that is unnecessary or impossible to attain should always be avoided.

Materials can be specified in one of three ways: by type, by British Standard, by proprietary name. Whichever is selected the minimum standard must be

Table 3.1 Example of specification clauses for soiling/cultivating/grading. (Reproduced with permission of NBS Services Ltd.)

This section covers:
- Preparation of subsoil
- Spreading of topsoil
- Initial treatment, cultivation and grading of in situ and spread topsoil.

For site clearance, excavation and stockpiling of topsoil see section C12.
For subsoil filling see section C21.
For seeding and turfing see section W21.
For planting see section W31.

The soiling/cultivating/grading work may be carried out:
- Entirely by the Main Contractor
- Entirely by a landscape Nominated Subcontractor
- Partly by the Main Contractor and partly by a landscape Nominated Subcontractor.

In the latter case Section W11 can be used to produce separate specifications for the Main Contractor (e.g. preparing subsoil and spreading topsoil) and for the Nominated Sub-contractor (e.g. cultivating and grading).

Y210
Topsoil is the original surface layer of grassland or cultivated land. It does not generally include soil from woodland, heathland moorland, bog or other special areas such as land impaired by industrial activity.
BS 3882 classifies topsoil in relation to the following characteristics:
- Texture: Insert 'light', 'medium' or 'heavy'

To be read in conjunction with Preliminaries and General Conditions.

PRODUCTS/MATERIALS

W11 : Y *SOIL/ADDITIVES/HERBICIDES*

Y210   Imported topsoil: to BS 3882.
Texture: . . .
Soil reaction: neutral.
Reasonably free of stones.
Maximum size of stones in any dimension: . . . mm.
Free of weed seeds, roots of perennial weeds, sticks, subsoil and foreign matter.
From an approved source.

Table 3.1 (contd)

- Soil reaction: pH value of neutral soil is 7.0
- Stone content: In assessing whether topsoil is reasonably stonefree, the natural local and site conditions should be taken into account
- Size of stones: for ordinary purposes stones up to 50mm in size are acceptable.

Y220   Imported topsoil: obtain approval of a sample load of not less than $5m^3$. Retain for comparison with subsequent loads.

Y230
Use this clause when the Contractor is required to import topsoil from a particular source, stating all relevant details, e.g. location, access, whether or not it has to be stripped or lifted from a spoil heap, price agreed (if any).

Y230   Imported topsoil: obtain from ...

Y410, Y420
Peat and sewage sludge are included in this section as additives to adjust the texture of topsoil when necessary.

Y410   Peat: to BS 4156.

Y420   Sewage sludge: friable, no large lumps, dry and containing not less than 6% nitrogen, 3% phosphate and 5% potash.

Y610   Lime: fine ground limestone containing not less than 50% of CaO equivalent.

Y810, Y820
Alternative clauses.
The ACAS list is published under the title of 'Approved Products for Farmers and Growers' published every year by HMSO for the Ministry of Agriculture, Fisheries and Food.

Y810   Herbicide: a type recommended for the purpose in the current list of the Agricultural Chemicals Approval Scheme.

Table 3.1 (contd)

Y820	Y820 Herbicide: . . .
Use this clause to specify herbicides by proprietary reference as required. Herbicides should be selected from the current list of the Agricultural Chemicals Approval Scheme. The clause can also be used to restrict use of herbicides to certain types for specific applications e.g. • Adjacent to watercourses lakes, ponds, etc • Adjacent to crops • Areas accessible to the public • Where existing flora and fauna are to be protected.	

clear, but it is always in the employer's interest to allow a contractor the maximum freedom of choice in the selection of his sources of supply compatible with the ability to lay down the minimum standards required.

In the case of plants it is clearly insufficient to specify just the type, e.g. to specify *Fraxinus oxycarpa* 'Raywood' or *Hedera colchica* 'Variegata' without any indication of age, size or source of supply.

Equally to specify that the plant be in accordance with 'the relevant' British Standard (see Table 3.2 and Appendix A) would be inadequate as alternative sizes are almost invariably included within the one Standard. The reference to the actual requirement has to be made clear, e.g. advanced nursery stock to BS 5236 : 1975. Even this allows both a 'heavy standard' tree to be provided to a stem circumference (measured 1 m from the ground) of between 12 and 14 cm, to be between 3.50 and 4.25 m high with a 1.8 m clear stem, and 'extra heavy' with a stem circumference of 14–16 cm and a height of 4.25–6.00 m.

The use of a proprietary supplier, while always to be used with caution, is often the only way of ensuring plants of an adequate standard are delivered. Just as the health of a child cannot be measured by its height, so the delivery of healthy plants can not be ensured solely by specifying their minimum size. While this practice removes the competitive element of pricing from the contractor (and its use should be avoided wherever possible) it does, at least, ensure the comparability of this part of the tender, with plants supplied to a minimum standard.

When an acceptable description intelligible to all parties can not be given

Table 3.2 Fifteen British Standards considered essential in landscape work. Many are unaware of the existence of the 83 British Standards for gardening, horticulture and landscape work listed in the February 1983 Sectional List of British Standards (SL 41) available free of charge from BSI at Milton Keynes (Tel. 0908 320066), or that 49 of them (i.e. 60%) are available in summary form. Fifteen of these Standards are considered essential references for all those concerned in landscape work; they are listed here and summarized in Appendix A.

---

1. NURSERY STOCK (FAC/1)

BS 3936 : Parts 1–11 : Specification for trees and shrubs, etc.

Part 1. Trees and shrubs
Part 2. Roses
Part 3. Fruit
Part 4. Forest trees
Part 5. Poplars and tree willows
Part 6. *not used*
Part 7. Bedding plants
Part 8. *not used*
Part 9. Bulbs, corms and tubers
Part 10. Ground cover plants
Part 11. Culinary herbs in containers

2. OPERATIONS BDB/5

BS 3998 : 1966	Recommendations for tree work
BS 4043 : 1978	Recommendations for transplanting semi-mature trees
BS 4428 : 1968	Recommendations for general landscape operations
BS 5236 : 1975	Recommendations for cultivation and planting trees in the extra large nursery stock category
BS 5837 : 1980	Code of Practice for trees in relation to construction
BS —	Ground maintenance (EPC/2)

3. MATERIALS FAC/2)

BS 3882 : 1965(78)	Recommendations and classification for topsoil
BS 3969 : 1965(78)	Recommendations for turf for general landscape purposes
BS 4156 : 1967(79)	Peat
*BS 5551 : 1978/81/82	Fertilizers

4. TERMINOLOGY

BS 881/589 : 1974	Nomenclature of commercial hardwoods and softwoods
BS 1192 : 1984	Part 4 Recommendations for landscape drawings
*BS 1831 : 1969	Recommended common names for pesticides
*BS 2468 : 1963	Glossary of terms relating to agricultural machinery
BS 3975 : 1966/69	Glossary for landscape work; Part 4 – plant description; Part 5 – Horticultural practice

---

*Not in Construction Digest Handbook.

without resorting to involved text or site inspection of plants in the nursery of the supplier, then it is either necessary to specify a single source suffixed by 'or equivalent' or 'or equal and approved', or by the more preferable alternative of listing, in the tender documents, three or four named suppliers from one or other of whom the Tenderer must obtain the material in question. When it is considered acceptable to add the suffix 'or equal and approved' to such a list, the proviso must be added that 'approval of the additional source must be obtained in writing from the specifier at least 7 days before the date for the submission of tenders'.

3.3 STANDARDS OF WORKMANSHIP

When specifying minimum standards of workmanship a choice of three ways apply: by finished effect, by British Standard Codes of Practice, and by method. By finished effect, with full responsibility for the method of achievement placed with the contractor, is clearly preferable but rarely practicable. 'Plant one semi-mature *Fagus sylvatica*' is clearly inadequate. Even the addition of 'in accordance with BS 4043 : 1966 – Recommendations for transplanting semi-mature trees' is rarely sufficient. Most specifiers will wish to rely on their own expertise and, while they may not specify the sequence and time of planting, they will almost certainly wish to specify the minimum dimensions and materials to be used and, the method of application in the construction of tree pits (even if, by strictly complying, the contractor may therefore be relieved of his responsibilities for their subsequent survival).

[handwritten margin note: Updated BS 4043:1987]

3.4 PROTECTION – SPECIFICATION CLAUSES

The protection of plants after they have been planted and before they become established always causes particular problems on landscape projects. Not only in respect of watering during the Defects Liability Period but equally in the provision of temporary protection. Such clauses as 'provide such temporary fencing to new shrub borders and grass areas during the works as is necessary and remove on completion of the Defects Liability Period' is today no longer good enough. While such a phrase might just possibly (but probably would not) suffice for the protection of an existing mature tree during the progress of the work, when applied to watering and the protection of new work, it is woefully inadequate.

When faced with such a loosely worded clause many contractors will conclude that the specifier does not rate this work of much importance nor rank it very high in the list of his priorities, and is therefore unlikely to enforce its provision with any vigour, if at all. Under such circumstances the prudent estimator who seriously intends to submit the lowest tender will allow little, if anything, in his tender, in the hope that he will be required to provide little more than a nominal amount of work for this item if any at all. Conscientious contractors will of course allow the proper amount and may, as a consequence, never submit the lowest tender and rapidly go out of business. The unscrupulous contractor, unexpectedly having the conditions enforced, will suffer serious financial loss, perhaps even going out of business himself. When the client then turns to the conscientious contractor to remedy the work he may find he no longer exists either; the project is, as a consequence, a disaster for all concerned.

As pointed out in JCLI practice note 1, where temporary protection such as fencing is considered necessary, this must be clearly specified and quantified at tender stage. Ownership of temporary protection, even if it is to be left in position during the Defects Liability Period, normally remains the property of the contractor unless stated otherwise in the contract documents; it is often an advantage if they are specified to become the property of the employer after practical completion.

3.5 STANDARD CLAUSES

It must by now be clear that there is no such thing, or there ought not to be, as a standard landscape specification. What all offices have, or should have, is a standard library of specification clauses from which the appropriate clauses can be selected for any particular project.

The use of standard clauses throughout the landscape industry obviously has the advantage of ensuring familiarity both on the part of the specifier and on the part of the contractor or supplier. Each knows from past experience the responsibilities and requirements of the clause, without the need for the careful scrutiny a new clause needs to ensure that the full obligations of the words used are fully understood and appreciated. This applies both to clauses in project specifications and to those used in trade preambles to measured items in Bills of Quantity. The Property Services Agency (PSA), the Greater London Council (GLC), and the National Building Specification (NBS, Table 3.1) all have libraries of standard specification clauses prepared specifically for landscape work. Grouped into sections, they include every alternative that is likely to be necessary on the full range of projects. They have comprehensive sets of preliminary clauses, with notes adjacent to each clause giving guidance as to the selection of the most appropriate alternative in any given situation. The various British Standards, Codes of Practice, and sources of other technical information are listed to assist in the selection of the appropriate clause. They all classify and codify clauses in the Standard Method of Measurement (SMM) -soon to be Common Arrangement - sequence and subdivide them into the two subsections referred to earlier: namely the specification of the materials to be used in each section, followed by the workmanship required in the various operations necessary for its location, assembly or planting. Those provided by NBS have the advantage of being appropriate to all landscape projects in both public and private sectors, and have the added advantage of having been edited by members of the LI, GLC and PSA whereas those of PSA are copyright and intended only for PSA projects. In addition NBS is available on subscription at a special rate to landscape offices which are not part of a larger architectural practice. All are regularly updated and revised to ensure that only the latest British Standard is referred to, and, where options exist within the standards themselves, these are identified to enable the appropriate choice to be made.

It is therefore obvious that there should be no such thing as a 'standard office landscape specification' as distinct from an office library of standard clauses from which those appropriate are extracted for each particular project. This will ensure that all aspects of the project are adequately specified, which rarely happens when the specification from a similar previous job is used, deleting (hopefully) those clauses that are inappropriate for the current job and neglecting to add those that are necessary for the new project but were not required on the previous one.

There is however one danger that arises from the selection of clauses from a fully comprehensive library: that of overspecifying. There is a great risk, particularly when inexperienced or unconfident, to include clauses 'just in case the need might arise'. When this happens the specification rapidly becomes out of balance and inappropriately large. The inexperience of the specifier is immediately apparent to the estimator, and the tender is increased accordingly to take account of the risk of possible increased costs arising as a result of this lack of experience.

Clauses from libraries of standard landscape clauses must always be copied out in full, either by copy typing from a list of clause numbers prepared by the specifier, or (now more commonly) by use of a computerized 'mark up' copy to be returned to the originator to print out. It is not considered sufficient or good practice to incorporate (by reference) the full library of clauses, or to give only headings and code references to identify the various clauses. This latter practice would involve the users – specifier, estimator and contract manager alike – to have to refer constantly to the source document which may or may not have been revised before or after the project specification was prepared, with the possibility of dispute and subsequent litigation which will inevitably arise in such instances.

It is now also possible to prepare a standard office library of landscape clauses based on a nationally accepted set of standard clauses in the same order of arrangement and coding, with one's own selection of the standard clauses and own special clauses inserted and coded accordingly. This is only practicable if suitable arrangements are made for the regular updating of the clauses, and obtaining the necessary licence where appropriate. However, in practice, it rarely causes problems; most computer agencies are able to offer this facility for even the simplest commercially available in-house microcomputers, such as those made by Apple, Commodore and ACT.

3.6   COMMON ARRANGEMENT (CCPI)

In 1979 a committee was set up at the instigation of the NCC Standing Committee to co-ordinate project information. It in turn established as a first
priority the need to devise a common array of up to 200 work sections grouped
into about 60 categories. These in turn could be brought together under 10–15
broad headings similar to the present trade headings. The intention was to
ensure that drawings, specifications, and Bills of Quantities were related to
each other with a common structure. In the event this resulted in Group D
(Ground work) with 5 subgroups and Group Z (Site surfacing/Planting/
Fencing) with 4 subgroups.

Those primarily affecting the landscape industry are D20 (Excavating and
soil/hard fitting) with 20 subsections, Z30 (Seeding/Turfing) with 15 subsections, and Z31 (Planting) with 20 subsections. These are listed in Tables 3.3–
3.5, and provided that those items in each section relevant to a particular
project are covered (in the same sequence) in drawings, specifications and Bills
of Quantity, estimators will then be able to submit tenders confident in the
knowledge that everything required of them will have been priced, and site staff
know the location and quality of materials and workmanship required of
them. Tables 3.3–3.5 are reproduced with permission of the Co-ordinating
Committee for Project Information. The information in the tables is taken
from a draft version of the Common Arrangement, the actual Common
Arrangement, is due to be published during 1986.

3.7   WATERING – SPECIFICATION CLAUSES

The specification for the provision of adequate water is essential for the
establishment and rapid growth of plants. A requirement to provide 'sufficient
water during the Defects Liability Period' is as inadequate as the similar provisions for temporary protection. Only a clause such as the following (also see
Figure 3.1) will ensure proper provision for watering in the contract
documents:

'The contractor is to water all trees, shrubs, grass and other planted areas at the time of
planting in order that the entire tree pit or planted area is moistened to field capacity.
Watering shall be undertaken on subsequent occasions when directed by the landscape
architect to ensure the establishment and growth of the plants.

To comply with this clause, the contractor is to allow for the provision of water, water
carts or hoses with a fine rose attachment or sprinklers at normal mains pressure,
allowed to run until the full depth of topsoil specified has reached a point where full
absorption is achieved over the areas of all trees, shrubs and grass on each occasion. The
contractor is to include and state in his tender the cost of compliance with this clause so
that the cost of visits can be deducted in whole or in part if not required to be
used.'

Table 3.3 Draft Common Arrangement: Subgroup D20 (Excavating and soil/hard filling).

Forming bulk, pit, trench and surface area excavations other than for m and e services. Filling holes and excavations other than those for m and e services. Making up levels by bulk filling or in layers, including hardcore but excluding bases to roads and pavings.

Included	Excluded
Applying herbicides to soil before excavating. Excavating topsoil, subsoil, made ground or rock.	Excavating and filling for temporary roads and other temporary works. (Preliminaries)
Breaking out existing substructures.	Ground investigation, D10.
Breaking out existing hard pavings.	Soil stabilization, D11.
Removing existing underground storage tanks and services.	Stabilizing soil in situ by incorporating cement with a rotovator.
Removing existing trees, shrubs, undergrowth and turf.	(Soil stabilization, D11)
Consolidating bottoms of excavations.	Site dewatering required to be executed by a specialist firm.
Trimming excavations to accurate shape and dimensions.	(Site dewatering, D12).
Keeping the excavations free of water (other than site dewatering).	Excavating, backfilling, beds and surrounds for engineering services, D21.
Temporary diversion of waterways and drains.	Excavating and backfilling for underpinning.
Benching sloping ground to receive filling.	(Underpinning, D40)
Making stockpiles of excavated material.	Filling internal plant containers. (Interior planting, N14)
Disposing of surplus excavated material.	Excavating and backfilling for below ground drainage.
Earthwork support.	(Drainage below ground, R12)
Filling with and compacting:	Excavating and backfilling for land drainage.
Excavated material (including selected);	(Land drainage, R13)
Imported material;	Hardcore/Granular bases to roads/pavings, Z10.
Rock;	Gravel/Hoggin roads/pavings, Z22.
Hardcore and granular material;	Cultivating and final fine grading of soil for seeding, turfing or planting.
Soil cement.	(Relevant sections, Z30, Z31)
Consolidating surface of filling with fine material.	Spreading peat, compost, mulch, fertiliser, soil ameliorants, including working in.
Preparing subsoil by ripping, grading, etc. before spreading topsoil.	(Relevant sections, Z30, Z31)
Transporting from stockpiles or importing and spreading topsoil.	Excavating and filling treepits. (Planting, Z31)
Filling external planters, beds, roof gardens with soil and drainage layers, including filter mats.	Excavating and filling post holes for fencing. (Fencing, Z40)

Table 3.4   Draft Common Arrangement: Subgroup Z30 (Seeding/Turfing).

Preparing soil and seeding or turfing to form lawns and general grassed areas.

Included	Excluded
Applying herbicides.	Earthworks and other preparation:
Cultivating topsoil, including removing large stones and weeds.	Clearing existing vegetation;
Fine grading topsoil.	Removing existing hard paving and obstructions;
Providing, spreading and working in peat, manure, compost, mulch, fertiliser, soil ameliorants, sand, etc.	Removing existing topsoil and stockpiling;
Edging strips for lawn areas.	General site contouring and adjusting levels;
Mesh reinforcement for grass areas.	Transporting from stockpiles or importing and spreading topsoil;
Seeding and rolling.	Filling external planters, beds, roof gardens with soil and drainage layers.
Turfing, including turf edges to seeded areas.	(Excavation and soil/hard filling, D20)
Hydro-seeding.	Land drainage, R13
Grass cutting.	Irrigation, S14
Work to existing grassed areas, including scarifying, forking, fertilising, applying selective weedkillers, local re-seeding or re-turfing, rolling, edging, etc.	Grass block paving: Sub-base (Hardcore/Granular bases to roads/ pavings, Z10);
Protecting new and existing grassed and planted areas with temporary fencing, etc.	Blocks and bedding (Slab/Brick/Block etc. pavings, Z24).
Watering, including during Defects Liability Period.	Special surfacings/pavings for sport, Z25.
Work specified to be executed during the Defects Liability Period.	Maintenance (as distinct from making good defects) other than that specified to be carried out during the Defects
Replacement seeding and turfing.	Liability Period.

It is important to then refer to this and the following item in the bills, schedules or tender summary, to ensure that it is included and priced for.

3.7.1 Drought conditions

Should emergency legislation restricting the use of water during drought conditions be imposed, the contractor will be required to ascertain, before planting, the availability of and arrange the collection and application of second-class water by bowser or other means from an approved sewage works, deliver to site and apply as specified. (See Fig. 3.2.)

Table 3.5 Draft Common Arrangement: Subgroup Z31 (Planting).

Preparing soil and planting herbaceous and other plants, trees and shrubs.

Included	**Excluded**
Apply herbicides.	Earthworks and other preparation:
Cultivating topsoil including removing large stones and weeds. Fine grading topsoil.	Clearing existing vegetation;
	Removing existing hard paving and obstructions;
Forming raised or sunken beds, borders, etc.	Removing existing topsoil and stockpiling;
Providing and spreading peat, manure, compost, mulch, fertiliser, soil ameliorants, and working in if required.	General site contouring and adjusting levels;
Planting herbaceous plants and bulbs.	Transporting from stockpiles or importing and spreading topsoil;
Planting shrubs and hedges.	Filling external planters, beds, roof
Planting nursery stock and semi-mature trees.	gardens with soil and drainage layers.
Excavating and backfilling tree pits.	(Excavation and soil/hard filling, D20)
Fence supports for hedges. Support	Interior planting, N14
wires, etc. for climbers. Tree stakes, tree	External prefabricated plant containers
guards, tree guys.	(Site/Street furniture/equipment
Wrapping and other protection of trees,	N30).
shrubs and plants.	Land drainage, R13.
Labelling.	Irrigation, S14
Applying anti-desiccants. Tree surgery,	Tree grilles.
thinning and pruning.	(Slab/Brick/Block/Pavior/Sett/Cobble
Protecting new and existing grassed and	pavings, Z24
planted areas with temporary fencing,	Seeding/Turfing, Z30.
etc.	Fencing, Z40.
Watering, including during defects	Maintenance (as distinct from making
liability period	good defects) other than that specified
Work specified to be carried out during	to be carried out during, the Defects
the Defects Liability Period.	Liability Period.
Replacement planting.	

6401
The number of waterings required will depend on the weather conditions and the number to be allowed for will depend on the anticipated time(s) of planting. Insert number required, which may vary for different types of plant, or the words 'as measured'.

6401   WATERING: ensure that sufficient water is applied to maintain healthy growth of trees/shrubs/plants. Suggest to SO when watering may be required and when instructed carry out using a fine rose or sprinkler until full depth of topsoil is saturated. Number of waterings to be allowed for:

- - - - -
- - - - -

6402   WATERING: spray crown of trees when in leaf during warm weather. Carry out in the evening.

Fig. 3.1 An example of specification clauses to cover watering requirements. (Reproduced with permission of NBS Services Ltd.)

1151
Use this clause only when the planting is to be done by a nominated sub-contractor.

1151   WATER will be provided by the Main Contractor up to Practical Completion of the Main Contract Works and thereafter by the Employer, always subject to availability of supply.

1201   DROUGHT CONDITIONS: if water supply is or is likely to be restricted by emergency legislation, inform SO without delay and ascertain availability and additional cost of second class water from a sewage works or other approved source.
1. If planting has not been carried out, do not do so until instructed.
2. If planting has been carried out, obtain instructions on supply of water.

Fig. 3.2 An example of specification clauses to cover action to be taken in drought conditions. (Reproduced with permission of NBS Services Ltd.)

4

Landscape quantities

4.1 MEASUREMENT OF LANDSCAPE WORK ON WITH- AND WITHOUT-QUANTITIES PROJECTS

The primary objective of any set of tender and subsequent contract documents is to ensure that everything that is required for the proper completion of the work is included by the contractor, and that tenders are submitted on a comparable basis (which is not to say that there may not be a wide range of different prices submitted by the individual tenders for the various elements of the work while the tender totals may not be dissimilar).

The secondary objective is to provide comparable rates for the landscape architect or quantity surveyor to value any variations to the contract and as a basis for valuations prepared in support of Interim and Final Certificates.

To achieve these two objectives it is essential on any project, large or small, to ensure that the tender and contract documents contain sufficient information for it to be priced by the contractor for this to be achieved. All standard forms of contract, therefore, contain provisions for the contractor to 'price the specification or schedules or schedule of rates' (JCLI, 2nd Recital).

Even when quantities are not provided by the employer it is advisable for specifications and tender summaries to state the overall areas of topsoil, grass and shrub borders, so that in the evaluation of tenders submitted it is certain that the areas included are comparable and that one tenderer has not included 60 square metres grass and 40 square metres shrub border, whereas another has taken 40 square metres grass and 60 square metres shrub border (both measured from the same drawing). To enter into a contract with such an error or discrepancy, albeit with the lowest tenderer, makes subsequent accurate financial control almost impossible.

Errors of this sort are most likely to arise when details at different scales are included on the same drawing. It is essential that the scales are clearly marked on each detail.

4.2 SCHEDULES

Even the smallest project will need a schedule in one form or another. BS 1192:

Part 1 defines a schedule as 'Tabulated information on a range of similar items' and gives separate tables for tree work, planting shrubs and climbers. (Tables 4.1–4.3 show examples of such schedules.)

Traditionally Bills of Quantities are provided by the employer for inclusion in the contract documents on only the larger landscape contracts, many contracts being let on a 'drawings and spec' basis.

To provide a uniform basis for measuring building works the committee set up by the quantity surveyors and contractors in 1922 has, over the succeeding years, produced a series of standard methods of measurement, the latest being the sixth edition (SMM6) which became operative in March 1979. (Table 4.4 quotes Section A.) This differed little from previous editions in the woefully inadequate treatment of landscape works dismissed summarily by thirty-one words in:

Clause D44 – Landscaping

'Soiling, cultivating, seeding, treating top surface, fertilizing and turfing to surfaces shall be given separately in square metres, stating the thickness of soil and the quantity per square metre of the seed or fertilizer. Any requirements for watering, weeding, cutting, settlement, re-seeding and the like shall be stated.' (Reproduced with permission of the Standing Joint Committee for the Standard Method of Measurement of Building Works.)

Against the often-repeated complaint – that 80% of a surveyor and estimator's time is spent measuring and pricing 20% of the value of a contract – it has to be admitted that the particular needs of landscape contracting require more than this if contractors are to be given sufficient information in a standard format and sequence for them to submit an accurately and comparably priced tender. Irrespective of the quality of the rules themselves a standard method is essential to establish the minimum information necessary to define the nature and extent of the work, items not listed being deemed not to have to be included in the tender, and any departures from the standard measurement conventions having to be specifically drawn to the attention of the estimator.

To resolve this deficiency BALI published in 1977 a 'Method of Measurement of Soft Landscape Works' which was subsequently adopted and published by JCLI in 1978 and was divided into the following seven sections (A–G).

A. Introduction.
B. Preamble.
C. Cultivation and preparation of ground for growing material.
D. Seeding and turfing.
E. Planting, including shrub and tree planting.
F. Thinning and pruning, tree surgery, grass improvement.
G. Protection of existing artifacts and growing material during construction.

31

Table 4.1 Example of tree work schedule (after BS 1192)

Tree No. and Tree Preservation Order (PTO) No.	Name	Protection
1 (113717)	*Quercus robur*	Barrier type . . . erected all round. No nearer the bole than the canopy drip line.
2	*Fraxinus ornus*	Barrier type . . erected where indicated on drawing no. . . .

*This column is optional.

Table 4.2 Example of tree planting schedule

Quantity	Name	Designation	Height/girth (where applicable*) cost
3	*Robinia pseudoacacis*	Tall standard	
5	*Betula pendula* 'Tristis'	Feathered	3.50 m (100 mm)

*Dimensions of standard trees as in BS 4043 and BS 3936 : Part 1.
†These columns are optional.

Work required	Cost*

Crown reduction to the South.
Remove dead wood.

Clean wound to the East; trim to live tissue
and treat with approved wound sealant.

Hand dig service duct trench.
Roots greater than 20 mm not to be severed.

Root system	Planting location			Unit rate † £	Total cost † £
	A1	A2	A3		
Bare root	3				
Bare root		2	3		

Table 4.3 Example of planting schedule for shrubs and climbers

| Quantity | Name | Root system/container volume | Height/spread* | Planting location | | | Unit rate £ | Total cost[†] £ |
				P1	P2	P3		
9	Rhus typhina	Container grown 2.5 L	900	–	3	6		
100	Vinca minor	Bare root	300 sp	–	30	70		

*When specifying spread use suffix sp.
[†]These columns are optional.

Table 4.4 SMM6 – Standard Method of Measurement of Building Works; Section A quoted. (Reproduced with permission of the Standing Joint Committee for the Standard Method of Measurement of Building Works.)

SECTION A

General rules

A.1 Introduction

This Standard Method of Measurement provides a uniform basis for measuring building works and embodies the essentials of good practice but more detailed information than is required by this document shall be given where necessary in order to define the precise nature and extent of the required work. This Standard Method of Measurement shall apply equally to both proposed and executed works.

A.2 Bills of quantities

1. Bills of quantities shall fully describe and accurately represent the quantity and quality of the works to be carried out. Work which cannot be measured shall be given as a provisional sum. Work the extent of which is not known shall be described as provisional or given in a bill of approximate quantities.
2. Rules of measurement adopted for little used forms of construction or not covered elsewhere in this document shall be stated.

A.3 Measurement

1. Unless the term metre used in this document is preceded by the words square or cubic it shall be deemed to be linear.
2. Work shall be measured net as fixed in position and each measurement shall be taken to the nearest 10 mm (i.e. 5 mm and over shall be regarded as 10 mm and less than 5 mm shall be disregarded). This rule shall not apply to any dimensions stated in descriptions.
3. Where minimum deductions of voids are dealt with in this document they shall refer only to openings or wants which are within the boundaries of measured areas. Openings or wants which are at the boundaries of measured areas shall always be the subject of deduction irrespective of size.
4. Where classification is given in this document as being between two limiting dimensions then the interpretation shall be as exceeding the first dimension and not exceeding the second.

A.4 Descriptions

The order of stating dimensions in descriptions shall be consistent and generally in the sequence of length, width and height. Where that sequence is not appropriate or where ambiguity could arise, the dimensions shall be specifically identified
2. Unless otherwise specifically stated in the bill or herein, the following shall be deemed to be included with all items:
   a. Labour and all costs in connection therewith.
   b. Materials, goods and all costs in connection therewith.

Table 4.4 (contd)

      c.   Fitting and fixing materials and goods in position.
      d.   Plant and all costs in connection therewith.
      e.   Waste of materials.
      f.   Square cutting.
      g.   Establishment charges, overhead charges and profit.

3. Junctions between straight and curved work shall in all cases be deemed to be included with the work in which they occur.
4. Notwithstanding the provisions in this document for labours to be given as linear items, such labours may be given in the description of any linear items of work on which they occur.
5. Notwithstanding the provisions in this document for labours to be enumerated, such labours may be given in the description of an enumerated item of work on which they occur.

A.5 Drawn information

1. Drawn information where required to be provided for the full implementation of this document is defined as follows:
   a. Location drawings
      i   Block plan. To identify site and outline of building in relation to Town Plan or other wider context.
      ii   Site plan. To locate the position of buildings in relation to setting out point, means of access and general layout of site.
      iii   General locating drawing. To show the position occupied by the various spaces in a building and the general construction and location of principal elements.
   b. Component details. To show all the information necessary for the manufacture and assembly of the component.
   c. Bill diagram. To be drawn information which may be provided with the bills of quantities to aid the description of the item. Information by way of dimensions or detail may be indicated, alternatively such information shall be included in the relevant description that accompanies the bill diagram.
2. The requirements of this document for detailed descriptions shall be deemed to have been compiled with if drawn information is provided and such information indicates fully the items required to be described.

A.6 Standard products

The requirements of this document shall be deemed to have been complied with if the item concerned is a product details of which have been published and to which reference has been made in the description.

A.7 Quantities

1. Where the unit of billing is the metre, quantities shall be billed to the nearest whole unit. Fractions of a unit less than half shall be disregarded and all other fractions shall be regarded as a whole unit.

Table 4.4 (contd)

2. Where the unit of billing is the tonne quantities shall be billed to the nearest two places of decimals.
3. Where the application of clauses A.7.1 and 2 would cause an entire item to be eliminated, such item shall be enumerated stating the size or weight as appropriate.

A.8 Provisional or prime cost sums

1. Where this document requires provisional or prime cost sums to be given in accordance with this clause, the choice of terms shall be made in conformity with the following definitions unless otherwise provided in the conditions of contract:
   a. The term 'provisional sum' is defined as a sum provided for work or for costs which cannot be entirely foreseen, defined or detailed at the time the tendering documents are issued.
   b. The term 'prime cost sum' is defined as a sum provided for work or services to be executed by a nominated sub-contractor, a statutory authority or a public undertaking or for materials or goods to be obtained from a nominated supplier. Such sum shall be deemed to be exclusive of any profit required by the general contractor and provision shall be made for the addition thereof.

A.9 Work in special conditions

1. Alterations and work in existing buildings shall be so described. Handling materials and getting them in or out of such buildings shall be deemed to be included with the items. Labours on existing work shall be so described.
2. Work carried out in or under water shall be so described stating whether canal, river or sea water and (where applicable) the mean spring levels of high and low water.
3. Work carried out in compressed air shall be so described stating the pressure and the method of entry and exit.

The first two sections deal with the provision of additional information and general requirements related to item descriptions, and the remaining five cover the measurement of the work under the various headings. (Table 4.5 quotes Section A.)

This has the effect of ensuring that landscape contractors being sent tender documents from a wide range of different sources, receive them in the same familiar format.

It is important to remember that civil engineering and building contracts have different ways of billing and specifying that which the contractor has to include in his tender. Each has its own rules and conventions and landscape contractors must remember this when preparing their tenders particularly with regard to the 'deemed to be included' items.

Table 4.5 JCLI Rules for the Measurement of Landscape Work; Section A quoted

SECTION A

General Rules

A.1 Application

The intention is that this document should be used for the measurement of all soft landscape work and that other rules of measurement should be used for other works and for preliminary and general items required of the landscape contractor and/or sub-contractor.

A.2 Definition of 'Schedules of Quantity'

'Schedules of Quantity' means a list of items giving quantities, as necessary, and brief descriptions of the work required. 'Bills of Quantities' as prepared by Quantity Surveyors using the building work standard method of measurement does not include soft landscape works. This document may therefore be used in conjunction with the 'Standard method of measurement for building works'. Detailed information on materials and workmanship shall be combined in the Specification, Planting Schedules or on the drawings. What is not detailed in the Schedules of Quantity will be deemed to mean not requiring to be priced by the tenderer.

A.3 General recommendations and requirements

1. In order to indicate the nature of the work, it is required, in addition to the Schedules of Quantity, that Drawings and Planting Schedules shall be provided as necessary to indicate size and number of areas, disposition of areas in relation to each other and an approximate location of obstructions with areas, together with an indication of existing items or areas to be protected within areas of new work.
2. The particular requirements of this document shall take precedence over the requirements of other rules of measurement with regard to soft landscape works.
3. Other rules of measurement used in conjunction with this document shall be stated in the Schedules of Quantity.
4. Where these and other rules of measurement are used for one contract, the general presentation of information shall be consistent with that required by these rules.

A.4 Item descriptions

1. Item descriptions in the Schedules of Quantity shall use, where apppropriate, the phrases and words indicated in this document.
2. Item descriptions for indentical quantities may be combined, only when it can be ascertained that all the operations will be required. Where it is customary for some operations to be omitted, or the number of times the operation has to be carried out varied, then separate items must be expressed.

Table 4.5 (contd)

A.5   Quantities

1.   The quantities shall be measured net from the drawings and no allowance shall
     be made for shrinkage, building or waste. Quantities may be rounded up or
     down, as appropriate, and fractional quantities should not be given. It is recom-
     mended that the unit of measurement for areas in excess of 15 000 m^2 shall be
     the ha.
2.   Items measured by m^2 or ha to a slope exceeding 1 in 3 shall be described as 'to
     slopes', which is also deemed to be the definition of a slope.

A.6   Classification of information

1.   Where possession of the site is required in stages, this shall be stated in the
     Schedules of Quantity and the work for each stage shall be kept separate under a
     suitable heading.
2.   Where there are varying defects liability periods required by the contract, work
     relating to each period shall be kept separate under a suitable heading which can
     be identified with the particular period.
3.   In addition to observing the requirements of A6 1 and 2 the work shall be
     grouped in the Schedules of Quantity according to the various major parts of the
     contract, where this is likely to affect costs.
4.   Having classified the work in accordance with A6.1, 2 and 3, work shall be
     further separated in accordance with the Sections indicated in this document,
     i.e. Sections B to G.

A.7   Section E

The rules contained in this Section may also be used for the aftercare of work
installed by the contractor, but which is not part of the contractor's defects liabilty
commitment. Work of this nature shall be kept separate under a suitable
heading.

SMM6 is only an interim edition pending a simpler but more radical
rearrangement, in an attempt to produce a document of more use to the
designer in communicating his intentions to the contractor, and more use to the
latter in production planning, control, materials ordering and cost analysis for
feed back. This information is at present available at taking off stage but is lost
in the subsequent stages of working up, quite apart from the need for the contractor to display his pricing concepts in such a manner to enable the quantity
surveyor to price valuations and variations without subsequent argument.

The publication of the draft SMM7 in 1984 has given the landscape industry
the opportunity of re-drafting its own proposals into a similar compatible
format incorporating the CCPI Common Arrangement for drawings,
specification and Bills alike. An example of SMM7 format, giving details of
'aftercare of soft-landscaped areas – grass cutting', is listed in Table 4.6.

Table 4.6 Example of JCLI Rules in draft SMM7 format

Classification table

1. Grass cutting	1. Area of grass per cut stated (m²)	1. Method of determination of frequency of cutting	1. Cut at a set interval of time stated
			2. Cut at a set height of grass stated
	2. Multiplier to the above representing the number of cuts stated (× Nr)		3. Cut at the Architect's instruction
	3. Level and to slopes ≤ 15° from horizontal	1. Disposal of cuttings	1. Spread cuttings evenly
			2. Box off cuttings and final disposal
	4. To slopes > 15° from horizontal		3. Rake up cuttings and final disposal

Table 4.6 (contd)

Measurement rules	Definition rules	Coverage rules	Specification information
1. Where cutting is to be at a set interval of time, the number of cuts stated shall be the total number required	Unless slowness of response leaves operations not 'used up" by end of season	1. Grass cutting is deemed to include stone picking and lightly rolling-in remaining projecting stones	1. Include all plan configurations and all types of mowing equipment
2. In all other cases the number stated shall be provisional and shall be so described			2. If a particular type of mower is required to be used this shall be stated
			3. Includes cutting up to all perimeters
			4. Excludes first cut

5

Landscape contract conditions

This chapter attempts only to summarize the salient features of the JCLI contract for landscape works. (For a full commentary see *The Shorter Forms of Building Contract*, Granada Publishing, London, 1984.)

5.1   THE NEED FOR A STANDARD FORM

Landscape contracts, like building contracts, differ from other contracts in that they are all 'work and material' contracts. They are not contracts solely for the sale of goods at common law, nor are they subject to the Sales of Goods Act 1979 even though the title in such materials as are required ultimately passes to the building owner. Equally, they are not contracts for services alone and are not therefore covered by the Supply of Goods and Services Act 1982, Part II.

Landscape contracts do not have to be in any special form, they can – and often are (for the smaller project) – by word of mouth. This inevitably causes problems, with misunderstandings as to what actually was agreed or what was to be done when circumstances arise that the parties have neglected to cover.

Frequently, 'contracts' are entered into by exchange of letters – the offer and its acceptance. While the terms of a standard contract can be incorporated by reference, e.g. *Modern Buildings v. Limmer & Trinidad (1975)*, this can also cause problems when the contract contains alternative provisions, e.g. fixed price or fluctuations. Problems also arise as to which edition was current at the time the contract was entered into when a contract has been subsequently amended.

If a new contract is drafted for each new project, or a local authority drafts its own, contractors will be suspicious of it and price accordingly. Also, by the Unfair Contract Terms Act 1977, some terms of a contract drafted unilaterally may be construed by the courts to be unenforceable and, where ambiguities arise, will be held to be *contra preferendem*, i.e. the meaning most favourable to the contractor will be adopted by the court. The courts have held, however, that where a contract has been agreed by all sides of the industry, this will not apply and it will not be considered an 'employer's' contract.

Fortunately for landscape contracts a Standard Form exists in the JCLI Standard Form of Agreement for Landscape Works (see Appendix C), with contract conditions covering the majority of situations considered likely to arise. Certain employers may, of course, find it necessary to annex their own special standard requirements but these should always be kept to the minimum.

5.2 THE JCLI STANDARD FORM OF AGREEMENT FOR LANDSCAPE WORKS

The Landscape Institute had published a Standard Form of Agreement for Landscape Work based on the JCT63 Form of Building Contract without Quantities edition in 1969 – followed by the 'with Quantities' version in 1973. The two forms were not however kept up-to-date with any of the subsequent JCT amendments. In April 1978 the JCLI, with the co-operation of the LI, prepared a new Form; this, with the additional clauses necessary for landscape work, was almost identical in context and format to the then current 1968 JCT Form of Agreement for Minor Building Works. This had been agreed with the JCT in order to reduce the proliferation of standard forms and to ensure the widespread acceptance of the JCLI Form by local authority and county councils who were also represented on the JCT. Since the designation of 'landscape architect' is not protected as is the use of the name 'architect' by the Architects Registration Acts, there is no need for the alternative 'supervisory officer' to be added to the word 'landscape architect' and the Form as printed is therefore equally suitable for unamended use by landscape scientists, ecologists, leisure and amenity managers.

The Form was revised in April 1981 to bring it into line with the new clauses and sequence of JCT 1980 Minor Works edition and was reprinted with minor corrections in April 1982 and again in 1985 to include the option of Bills of Quantities and to enable the form to be used in Scotland. It is now the recommended form of contract for all public local authority and private sector landscape contracts (landscape works executed as subcontracts are dealt with in the following chapter).

The 1981 edition provided the requirement for the contractor to price any Schedules or schedules of rates included as contract documents in the 1st and 2nd Recitals, so that the Form was suitable both for those contracts with quantities and those with only drawings and specifications, (but without the requirement for quantities to comply with the SMM previously described as inadequate). It provided for the option of naming any quantity surveyor the employer intended to appoint, e.g. for the valuation of variations, but, as in the JCT Minor Works Contract, did not specify any particular duties and also specifically excluded from the contract sum the value added tax that was always due from the employer on landscape contracts.

5.3 ARBITRATION

It is essential to realise that since *Sutcliffe v. Thakrah* the landscape architect is no longer considered a 'quasi-arbitrator' since he is an employee of the client with only the duty under the contract to act 'fairly and reasonably'. Only when the contractor gives notice that he considers this to be no longer the case is a 'dispute' considered to have arisen. Then the provisions of the arbitration clause for the appointment of an independent arbitrator under the 1950 and 1979 Arbitration Acts come into force. The effect of this is therefore that the landscape architects' decisions are no longer inviolate and can always be challenged if the landscape contractor feels sufficiently aggrieved and if he considers the amount or principle involved to justify the not-inconsiderable costs of arbitration proceedings.

Regrettably, from time to time the parties to the contract – namely the employer, or the landscape architect on his behalf, and the contractor – cannot reach agreement on some dispute that has arisen between them, such as the valuation of a particular variation or an extension to the contract period for completion of the works. Most contracts provide for this eventuality by the inclusion of a clause providing for disputes to be submitted to one or more impartial persons to settle the matter.

The JCLI Contract is no exception and sets out in Article 4 for such disputes to be submitted to the binding decision of an arbitrator agreed between them or should this not be possible, appointed by the President or Vice President of the Landscape Institute. Under these circumstances the courts are reluctant to interfere and hear the case, unless there is some specific question of law involved. Such arbitrations are governed by the Arbitration Acts of 1950 and 1979, when the arbitrator's decision, published in the form of an Award, is final and binding on both parties and without the right of appeal. Arbitrations usually take place after practical completion. Should this situation arise, a letter on the lines shown in Fig. 5.1, setting the necessary procedures in motion, should suffice.

An arbitration will usually take the following form:

1. After a preliminary meeting between the parties the Arbitrator will issue directions for the exchange of 'pleadings' and the arrangements for the place, date and time of the hearing.
2. When the parties have submitted to each other in writing a short summary of their claim, the defence and counter claim, reply, any further or better particulars, and have inspected the supporting documents and evidence,

the Arbitrator fixes a date and time for the hearing.

3. At the hearing, each side presents his case with full supporting evidence, witnesses and experts. A hearing will normally last two or three days although hearings of six months or even a year are not unknown.

4. After the close of the hearing the Arbitrator draws up his Award, giving his decision in writing, and directs which of the parties is to pay their own and the other's costs.

Some of the advantages for landscape contracts of submitting disputes to arbitration rather than submitting them to the courts, particularly if the dispute is on technical matters, are:

1. The hearing is private with only the parties to the dispute, their lawyers, witnesses and experts present.

2. The time and place of the hearing can be arranged to suit the convenience of all concerned.

3. If the parties so wish, a decision can be arrived at more quickly and cheaply than through the courts.

4. The person chosen as Arbitrator will usually be fully conversant with the technical aspect of the problem.

```
Dear Sirs,

Whereas disputes and differences have arisen between you and ourselves
within the meaning of Article 4 of the Contract dated ...............
between ..................... and .................... I here give
you notice of our intention to have such differences settled by
arbitration in accordance with the provisions of the Article.

Yours faithfully,
```

Fig. 5.1 Example letter setting arbitration procedures in motion.

5.4 THE CONDITIONS

Having left space blank at the top of the contents page of the contract, for the parties to enter into the contract under seal (should they desire to extend the statutory period of Limitation from 6 to 12 years) the actual Conditions of the contract are contained on four A4 pages under eight headings. (Appendix C contains a specimen copy of the JCLI Standard Form.)

1 The intentions of the parties

1.1 The *contractor* is obliged to carry out and complete the works in a good and workmanlike manner, only being relieved of his obligation to comply with the contract documents where the landscape architect has reserved to himself the approval of the quality of certain materials and workmanship. (This is of course irrespective of the landscape architect's responsibilities to his client to monitor the work of the contractor.)

1.2 The *landscape architect* (who is not a party to the contract) is made specifically responsible for supplying, on the employer's behalf, any necessary further information, issuing certificates and confirming all instructions in writing.

2 Commencement and completion

2.1 Space for inserting the date given in the tender documents on which the work *may* be commenced (there is no obligation on the contractor to do so) is left, as is space for the date by which the contractor is obliged to complete the work.

2.2 The landscape architect is responsible for *extending* in writing the period for completion of the works by a reasonable amount of time for reasons which the contractor has notified him as having delayed completion (not progress) and which were not under his (the contractor's) control. Most landscape architects will consider the 'relevant events' in JCT80 clause 25 as being reasons beyond the control of the contractor. There is however no requirement for the landscape architect to justify what he considers to be reasonable nor to quantify and total each individual reason.

2.3 Pre-estimating the amount of *damages for non-completion* (never, it must be remembered, to be punitive) in this way saves the necessity of proving in court the amount of damages suffered – which would otherwise be required if the damages were left at large. In assessing the amount of such damages, allowances must be made for:

'notional loss of interest on capital'
'inconvenience or any actual consequential loss'
'additional professional fees'.

It is generally accepted that the amount of notional loss of interest per week is arrived at by such a formula as:

$$\frac{\text{Contract sum}}{52 \text{ weeks}} \times \frac{\text{bank rate}}{100} = \pounds \ldots \text{ per week}$$

To this should be added any consequential loss (rare on landscape projects) together with a pre-estimate of the weekly cost of any additional professional fees.

2.4 The *completion date* to be certified by the landscape architect is that when in his opinion the works have reached 'practical completion'. Not 'practically' (i. e. almost) complete but 'practical completion of the works,' which is generally accepted as being when the works are sufficiently complete for them to be safely and conveniently used for the purpose for which they have been designed. No strict definition of these words, in the restricted use to which they are put, has ever been laid down in the courts (and it is hoped never will be since were this to happen it would restrict the judgment of the landscape architect), every particular situation at the moment being considered on its merits.

2.5 *Defects* to all items of work - other than the failure of trees, shrubs, grass and other plants - are to be made good at the contractor's expense within three months (or such other period as is stated in the tender documents and inserted here) and the landscape architect is to certify when in his opinion these have been made good.

2.6 *Partial possession* is not provided for in the JCT Form since it was not considered likely to arise in the type of project for which the form was intended. On landscape projects however, it was appreciated that circumstances could arise such as when the work was completed in all respects, except that the seeding of grass areas would have to be postponed until such time as its germination could be ensured, or the planting of tree clumps postponed until bare root stock could be safely lifted. Under these circumstances, rather than issue a certificate of practical completion and exclude the grass or trees as 'an outstanding item' under this clause, it is possible in landscape contracts to leave part of the site in the possession of the contractor. He will therefore remain responsible for its security and protection from malicious damage etc., and the employer (with the consent of the contractor), for reasons not envisaged at the commencement of the contract, to take possession and have use of and pay for that part of the site that has been finished, to release half the retention on the part handed over and to start the Defects Liability Period from the date that the part was taken over.

2.7 *Plant failures* prior to practical completion of the works are always to be replaced by the landscape contractor entirely at his own cost, with the exception of those found to be missing as a result of theft or malicious damage, which are dealt with under a separate clause.

JCLI Practice Note 1 deals with plant failures at practical completion as follows:

'All plants which have failed prior to Practical Completion or within six weeks of the first leafing out in the case of trees, shrubs or grass at the first cut and roll whichever is the later, are to be replaced by the Contractor entirely at his own expense unless it arises from theft or malicious damage after Practical Completion.'

At an appropriate time, the contractor and landscape architect should meet to establish the extent of any defects and failures. The landscape architect will then prepare a schedule of these defects and send it to the contractor within fourteen days. The contractor will inform the landscape architect when the work has been rectified.

After practical completion, plant failures are dealt with in one of two ways.

(a) If the upkeep of the site during the Defects Liability Period, inserted in the tender and contract documents for the various types of plants, is to be undertaken by the landscape contractor then he is made responsible for the replacement (at his own cost) of any of them that have died or are found to be dying while he has been responsible for their maintenance. The landscape architect is required to certify at the end of the period when this replacement has been satisfactorily completed.

(b) Alternatively, if the employer is responsible for the upkeep after practical completion, then the contractor is relieved of further responsibility and should any plants subsequently be found to be dead or dying, since injudicious or inadequate maintenance by the employer could clearly have resulted in the early demise of the plants concerned, the employer will have to make his own arrangements and pay for the replacements whether through the initial contractor or another.

In early drafts of the contract the above word 'upkeep' was used instead of maintenance, it being considered this would differentiate it from the maintenance of the hard landscape and buildings; but it was decided by the LI that more common usage used to describe the Defects Liability Period should prevail.

3 Control of the works

3.1 *Assignment* of the whole contract either by the employer or by the landscape contractor without the consent of the other is precluded by this clause (which did not appear in the 1978 edition but was added in 1981 to conform with MW80.)

3.2 *Subcontracting* without the consent of the landscape architect (which shall not be unreasonably withheld) is similarly precluded. It should be noted that there is no provision in this Form for work to be carried out concurrently on the site by others directly employed by the employer.

3.3 The contractor is obliged to keep a *competent person* in charge on site at all reasonable times, who is specifically authorized to receive instructions on the contractor's behalf. There is no provision for the right of access to the works either for the architect or a clerk of works this being an implied condition, since the landscape architect could not otherwise carry out the various duties required of him in the other conditions in the contract.

3.4   The landscape architect may *object to the employment* of certain individuals on site (not their employment by the contractor, which might conflict with the Employment Protection Act of 1975), should he consider them to be incompetent, or their behaviour to be offensive.

3.5   The landscape architect is empowered to issue variations and *instructions*, which by implication include those concerning opening up and the removal of defective work. These must be in writing. In addition, the 1981 edition carries the option for the employer to instruct others to do any work which the contractor has neglected to do in compliance with an instruction, and to deduct the cost from any money due to the contractor.

3.6   *Variations* may be ordered by the landscape architect (and are therefore legally binding on the employer), to add, omit or change the works or the order or period when they are to be carried out, and for these to be valued by the landscape architect (not the contractor) on a fair and reasonable basis using the prices referred to in the First and Second Recital.

There is also the proviso, which does not exist in the JCT Minor Works Contract, that if any omission substantially varies the scope of the work, this shall take into account the effect on the cost of the remainder of the work. There is also the option for the landscape architect and the contractor to 'agree' the price of a variation prior to carrying it out – this is always to be recommended, if possible.

3.7   *Provisional and P C sums* are defined in *SMM*. Provisional sums are for work or costs which cannot be entirely foreseen, defined or detailed at the time of issuing the tender documents. Prime cost (p.c.) sums are those for work by a nominated subcontractor, statutory authority, public undertaking or materials or goods to be obtained from a nominated supplier, the sum to be exclusive of any profit required by the general contractor, for which provision should be made for it to be included in the tender. When making such provision it is recommended that a clause such as the following be used:

'Include the p.c. (provisional) sum of £... for... to be executed by a specialist subcontractor selected by the landscape architect. Add for profit and attendance.'

Additionally, if the identity of the subcontractor proposed is known at the time of the invitation to tender, his name can be inserted and equally important when appropriate the period of time the subcontractor needs to carry out and complete the work. This eliminates the possibility of any future claim from the main contractor. When the identity of a subcontractor is not known to him at the time of tender and consequently he has no way of finding out how long he needs to execute the subcontract work.

There is no provision in the form for any cash discount from a

49

nominated subcontractor or supplier, nor for any direct payment by the employer in the event of default by the main contractor.

Should it be possible to draw and/or describe the work to be carried out or supplied by specialists sufficiently accurately for it to be included in the tender and contract documents for it to be priced, it is often preferable to include the names of those firms the contractor is restricted to use, by including a clause such as the following.

'The landscape work, in accordance with this specification and drawings no. ...,
shall be carried out by one of the following registered members of the British
Association of Landscape Industries (BALI):

> 1 . . . .
> 2 . . . .
> 3 . . . .
> 4 . . . .
> 5 . . . .

or other landscape contractor approved prior to the submission of tenders.'

There are no Standard Forms of subcontract that the main contractor is obliged to use or that is available for use for nominated, named or 'domestic' (i. e. chosen entirely at the discretion of the main contractor under clause 3.2) subcontractors in connection with the JCLI Form; that included in Appendix B may be appropriate, landscape architects and contractors must however ensure that it meets their own requirements, and if necessary take legal advice before adopting it.

3.8 *Objections to a nomination* may be made by the main contractor but this clause will not apply if the identity of the subcontractor(s) have been made known to him at the time of tender in accordance with the previous clause.

3.9 *Disturbance of regular progress* for reasons within the control of the employer, his agents or servants (and no other), entitle the contractor to be reimbursed by such sum as the landscape architect ascertains and which he includes in progress payments as being due.

Neither of the above two clauses exists in the JCT Minor Works Form.

4 Payment

4.1 The correction of any inconsistencies that may be discovered, in or between the contract documents, is acknowledged in the Contract and is provided for with the simple statement that they shall be corrected and, if this involves a variation, valued as such, leaving every case to be treated on its merits. The question of precedence is dealt with by the statement that the contract conditions shall prevail over all others, leaving by implication the accepted convention that drawings take precedence for location, Bills for quantity, and the specification for quality.

4.2   *Progress payments* are provided for: 'when requested by the contractor at intervals of not less than 4 weeks from the date of commencement' (the actual date *not* the one in the contract after which the works *may* be commenced) without any limitation on the minimum amount claimed. The landscape architect has only to include for work 'properly' executed. This does not relieve the contractor of his obligations under clause 1.1 to complete the works in accordance with the contract documents nor place any contractual obligation on the landscape architect to ensure that he does so. It does however enable him to deduct the value of any work not in accordance with the contract, from an Interim Certificate and, as they are continuing valuations, any work included in a previous certificate and subsequently found to be defective can be also deducted from the Certificate.

There is no specific provision for the removal of defective work; when this arises the landscape architect issues the necessary instructions under clause 3.5 and, in the event of non-compliance, the employer may arrange for the work to be carried out by others.

The clause also provides for unfixed materials on site to be included in Interim Certificates notwithstanding the fact that legally possession does not otherwise pass to the employer until they are fixed. To prevent problems of retention of title (such as those which arose to the Romalpa and Dawber Williamson cases, in neither of which was there any contract between the supplier of the goods in question and the employer) it is always advisable to include in the contract documents a clause such as the following:

'At the time of each valuation the contractor is to disclose to the landscape architect which of the unfixed materials and goods on site are free from, and which are subject to, any reservation of title inconsistent with the passing of property as required by clause 4.2 of the Conditions of Contract, together with their respective values. When requested provide evidence of freedom from reservation of title'. ©NBS Services Ltd.

This is particularly important in the case of plants delivered to site and temporarily stored pending planting in their final locations. Equally, problems may arise with materials stored 'off site' until required, i.e. in the landscape contractor's nursery. In these instances they must be both properly insured and clearly identified if the landscape architect is to be asked to use his discretion and include them in an Interim Certificate.

Retention is provided by the deduction of 5% from each certificate without the option of the insertion of any other amount, nor with any requirement for it to be identified and held in trust for the contractor. Amounts previously certified (not paid) are also to be deducted from the valuation for each certificate and the certificate is to be honoured within

Askham Bryan College
of Agriculture and Horticulture
LIBRARY BOOK

14 days of issue (not receipt). It is now usual for the certificate to be forwarded to the client direct with a copy sent concurrently to the contractor (see Chapter 9).

4.3   *Penultimate Certificates* are to be issued within 14 days of practical completion, releasing half the amount of the retention and based on the contract sum adjusted to include the value of any variations and the adjustment of p.c. and provisional sums. For this reason if the contractor is to be responsible for the subsequent upkeep of the landscape work this should be valued separately (see Chapter 9) and not be included in the main contract sum.

For the same reason there is provision in this clause for the amount of retention to be increased if the amount of plant failures are considered to be in excess of 10%, when the amount retained is to be adjusted accordingly by increasing the retention by the amount of the Bill rates for the defective items. This Certificate is also to be honoured within 14 days of issue.

4.4   The *Final Certificate*. Under both JCT and JCLI Forms the contractor is obliged to provide all the financial evidence the landscape architect needs to complete the final valuation, within 3 months (or such other period as is inserted) of the certificate of practical completion. The landscape architect must then issue his Final Certificate within the following 28 days *provided* the Defects Liability Period has expired, and the landscape architect has certified that all defective items have been made good in accordance with clause 2.5.

It must be emphasized that in this instance, although the architect has a duty to act fairly and has a duty to his client not to over-certify, he must not be subjected to improper pressures from his client to withold the certificate (*Hickman v. Roberts*, 1913). Nor is he immune from charges of negligence in the issue of a final certificate, it having been held since 1974 (*Sutcliffe v. Thakrah*) that he is no longer a 'quasi-arbitrator' as had been thought to have been the case since *Chambers v. Goldthorpe* in 1901.

The duty of the landscape architect to issue certificates is clearly laid down in the conditions of the contract. If he does not do so at the proper time the landscape contractor's remedy is to submit the matter to an arbitrator appointed by the current President of the Landscape Institute. This need not be an expensive or lengthy procedure and if the certificate is still not forthcoming it can be enforced by the courts.

4.5   *Contributions, levies and tax changes.* If any unforeseen changes are suddenly imposed by the Government they could impose considerable burdens on a contractor since, under a fixed-price contract, he could in no way pass them on to the employer. This eventuality is therefore covered by Part A of the supplementary Memorandum and incorporated by reference in clause 4.5. Since this covers only 'work people', and excludes site and head office supervisory staff, levies and taxes on materials are covered by an additional percentage to be added to cover the cost of these items: 20% being generally considered appropriate for fluctuation contracts in excess of 12 months, 10% for fixed-price contracts of 12 months or less. There is the option of deleting the whole clause if the contract is of such a limited duration as to make it inappropriate.

4.6 *Fixed price/fluctuations.* Many landscape projects are of a duration of 12 months or less, when it is reasonable for a contractor to provide in his tender for any change in the cost of labour, materials, plant or other resources subsequent to the submission of his tender. There are many other instances, such as when planting has to be postponed until the beginning of the next planting season or when the needs of the project are such that it has to be spread over two seasons from the outset, and it is then prudent to allow the contractor to recover the actual cost of any increase that may arise. This is done by using category 48 of the Board of Trade (NEDO Formula) monthly index of costs of landscape work in accordance with Part D of the Supplementary Memorandum and Formula Rules which are incorporated by reference in the alternative clause 4.6B having deleted clause 4.6A.

Where provided for in the tender documents, the *recovery of unforeseen increased costs* arising during the progress of landscape works is achieved by the use of the 'Formula Rules' (clause 4.6B of the JCLI Form of Contract).

The Government's decision on the use of the Formula Method of calculating fluctuation in public sector work (DoE Circular 158/73, Welsh Code 313/73 and Scottish Office 2/1974, the preparation of cost indices prepared for NEDO by the EDC for Building) resulted in the publication of the HMSO booklet *Price adjustment formulae; guide to application and procedure (series 2)* and the *Description of indices,* using indices compiled and maintained by the Property Services Agency of the DoE as monthly bulletins.

The Formula Rules for work category indices (series 2) published by the Joint Contracts Tribunal are obtainable from the RIBA, the RICS and the NFBTE. They set out the method of adjusting the contract sum at each interim valuation by adjusting the value of work included in that valuation in accordance with the movement of the index numbers in the monthly bulletins (series 2) referred to above, together with a practice note (33) and worked examples giving guidance on the application of the rules for the Standard Form of Building Contract.

With regard to the JCLI Standard Form for Landscape Works this is covered in Category 48 (series 2) 'soft landscaping' and is included in the list of indices published monthly. These are available from HMSO and

53

are also published monthly in the building business section of *Building* magazine.

The application of the index follows the normal lines, e.g.

Increase =

$$\frac{\text{Valuation month index} - \text{base month index} \times \text{value of work done in month}}{\text{Base month index}}$$

Costs are based on June 1976 = 100.

5 Statutory obligations

5.1 *Statutory obligations, notices, fees and charges* are the responsibility of the contractor, whether specifically referred to in the contract documents or not. If the contractor finds anything in them that he considers will involve him in a contravention, the contract requires him to notify the landscape architect. Should he comply with the contract documents and a contravention is subsequently discovered, the contract provides for the cost of compliance to be recovered from the employer.

5.2 *Value added tax* on landscape work is nearly always due at the standard rate. Customs and Excise Note 708 specifically excludes 'site restoration' which is defined as 'the clearance of rubble, levelling the land, the application of topsoil and the laying of grass and simple paths, the planting of trees or shrubs or elaborate ornamental work apart from new building work which was otherwise zero rated'. The contract sum being exclusive of value added tax, this is to be collected by the contractor separately from the employer, in accordance with Part B of the Supplementary Memorandum; this also provides the necessary procedures for the employer (through the contractor) to challenge any tax which he considers to have been incorrectly imposed.

5.3 *Statutory tax deduction scheme* legislation makes the employer liable for any tax on the income of a self-employed person in the building industry which he may not have disclosed. It is therefore essential that employers, or landscape architects on their behalf, obtain copies of, or sight of, the current certificates of exemption from all the contractors and subcontractors they intend to employ, and to establish the necessary procedures at the outset of the contract so that they are not subsequently held responsible for the unpaid tax of the firms they employ.

5.4 Although the *Fair Wages Resolution* has now been rescinded this clause is still necessary to cover the eventuality of it remaining in some local authority standing orders.

5.5 *Prevention of corruption.* By the use of the words 'shall be entitled to' this clause allows the employer the option of cancelling the contract and recovering the amount of any loss which he may have incurred as a result

54

of the contractor having made any gift or consideration covered by the various Prevention of Corruption and Local Government Acts.

6 Injury, damage and insurance

6.1 *Injury to, or death of, persons* arising from carrying out the work is the sole responsibility of the contractor who has not only to indemnify the employer, but also to take out sufficient insurance to ensure that he has the financial resources to meet any claim which may arise (even after the work is finished) unless it arises from any act or neglect of the employer or any person for whom the employer is responsible.

6.2 *Damage to property* is similarly the sole responsibility of the contractor, for which he must also have the necessary insurance to ensure he can cover his liabilities. In this instance however he is responsible only for claims arising from his own negligence; there is no provision for any insurance under this contract to cover any damage arising from the negligence of the employer, nor is there provision for the amount of the limit of the indemnity to be inserted (e.g. £50 000 for any one occurence). The requirement is for 'any damage whatsoever'. Should employers doubt that the contractor has sufficient insurance on a particular project to cover his obligations, this can be remedied by use of the powers under the later clause 6.4 requiring the contractor to provide the necessary evidence.

6.3 *Insurance of the works* against damage arising from the normal perils of fire, flooding, etc. is usually made the responsibility of the contractor for new work, and the employer for alterations. On new work the employer's interest should be endorsed on the policy for the full value of the works including landscape architects fees, unfixed materials, removal of debris and reinstatement and current costs. Any consequential loss to the employer, and to the contractor's temporary buildings and plant are excluded.

6.4 The clause on *evidence of insurance* provides for the production of such evidence as the employer may reasonably require 'that the necessary insurances have been taken out and are in force'. Although not specifically required, a formal 'Certificate of Insurance' is normally the best way of dealing with this.

6.5 *Malicious damage*, both before and after practical completion, is an increasing problem on landscape projects. Clause 6.5A makes the landscape contractor entirely responsible for making good, at his own expense, all damage arising from theft and malicious damage prior to practical completion. On sites where the risk of such damage to the work is considered to be abnormally high (and the nature of landscape work makes this more common than on building contracts), it may be in the employer's interest to include a provisional sum in the tender conditions to cover the anticipated cost of making good such damage. This is provided for in clause 6.5B. While the contractor is still required to take all steps as are reasonable to minimize the risks of such damage in the event of it occuring, he is then paid no more and no less than the actual cost of the necessary reinstatment without any increase in the total contract sum.

7 Determination

The employment of the contractor (not the contract – an entirely different matter) can be terminated by either the employer or the contractor under the provisions of clauses 7.1 and 7.2. Notwithstanding the apparent simplicity of these two clauses, meticulous and informed legal advice is essential in the drafting and delivery of the necessary notices if the required determination is to be properly delivered and not repudiated.

7.1 *Determination by the employer* can only be made for one of two reasons: either if the contractor has failed 'to proceed dilegently' or has wholly suspended the carrying out of the works, or in the event of his having failed financially. In the first case the employer has to prove that the contractor has not merely 'postponed' the work; in the second case it is a matter of fact. In both cases the employer (not the landscape architect) has to 'serve' the notice and the contractor then has to give up the site immediately.

7.2 *Determination by the contractor* can be effected for only one of four reasons:

1. If the employer is more than 14 days late in making progress payments.
2. If the employer obstructs the carrying out of the works.
3. If the employer suspends the work for over a month.
4. If the employer fails financially.

Should any one of these occur then the employer has 7 days from receipt of the notice in which to put matters right.

8 The Supplementary Memorandum

This sets out in detail the provisions regarding tax changes, value added tax and the statutory tax deduction scheme which are incorporated by references in clauses 4.5, 5.2 and 5.3.

5.5 USE OF THE FORM IN SCOTLAND

The JCLI form was noted as 'not for use in Scotland', it having been drafted in accordance with the provisions of English and not Scots law. The primary difference is that effecting the legally binding nature of the offer and its acceptance. The JCLI form can now be used in Scotland the line 'subject to the proper law of this contract being English law' having been inserted in the 1st Recital. The parties to any contract can choose the law to apply to it, e.g. civil engineering work in the Middle East is often carried out subject to English law.

It is also necessary to distinguish the law of the place where the work is to be performed, e.g. for the contractor to comply with the statutory obligations, building regulations, and the law of the place where the arbitration referred to in Article 4 is to take place, although this could well follow Scots procedures if required without causing any difficulty.

Similar provisions may apply to work carried out under the laws applicable to Northern Ireland.

5.6 THE JCT INTERMEDIATE FORM IFC84

The JCLI Agreement for Landscape Works was first issued in April 1978 at which time the 1968 JCT Minor Works Form on which it was based had no provision for 'Plant failures' nor 'Malicious damage', neither did it cover:

2.6   Partial possession;
3.6   The valuation of variations using tender rates;
3.8   P.C. Sums and objections to nominations;
3.9   Direct loss and expense if progress is disturbed;
4.6   Fluctuations;

and detailed provisions were therefore incorporated to cover these aspects.

While suitable for the majority of landscape contracts over the six years since it was first published, instances have occured of local authorities expressing reluctance to use the Form on landscape contracts in excess of £75 000.

The JCT has now published an 'Intermediate' Form (IFC84) for use on all contracts both private and public sector, local authority, with or without quantities, prepared in accordance with the Standard Method of Measurement (SMM6). While it still does not cover plant failures and malicious damage, the remaining aspects previously ommitted are now provided for.

For those larger landscape contracts where the detailed provisions of the JCT Intermediate Form may be appropriate the following supplementary clauses (which are detailed in Appendix D) may be incorporated:

Partial possession by the employer – use IFC84 clause 2.11 (note this is optional in IFC84).
Failures of plants – use JCLI clauses 2.7A and 2.7B, with the last three lines of 4.3.
Malicious damage – use JCLI clause 6.5A.

As with JCT 80, obligatory forms of tender and subcontract are required to be used for 'named' subcontractors (Forms NAM/T and NAM/SC). In this instance, however, the NAM/SC subcontract conditions are incorporated by reference and are not required to be signed as part of the subcontract document.

5.7 THE ICE FORM

While the JCLI conditions are applicable to most landscape projects, those for large amounts of earth moving, roads, and footpaths are often executed under the ICE Form. This is a re-measurement contract with all the work re-measured, valued and paid for on completion irrespective of the amounts given in the tender and contract document (clauses 56). The engineer has far greater powers under this Form than any other, and has wider discretion with regard to the programme and sequence for the progress of the work. The other main difference are as follows.

Clause 10 makes provision for securities for due performance if required.

Clauses 11 and 12 acknowledge the possibility of any unforeseeable physical conditions or artificial obstructions.

Clause 19: the contractor must provide watching and lighting to the site.

Clauses 20–24 require the contractor always to insure for all risks except hostilities, civil strife, etc. and damage to the works arising from the supervising officer's (S.O.'s) design.

Clause 26A: the employer must serve notices under the Public Utilities Street Works Act when notified by the contractor that work is commencing.

Clause 26 provides for the reimbursement of rates and taxes on temporary buildings.

Clauses 29 and 33 prohibit nuisance and require the removal of rubbish.

Clause 30: the employer accepts responsibility for damage to roads by extra-ordinary traffic.

Clause 35: regular labour returns are to be made if requested.

Clause 38: work shall be opened if notified and made good, at the contractor's expense, if not in accordance with the contract.

Clauses 45–46: night or Sunday work forbidden unless the work is behind schedule and then at no extra cost and no extension unless permission is refused.

Clauses 47–48: only liquidated damages are reduced if partial occupation arises.

Clause 52 allows the S.O. to vary contract rates for variations.

Clause 53 defines plant becoming the property of the employer, and makes special provision for hired plant and hire purchase.

Clauses 58–59: nominated subcontractors and suppliers must pay 2.5% cash discount, and must allow payment to be withheld by the contractor.

Clause 60: interest becomes due on Certificates not honoured by the due date. (But watch out if only the interest is paid and no capital.)

Clause 64: the employer may execute emergency work to prevent accidents.

Clause 65 covers fluctuations of price arising on the outbreak of war.

Clause 66: the engineer's decision is final and binding on both the employer and the contractor.

Clause 67: Contracts executed in Scotland are allowed for.

5.8 GC WORKS 1

Should the project be for a Ministry or Government Department then the work will almost certainly be executed under the GC Works 1. While similar to the JCLI, JCT and ICE Forms it differs in the following respects.

Clause 2 requires the contractor to be wholly responsible for satisfying himself as to site conditions affecting the works.

Clause 3: ownership of all materials, plant and equipment becomes the property of the employer.

Clause 7: Sunday work may be allowed at an extra cost to the employer.

Clause 9 makes no provision for rates to be ever varied in valuing variations.

Clause 13 requires that the contractor provide all facilities for testing, except the cost of work found satisfactory by independent experts.

Clause 14: the contractor must include in his tender for the cost of all notices and fees.

Clauses 17 and 19 cover watching, lighting, nuisance, and the removal of rubbish.

Clause 20: proper provision is made for the use of excavated material in the works.

Clauses 25 and 26: the risk of fire, flood and earthquakes are accepted by the employer, but the contractor must take all reasonable precautions to prevent any damage from them.

Clause 34 requires labour returns to be made daily.

Clause 38: 2.5% cash discount is payable on subcontractors and suppliers but no retention.

Clauses 40–41 The employer may order and pay direct but there is no provision in the event of earlier certified sums being unpaid. Payment can be certified fortnightly on contracts in excess of £50 000. The contractor is paid 95% of the value of work executed, and 80% on materials. One-third of sums is released on 'completion'. The balance when the final account is certified.

Clause 43 allows the employer to recover money outstanding on other contracts from the contractor.

Clause 44: the employer has special powers to determine in the event of the outbreak of war.

Clause 49: the employer also has power to execute emergency work to prevent accidents.

Clauses 56–59 are requirements covering admission to the site, passes, photographs, and the Official Secrets Act.

Clause 61 precludes the Arbitrator from dealing with matters covered in clauses 3, 7, 9, 13, 36, 37, 40, 44, 46, 55 and 56.

The main Forms of Contract (apart from JCLI Standard Form – which is fully covered in Section 5.4) are compared in Table 5.1.

Table 5.1 Forms of Contract and subcontract

ICE Form	Designed for large civil engineering contracts (i.e. bridges, motorways, slagheaps, sewage works, etc.). A very simple form for few trades with wide powers, i.e. engineer can dictate sequence of execution. Simple quantities, e.g. 's & f 1 no. manhole'. All work re-measured as it proceeds.
GC Works 1	A very one-sided contract designed for government (as distinct from local authority) building contracts. Gives wide powers to the architect (S.O.). Comes about half way between ICE and S.F.B.C.
JCT Standard Form of Building Contract (S.F.B.C.)	Incorrectly known as RIBA Form. By now a very complex document in a variety of Forms. i.e. with/without Quantities, Private/Local Authorities (virtually the same), Approximate Quantities, Phased Completion, etc. variants.
JCT Minor Works	The smaller version designed for 3-month contracts up to £30 000 value for use on private, local authority, new and alteration *fixed-price* contracts. Very useful for a wide variety of projects including landscape.

6

Landscape subcontracts

This chapter covers only the general principles of subcontract documentation, highlighting those special characteristics affecting landscape subcontracts. (For detailed consideration of building contracts and subcontracts see *The Standard Form of Building Contract* by John Parris, and *Building Subcontract Forms* by Dennis F. Turner.)

If landscape projects can be carried out under the direction of a landscape architect as a direct contract such as that envisaged by the JCLI conditions between the employer and the landscape contractor this is sometimes in the best interests of all concerned.

6.1 DIRECT SUBCONTRACTS – CONSECUTIVE

It is not always possible to execute projects in this way, and many (such as those connected with buildings) are carried out concurrently with the work of another contractor on the same site at the same time.

Clearly it is simpler if one contractor waits until the other has finished and left the site before starting his own work. This is often possible on projects such as those connected with industry, civil engineering and hospital work, when not only can the landscape work be delayed until the main contractor has cleared up and left the site, but it can also be delayed until the planting can be carried out at a time of year best suited to the establishment of strong and healthy plants.

On landscape work in connection with housing and schools, however, it is essential to have all planting complete and well established before the site is handed over to the future occupants if the plants as well as the buildings are to be treated with the respect to which they are entitled, and the risks of malicious damage minimized.

6.2 DIRECT SUBCONTRACTS – CONCURRENT

'Artists and tradesmen' would seem to be an odd description for a landscape contractor but that was the side heading of the 'Epstein' clause introduced into the earlier forms of the JCT contracts for building work. Under clause 29 of the current form, the employer may, provided that it is described in the tender and contract documents, arrange for others (such as landscape contractors) to enter the main contractor's site and carry out landscape work concurrent with that of the main contractor. Such a division of responsibility must inevitably run great risks of possible dispute on all but the simplest of projects, each side blaming the other – let alone the employer or landscape architect – when something goes wrong. Even when the work is to be carried out by the employer's own staff, e.g. a parks department, great care must be taken to ensure that the main contractor is explicitly informed in the tender documents of the full details of the work involved, if subsequent disputes, claims and arguments are to be avoided.

6.3 DOMESTIC SUBCONTRACTS – CONCURRENT

By far the simplest procedure, therefore, is to arrange for the landscape work to be carried out by the main contractor using his own staff or subcontractor of his own choosing. This however (unless included as a provisional sum) requires all the decisions with regard to planting – including the preparation of detail drawings, planting layouts, schedules and specification – to have been prepared and included in the tender documents. If Bills of Quantities are involved the work must be properly measured and included in the Bills. Clause 19 of the JCT Standard Form of Building Contract then permits the main contractor either to carry out the work himself or to subcontract the work to a firm entirely of his own choosing, possibly one with whom he has already established a good working relationship in the past. Should he decide to subcontract the work this is then subject to the right of reasonable objection by the employer, but the main contractor still accepts full responsibility for its satisfactory completion; he has to arrange for it to be carried out at a time to suit his own convenience and programme, compatible with the needs of the plants for seasonal lifting and their subsequent establishment.

It is important to note that by including the work within the main contract in this way, the employer can withhold his Certificate of Practical Completion should he wish, until the landscape works are also complete.

The advantages of having a standard form of subcontract for use under these circumstances are obvious, each party knowing that it is compatible with the main Form, in time becoming familiar and experienced with its usage, knowing that all aspects and their own requirements are fully covered, and that any special requirements are clearly identified. Such a Form exists for use with the JCT 80 Standard Form of Building Contract. The standard form of subcontract, for Domestic Subcontractors appointed under clauses 19.2 and 19.3 of the 1980 JCT Standard Form of Building Contract, is suitable for use in all editions: Local Authorities or Private, With or Without Quantities. Although prepared by the NFBTE, the Federation of Associations of Specialists and Sub-Contractors, and the Committee of Specialist Engineering Contractors, its use ensures that the obligations of the main contractor are effectively transferred to the subcontractor and are therefore equally appropriate for landscape subcontractors on building contracts.

The actual form is published in two parts, the first being the Articles of Agreement comprising the four Recitals, identifying the scope of the subcontract works, the main contract works, and the right of inspection of the main contract conditions. The three Articles cover the main and subcontract provisions, obligations and conditions, the subcontract sum (either lump sum or re-measured), an arbitration clause providing for an Arbitrator appointed by the president of the RICS, and for the law of subcontract to be the law of England unless otherwise stated. The form provides also for the subcontract sum to be entered into the Form and for it to be signed by the main contractor and subcontractor, under hand or seal as required.

The second part comprises the subcontract conditions which can be incorporated by reference under Article 1.3. The Conditions run to 37 clauses over 44 pages which, although they adopt decimal numbering, are neither section-headed nor follow the same sequence as JCT 80. They do, however, deal exhaustively with all aspects of subcontract work likely to arise on the larger building and specialist engineering subcontract under the headings listed in Table 6.1.

The NFBTE (BEC) also published in August 1984, as Amendment No. 1, an additional clause 21.4.5 relating to the ownership of unfixed subcontract materials and goods on site which have been included in an Interim Certificate so that they become the property of the Employer when the Employer has honoured the certificate and paid the main contractor. This effectively overcomes the Romalpa problems of the Dawber Williams case relating to roofing tiles – although this view is not universally held.

The JCLI has now prepared a standard form of subcontract (Appendix B) for use with the JCLI Standard Form of Agreement for Landscape Works (Appendix C). This form incorporates, for the information of subcontract tenderers, the conditions of the Main contract and on the reverse the Form of Tender for the subcontractor works on which the subcontractor enters his price, to this are attached the Conditions drafted to mirror the obligations of the Employer and Main Contractor into the subcontract.

6.4 LISTED SUBCONTRACTORS

The particular nature of landscape works, with the problems of plant supplies and the difficulties in the precise specification of workmanship and materials, often make it advisable to restrict the main contractor's choice of subcontractors for the landscape work to only those of proven experience and ability. To

Table 6.1 Standard form of subcontract for use with JCT 80 Standard Form of Building Contract – main clause headings.

1.	Interpretation.	20.	Finance (No. 2) Act 1975.
2.	Subcontract documents.	21.	Payment of subcontractor.
3.	Subcontract sum additions.	22.	Benefits under main contract.
4.	Directors for subcontract works.	23.	Right to set off.
5.	Subcontract liability.	24.	Adjudicating subcontract claims.
6.	Injury to persons/property.	25.	Right of access.
7.	Subcontract insurance.	26.	Assignment of subletting.
8.	Clause 22 perils.	27.	Attendance.
9.	Insurance policies.	28.	Interference with property.
10.	Responsibility for subcontract plant.	29.	Determination of subcontract by main contractor.
11.	Subcontract date for completion.	30.	Determination of subcontract by subcontractor.
12.	Failure to complete.		
13.	Direct loss and expense.	31.	Determination of main contract.
14	Subcontract Practical Completion.	32.	Fair wages.
		33.	Loss and expense by strikes.
15.	Subcontract price.	34.	Fluctuations method.
16.	Valuation of variations.	35.	Contractors' levies and taxes.
17.	Valuation of subcontract works.	36.	Fluctuations in cost.
18.	Bills of Quantities – SMM.	37.	Formula adjustment.
19.	Value added tax.		

ensure some control over the choice of suitable landscape subcontractors, employers and their landscape architects often specify – as suggested in Section 5.4.3 – a list of three or four firms of an acceptable standard restricting the choice of main contractor to the firms named from whom he is to obtain tenders. At the same time he is allowed, at his sole discretion, to choose the one to carry out the work, then accepting full responsibility for their satisfactory performance, making his own arrangements for payment, and deciding when the subcontract work is to be carried out.

This is also covered by clause 19 of the JCT Form of Building Contract. Although it provides for either party with the consent of the other (which shall not be unreasonably withheld) to add additional firms to the list at any time, the specification should include a clause requiring the main contractor to request approval to any addition or substitution 10 days prior to the tender date. A suitable form of enquiry to take up references on subcontractors put forward by main contractors is shown in Fig 6.1. It is important to ensure that when submitting their tender, contractors should be asked to name which of the listed subcontractors they have chosen and included.

A subcontractor selected by the main contractor in this way remains a domestic subcontractor, so that the main contractor has no right to an extension of time for any delay on the part of the subcontractor and also accepts full responsibility for the performance of the subcontractor he has selected. He accepts sole responsibility for conduct and execution on site, having also to sort out any delayed starting dates, sequence of trades, and disputes with others employed on the works at the same time. This is a most valuable provision in building contracts, and may become the standard way of selecting subcontractors for work on building contracts in the future. It has been suggested that it may not produce the lowest tenders, but as there is every incentive for the main contractor to select not the lowest but the most reliable subcontractors, this would appear to be unlikely, and the knowledge that the lowest tenderer has included the most reliable and suitable subcontractors at the same time accepting responsibility for their proper performance would suggest its increasingly widespread adoption.

6.5 NOMINATED SUBCONTRACTORS ON LUMP-SUM BUILDING CONTRACTS

On those occasions when for one reason or another it has not been possible to measure and accurately describe the landscape work in the tender documents, or it is necessary to restrict the work to a *single* landscape subcontractor chosen by the employer or his landscape architect, for one of the three reasons said by Banwell to justify nomination, i.e. (1) when special techniques are required; (2) when early ordering is necessary; or (3) when a particular quality of work is essential (all of which apply to landscape work), then under clause 19 of the JCT Standard Form, this requires the inclusion of a prime cost sum in the tender documents and for the work to be carried out as a nominated subcontract under clause 35.

As the procedures to be followed when a landscape subcontractor is nominated under clause 35, had been devised so that they may be applied to all

Spon's Landscape Contract Manual

PRIVATE & CONFIDENTIAL

Dear Sirs,

We have been given your name by the above in connection with their request to be considered for work to be carried out under our direction.

We would be very grateful if you would complete the attached copy of the following questionnaire and return it to us in the envelope provided as soon as possible.

(Please indicate by ✓)   Below Av./Average/Above Av.

1. Office and site organization			
2. Standard of workmanship			
3. Observance of completion dates			
4. Availability of labour and co-ordination of sub contractors and suppliers			
5. Willingness to make good defects			
6. Absence of unreasonable claims and prompt settlement of accounts			

7. What would you consider to be the maximum value of any one contract they could undertake?   £ ....

8. Would you use them again?   YES/NO

9. Any other comments:

Yours faithfully,

Fig. 6.1 Example letter of enquiry to take up references on subcontractors.

building nominated subcontracts, e.g. heating and electrical engineering, piling, fixing external cladding and the like, much of the detail such as that relating to shop drawings is inapplicable to landscape work, but even had the procedures not been made obligatory, landscape subcontractors on building contracts would still have needed the same information to be provided in their tender documents.

6.5.1 Clause 35

The effect of this is that, in return for the right to restrict the work to a single landscape subcontractor of his own choosing, the employer loses his right to liquidated damages if the main contract completion is delayed by the landscape subcontractor, and the landscape subcontractor is entitled to direct payment if the main contractor does not pay amounts stated as being due to him in Interim Certificates.

6.5.2 NSC2

The problem of the loss of liquidated and ascertained damages is overcome in clause 35 by the use of a separate agreement between the employer and subcontractor in which they enter into a direct contractual arrangement (NSC2) where clause 3.4 states that:

'The subcontractor shall so perform the Subcontract that the Contractor will not be entitled to an extension of time for completion of the Main Contract works by reason of the Relevant Event in clause 24.4.7 of the Main Contract conditions'.

NSC2 also requires the subcontractor to warrant that he has exercised, and will exercise, all reasonable skill and care in the design of any of the work, in the selection of any goods or materials, and in the satisfaction of any performance specification for which he is responsible.

The employer is then entitled to recover from the subcontractor the liquidated and ascertained damages he has lost as a result of having had to grant an extension to the contract period of the main contractor by reason of the delay caused by the nominated landscape subcontractor. For this reason – so that the nominated subcontractor is aware of the amount of liquidated damages and the contract period in the main contract – the use of a standard from of tender containing this information (NSC1) is also made obligatory.

6.5.3 NSC1

This 12-page standard Form of Tender the use of which is obligatory (unless the alternative method using NSC2a/4a is used) thus ensuring that all the information required both by the main contractor and the subcontractor is known to each other before they enter into their subcontract.

The key sections of this document are in the two pages (9 and 10), comprising the second schedule completed in turn by the landscape architect, the landscape subcontractor, and the main contractor – before the subcontract is entered into. As can be seen from the following worked example (Fig. 6.2):

First, in Section 1A: the landscape architect, before sending the Form of Tender to the subcontractor(s), inserts the period during which he estimates the site will be available for the landscape works to be carried out on site.

Secondly, in 1B2: the landscape subcontractor inserts the period he estimates he will actually need to complete satisfactorily the work for which he is tender-

Schedule 2: Particular Conditions

Town and Country Landscapes Ltd.
Dukes Meadows
Mortlake, SW14

Note: When the Contractor receives Tender NSC/1 together with the Architect/Supervising Officer's preliminary notice of nomination under clause 35·7·1 of the Main Contract Conditions then the Contractor has to settle and complete any of the particular conditions which remain to be completed in this Schedule in

agreement with the proposed Sub-Contractor. The completed Schedule should take account not only of the preliminary indications of the Sub-Contractor stated therein, but also of any particular conditions or requirements of the Contractor which he may wish to raise with the Sub-Contractor.

1.A   Any stipulation as to the period/periods when Sub-Contract Works can be carried out on site:[s]

to be between ___3rd October, 1984___   and ___3rd March 1985___

Period required by Architect to approve drawings after submission

Not Applicable

1.B   Preliminary programme details[t] (having regard to the information provided in the invitation to tender)

Periods required:

(1)   for submission of all further sub-contractors drawings etc. *(co-ordination, installation, shop or builders' work, or other as appropriate)*[u]

Not Applicable

(2)   for execution of Sub-Contract Works: off-site   12 weeks

on-site   6 weeks

Notice required to commence work on site   4 weeks

1.C   Agreed programme details (including sub-contract completion date: see also Sub Contract NSC/4, clause 11·1)[v]

COMMENCE ON SITE   7th FEBRUARY 1985

COMPLETE BY 30th MARCH 1985

2.   Order of Works to follow the requirements, if any, stated in Schedule 1, item 11[w]

COMPLETE 1 courtyard at a time commencing at the Northend of the site and working southwards

---

Fig. 6.2   Worked example from Tender NSC/1, Schedule 2. (Reproduced with permission of RIBA Publications Ltd.)

ing, together with other timetables for ordering material and the notice he requires to commence work. He then returns the Form to the landscape architect.

Thirdly, in 1C: the main contractor, before entering into the subcontract, inserts any further details as to the sequence of work he may wish to impose and any revisions to the programme for the execution of the work.

On the next page (Page 10) the landscape subcontractor is required to insert any special attendance requirements he needs from the main contractor and which has not been included in his tender.

The actual procedure is carried out in eight stages as follows:

1. Stage 1: the architect completes those parts of NSC1 he can, and sends it with two copies and NSC2 to the landscape subcontractor(s).
2. Stage 2: the subcontractor(s) completes as much as he can, and sends them all back to the architect.
3. Stage 3: the architect approves and signs NSC1 and obtains the signature, on NSC2, of the employer who keeps the original, the contractor taking a copy.
4. Stage 4: the architect sends a copy of the signed NSC2 to the subcontractor and issues to the main contractor a preliminary notice of his intended nomination with all copies of completed NSC1 and NSC2.
5. Stage 5: the main contractor agrees and completes NSC1, signs all three copies and sends them back to the architect.
6. Stage 6: the architect then sends NSC3 to the main contractor nominating the subcontractor with the original NSC1.
7. Stage 7: the architect sends copies to the subcontractor.
8. Stage 8: the contractor and subcontractor enter into their subcontract (NSC4).

Note: should NSC1 not have been used to obtain the landscape subcontract tender(s) then an alternative method using NSC2a/4a exists ensuring that the information, regarding liquidated damages and programmes, are known to, and agreed between, the main contractors and subcontractors concerned before the nomination is made.

6.5.4 The JCT standard form of nominated subcontract (NSC4)

NSC4 is the standard form of subcontract for nominated subcontractors the use of which is obligatory for all such subcontracts entered into under JCT80 contracts, landscape and air-conditioning alike. It is specifically designed to reflect in every respect the provisions of the main contract, particularly those dealing with insurance, disturbance to progress, and tax certificates. No such JCT subcontract previously existed, and its use has caused few (if any) problems to date.

The subcontract includes three contents pages setting out headings of the 34 main clauses, and runs to 42 pages. It is intended that separate NSC4 subcontracts will be signed for each nomination, i.e. they will not be incorporated by reference, as the Intermediate Form subcontract conditions are. For full details the BEC (NFBTE) 10-page guidance notes should be referred to; but in general terms the same provisions for nominated subcontractors, as were included in the 1963 JCT Edition, are unchanged – i.e. those affecting direct payment, early release of retention, responsibility for attendance, making good defects, extensions to the contract period, adjudication, and determination.

The provisions for the right of set-off by the main contractor are set out in clauses 23 and 24; they deal both with the case when it has been agreed with the contractor and subcontractor, and when it has been awarded by the court in litigation or arbitration. The payment of the costs of both an arbitrator and an adjudicator are also covered.

The subcontract also provides, under clause 29, for the architect to determine the subcontract if he considers the subcontractor to be in default, if the subcontractor becomes insolvent, or if the subcontractor himself has validly determined the subcontract. The architect then is obliged to make a further nomination and, if this is because of a valid determination by the subcontractor, then any extra cost to the employer arising from the new nomination has to be borne by the main contractor.

6.6   SUBCONTRACTS EXECUTED UNDER THE ICE FORM OF CONTRACT

The standard form of subcontract prepared for use with the ICE Form is relatively simple, with the conditions of the main contract incorporated by reference. Nineteen short clauses on seven pages are followed by five schedules detailing:

1.   The particulars of the main contract.
2.   The subcontract documents and scope of the works.
3.   The price, retention, and period for completion.
4.   Facilities provided by the contractor.
5.   Insurances.

The subcontract clause headings are listed in Table 6.2

Table 6.2 Standard form of subcontract for use with ICE Standard Form – main clause headings.

1.	Definitions.	11.	Property, materials, and plant.
2.	General.	12.	Indemnities.
3.	Main contract.	13.	Insurances.
4.	Contractors facilities.	14.	Maintenance and defects.
5.	Site working access.	15.	Payment.
6.	Commencement and completion.	16.	Determination of main contract.
7.	Instructions and decisions.	17.	Subcontractors' default.
8.	Variations.	18.	Disputes.
9.	Valuation of variations.	19.	Value added tax.
10.	Notices and claims.		

7

Plant supplies

The success of any landscape project is dependent on the satisfactory synthesis of the following:

1. The choice of the appropriate plant.
2. The cultivation of sufficient quantities of healthy stock by the nurseryman.
3. Its successful lifting, packaging and delivery to site.
4. The proper handling of the plants after they have been delivered.

The failure of any one aspect will inevitably result in the death of the plant and possibly the failure of the project even before the date of practical completion.

Choosing the appropriate plant requires a combination of an appreciation not only of the physical aspects of the plants such as the height, spread and seasonal changes of colour of leaves, flowers, bark and fruit, but also of the micro-climatic conditions, the preferred type and pH value of the soil, the requirements for sun and shade, and toleration of wind, frost, salt, draught and urban pollutants, on which its survival depends.

No doubt all this information will be shortly available on instant access from a computerized data bank. At present one must depend on memory and a variety of sometimes-conflicting technical references, never fully comprehensive and often having to resort to experience and skilled judgement – usually known as plantsmanship, an attribute sometimes thought to be possessed by a rapidly declining number of people.

7.1 CHOOSING THE APPROPRIATE PLANT – USING THE JCLI PLANT LISTS

To ensure that, having selected the appropriate plant, it is available in sufficient quantities when required, it is necessary to rationalize cultivars — particularly those with a genus where previously many almost identical cultivars, e.g. rhododendron, azalea and roses, have been on offer by nurserymen.

Landscape designers and managers, both in the local authority and private sectors, need a list from which they can confidently select plants in the knowledge that they are likely to be generally available in quantity from most reputable nurserymen throughout the country. Garden centre operators need to know which species to stock in quantity to meet current and future demands. Nurserymen require long-term guidance on the plants they will be required to supply two or three years hence. Landscape and horticultural students need to learn the characteristics of a basic list of plants, to be supplemented in later years as the students' range of experience and skill grows.

To meet these demands JLCPS and JCLI have prepared two lists of plants – the herbaceous list (Fig.7.1), and the tree and shrub list (Fig. 7.2) – selecting from the 12 000 plants that can be grown in this country, over 750 herbaceous and 1000 trees and shrubs which should usually be readily available.

In the trees and shrubs list, those that may be in short supply due to difficulties of propagation, those raised from seed too quickly reach saleable size in the nursery and then tend to deteriorate, those that are too tender for exposed positions in all but the mildest localities, and those that will not tolerate alkaline or chalky conditions, are all indicated separately.

In choosing from the herbaceous plant list, specifiers must always remember that should the microclimate of the proposed location be in any way susceptible to frost the following five species will always be at risk: *Choisya ternata, Eucalyptus gunii, Hebe* spp., *Senecio greyii*, and *Garrya eliptica.*

Specification of those plants available in containers are laid down in the British Container Growers Group List, which sets out the standards to which the majority of container-grown plants are available, giving both the minimum and recommended capacities of the containers and/or the minimum heights or the diameters of the plant (see Fig. 7.3). It also describes the physical shape of the plants when offered for sale: branched or bushy, single leader, side shoots or, if multi-stemmed, with details of the number of breaks in the lower third of the plant: whether terminals and/or laterals should have been pruned and if caning is to be provided. Details are given of the normal method of raising: by budding, stem cutting, division, graft, layering, root cuttings, by runner or seed. It is thus possible for the specifier to be confident that not only the size but also the shape and method of propagation of container grown stock are known and ensured for the more common cultivars. In general it should always be borne in mind that most plants grown in containers are unlikely to be safely transplanted if the containers in which they are sold are less than 3 litres; 4–5 litres are usually more advantageous, and in some circumstances even 7–10 litres are necessary.

The success of any landscape project stands or falls on the supply to site of good quality healthy plants by the nurseryman. The well-known reputable

HERBACEOUS PLANTS

EXOTIC &
BRITISH NATIVE

CHRIS HODGSON
1981

As Recommended by

Joint Liaison Committee on Plant Supplies

Fig. 7.1   JLCPS/CPSE Herbaceous plant list.

FOREWORD

Two lists are included in this publication —

    A.   Exotic herbaceous plants (pages 1 - 19)

    B.   British Native herbaceous plants (pages 20 - 28)

The objectives of both lists are:

1.   To promote the more widespread use of herbaceous plants by means of two definitive, informative lists which summarise useful information not readily available elsewhere.

2.   In the Exotic List to rationalise cultivars, hybrids or strains as far as is possible excepting that in the case of those Genera marked thus * a selection of the many and often ephemeral cultivars etc. is advised in consultation with reputable suppliers.

3.   To improve the future availability of these plants in Britain particularly of native species considered to be increasingly in demand during the next few years.

(A) EXOTIC HERBACEOUS PLANTS

EXPLANATORY NOTES

1.   This list includes 'typical' herbaceous plants, non-woody ground cover and the more vigorous rock plants; clump-forming bulbous species, ornamental grasses and sedges, ferns and aquatics. It excludes annuals, biennials and most bulbous species and most herbs. The majority of plants are introduced species and cultivars or hybrids (i.e. **exotic** or non-native). Some native aquatic plants are included.

2.   The alphabetical lists are printed in bold and in normal type to distinguish priority and important plants from the other selections.

3.   The column heading used in conjunction with the category markings as denoted should be used as guidelines only. In some cases information is not available for every plant species listed. This is particularly the case with the last column that refers to the use of the herbicide Lenacil.* It should be emphasised that any herbicides, including Lenacil should be used with caution on herbaceous plants but as Lenacil probably has the greatest tolerance in this respect its use can be advised with care as indicated. Simazine may also be used with great care and discrimination on some herbaceous plants.

4.   Where it is considered inadvisable or misleading to specify or recommend named cultivars or hybrids of genera such as Delphinium and Lupin marked thus *, a selection from a current reputable supplier's list is recommended.

*Information kindly supplied by the Weed Research Organization.

2

Fig. 7.1 (contd)

JLCPS HERBACEOUS

(A)   EXOTIC HERBACEOUS LIST

heavy type indicates priority plants

plant falls clearly into category shown   ●

plant may be suitable for category shown   ○

Lenacil column   ○   Some tolerance

●   Tolerant

	Type					Best Growth Conditions						Other factors					
	Rock Plant	Typical herbaceous plant	Fern	Grass, ornamental/sedge	Aquatic	General purpose	Sun	Shade	Dry	Moist	Waterside, Marginal	Winter effect	Ground cover	Long lived	Invasive	Spring or ex-pot planting	Tolerant of Lenacil
ACAENA 'Blue Haze'	●					●			●				●		○	●	
microphylla	●					●			●				●		○	●	
ACANTHUS mollis		●				●	●	○	●	●		○		●	○		○
spinosus		●				●	●	○	●	●		○		●	○		○
ACHILLEA 'Coronation Gold'		●				●	●	○	●			●					○
'Moonshine'		●				●	●	○	●			●					○
ptarmica 'The Pearl'		●				●	●	○	●			○					○
millefolium 'Cerise Queen'		●					●	○	●				●		○	●	○
ACONITUM x cammarum 'Blue Sceptre'		●				●	●	○	○	●				●			●
(Monkshood) 'Bressingham Spire'		●				●	●	○	○	●				●			●
ACTAEA spicata		●					○	●		●							
AETHIONEMA 'Warley Rose'	●					●	●		●				○			●	
AGAPANTHUS Headbourne Hybrids		●				●			●							●	○
AJUGA reptans 'Burgundy Glow'							○	●	○	●		●	●			●	
(Bugle) 'Purpurea'							○	●	○	●		●	●			●	
'Variegata'							○	●	○	●		●	●			●	
ALCHEMILLA mollis		●				●	●	●	●	●			●	●	○		●
ALISMA plantago aquatica (Water Plantain)					●	●					○					●	
ALSTROEMERIA Ligtu Hybrids		●				●	●		●						○	●	
ALYSSUM saxatile citrinum	●					●			●			○	○				
ANAPHALIS triplinervis		●				●	●	○	●	●		○					●
ANCHUSA azurea 'Loddon Royalist'		●				●	●		●							●	●
ANDROSACE sarmentosa	●					●	●		●				○			●	
ANEMONE x hybrida (including A. hupehensis and A. japonica) 'Honorine Jobert'		●				●	●	○	○	●				●	○		○
'September Charm'		●				●	●	○	○	●				●	○		○
'White Queen'		●				●	●	○	○	●				●	○		○

3

Fig. 7.1 (contd)

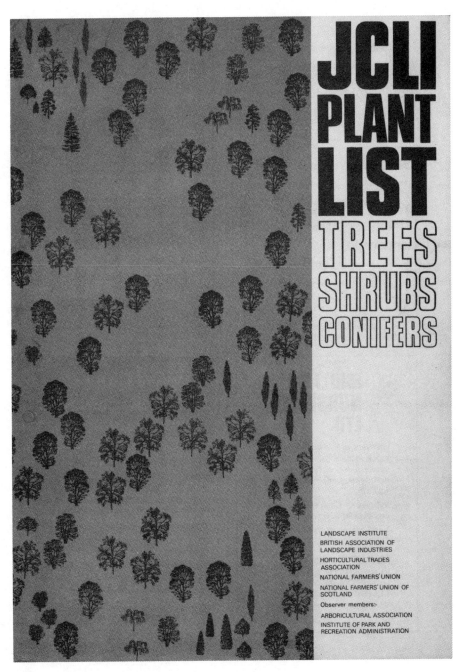

Fig. 7.2 JCLI tree and shrub list.

F O R E W O R D

The objectives of this standard list of trees, shrubs, climbers and conifers, arranged alphabetically, are twofold:-

Firstly, to improve the availability of these plants in Britain over the next several years.

Secondly, to rationalise cultivars within a genus where previously many similar cultivars have been offered.

The list has been prepared and agreed by the Bodies comprising the Joint Council of Landscape industries which are:-

The Landscape Institute

The British Association of Landscape Industries

The Horticultural Trades Association

The National Farmers' Union

The National Farmers' Union of Scotland

Observer Members :—

The Arboricultural Association

The Institute of Park and Recreation Administration

Landscape Designers and Local Authorities are expected to select plants primarily from this list in the knowledge that plants not included in the list may not be available generally, or in any quantity.

Garden Centre Operators are expected to bear this list in mind when deciding what varieties to stock.

Nurserymen are expected to give this list due attention when preparing their propagating programmes.

Landscape and other Students should find this list particularly helpful.

KEY

S   —   Indicate plants which are more difficult to propagate than others, so supplies may often be limited.

0   —   Indicates plants raised from seed which quickly reach saleable size, but then rapidly deteriorate in the nursery; it is uneconomic to propagate quantities of such plants at random, and they are best grown under some form of contract.

*   —   Indicates that the plant is evergreen

†   —   Indicates that the plant is too tender for exposed positions in all but the mildest localities, though most of them are hardy on walls, or when given evergreen, woodland, or similar protection.

‡   —   Indicates that the plant requires lime-free or neutral soil, and will not tolerate alkaline or chalky conditions.

NOMENCLATURE

Familiar plants may appear under new names as botanists reclassify or discover an earlier legitimate name. Nomenclature follows Hilliers Manual of Trees and Shrubs.

....   Further copies of the list may be obtained, free of charge, from the H.T.A., 18 Westcote Road, Reading. RG3 2DE Please enclose a stamped addressed envelope.

Fig. 7.2 (contd)

TREES AND SHRUBS

	ABELIA	x grandiflora
	ACER	campestre
.	,,	cappadocicum 'Rubrum'
S	,,	davidii 'George Forrest'
S	,,	griseum
S	,,	heldreichii
S	,,	japonicum 'Aconitifolium'
S	,,	,, 'Aureum'
	,,	x lobelii
	,,	negundo
	,,	,, 'Variegatum'
	,,	palmatum
	,,	,, 'Atropurpureum'
	,,	,, 'Dissectum'
	,,	,, 'Dissectum Atropurureum'
	,,	,, 'Heptalobum Osakazuki'
	,,	,, 'Senkaki'
	,,	platanoides 'Columnare'
	,,	,, 'Crimson King'
	,,	,, 'Drummondii'
	,,	,, 'Schwedleri'
	,,	pseudoplatanus
	,,	,, 'Atropurpureum'
		(Purpureum)
		Spaethii) budded
S	,,	,, 'Brilliantissimum'
	,,	,, 'Erectum'
	,,	,, 'Leopoldii'
	,,	,, 'Worleei'
‡	,,	rubrum
‡	,,	saccharinum (dasycarpum)
	,,	,, 'Pyramidale'
	AESCULUS	x carnea 'Briotii'
	,,	hippocastanum
	,,	,, 'Baumannii'
		('Flore Pleno')
S	,,	indica
S	,,	parviflora
	AILANTHUS	altissima (glandulosa)
	ALNUS	cordata
S	,,	firma hirtella
	,,	glutinosa
	,,	incana
	AMELANCHIER	lamarckii (x grandiflora)
		(canadensis of the trade)
S	ARALIA	elata
*	ARBUTUS	unedo
	ARONIA	arbutifolia
	ARTEMISIA	abrotanum
†	,,	arborescens
O	ATRIPLEX	halimus
*	AUCUBA	
S	,,	japonica
	,,	,, 'Crotonifolia'
S	,,	,, 'Nana Rotundifolia'
	,,	,, 'Variegata' (Maculata)

† *	AZARA	microphylla
	BERBERIS	'Barbarossa'
	,,	buxifolia 'Nana'
*	,,	candidula
*	,,	darwinii
*	,,	gagnepainii
*	,,	julianae
S *	,,	x lologensis
	,,	x ottawensis 'Purpurea'
*	,,	panlanensis
*	,,	x stenophylla
	,,	,, 'Irwinii'
	,,	thunbergii
	,,	,, atropurpurea
	,,	,, 'Atropurpurea Nana'
S	,,	,, 'Rose Glow'
*	,,	verruculosa
	,,	wilsoniae
S	BETULA	costata
	,,	jacquemontii
S	,,	nigra
	,,	papyrifera
	,,	pendula (verrucosa)
S	,,	,, 'Dalecarlica'
	,,	,, 'Tristis'
	,,	,, 'Youngii'
	,,	pubescens
	BUDDLEIA	alternifolia
	,,	davidii 'Black Knight'
	,,	,, 'Empire Blue'
	,,	,, 'Fascinating'
	,,	,, 'Royal Red'
	,,	,, 'White Bouquet'
	,,	globosa
	,,	'Lochinch'
*	BUXUS	
	,,	sempervirens
	,,	,, 'Handsworthensis'
	CALLICARPA	bodinieri
‡ ‡	CALLUNA	
O	,,	vulgaris
	,,	,, 'Alba Plena'
	,,	,, 'Alportii'
	,,	,, 'Blazeaway'
	,,	,, 'County Wicklow'
	,,	,, 'H. E. Beale'
	,,	,, 'Mairs's Variety'
	,,	,, 'Peter Sparkes'
	,,	,, 'Robert Chapman'
	,,	,, 'Rosalind'
	,,	,, 'Serlei'
	,,	,, 'Silver Queen'
	,,	,, 'Sister Anne'
‡ *	CAMELLIA	
	,,	japonica 'Adolphe Audusson'
	,,	,, 'Alba Plena'
	,,	,, 'Alba Simplex'
	,,	,, 'Contessa Lavinia Maggi'
	,,	,, 'Donckelarii'
	,,	,, 'Elegans'
		(Chandleri Elegans)
	,,	,, 'Gloire de Nantes'

Fig. 7.2 (contd)

THE BRITISH CONTAINER GROWERS GROUP

Specification of Standards

for the Production of

Hardy Container Grown Plants

EDWARD BACK	FARGRO LTD, CANTERBURY ROAD, WORTHING
PETER BULLOCK	J. & W. BLACKBURN LTD., SHELLEY, HUDDERSFIELD
DAVID CLARK	NOTCUTTS NURSERIES LTD, WOODBRIDGE, SUFFOLK
MIKE CLIFT	WATERERS NURSERIES, BAGSHOT, SURREY
LIN DEMPSTER	BOULTON BROS. MODDERSHALL LTD., STONE, STAFFS.
MIKE DUNNETT	BLAKEDOWN NURSERIES LTD., KIDDERMINSTER, WORCS.
BRIAN HUMPHREY	HILLIERS NURSERIES (WINCHESTER) LTD., HAMPSHIRE
BARRY LOCKWOOD (Chairman)	ROSES AND SHRUBS LTD., WOLVERHAMPTON, STAFFS.
ROBIN TACCHI	TACCHI'S NURSERIES, HUNTINGDON
	MIDLAND NURSERIES LTD., SOLIHULL, WARWICKSHIRE
	BERNHARDS RUGBY NURSERIES LTD., RUGBY, WARWICKSHIRE.

Fig. 7.3 Specification of standards for container-grown plants, issued by the British Container Growers Group.

INTRODUCTION

This document is intended to provide a definition of standards to which a range of Container Grown plants should be produced.

The majority of plants produced in quantity are represented, if not specifically, then by a comparable plant.

COLUMN No. 1   **PLANT GENERA** – represented with additional vigor categories for larger Genera.

COLUMN No. 2   **'MINIMUM STANDARD'** – below which stock should not be offered. The figures are shown thus – e.g. 2/30. The first figure 2 indicates the volume capacity of the container in litres, followed by the minimum height of the plant in centimetres, measured from the surface of the compost. 'D' refers to the diameter measurement where applicable.

COLUMN No. 3   The **'RECOMMENDED STANDARD'** is stated also in Container Volume and Height. It is proposed that this column should be the standard to which growers should progress and would, in time, replace the 'Minimum Standard Column.'

COLUMN No. 4   **'PLANT HABIT'** – describes the physical appearance of the plant with the following definitions:

    Branched – A branched plant with few shoots arising from the branches.

    Bushy – A branched plant with several shoots arising from the branches.

    Leader and Laterals – A single dominant shoot with significant side shoots.

    Single Leader – A single dominant shoot with few, if any, side shoots.

    Several Shoots – A number of shoots arising from ground level.

COLUMN No. 5   **NUMBER OF BREAKS IN LOWER THIRD OF THE PLANT**

COLUMN No. 6   **PRUNING CODE** – refers to the type of pruning required to achieve the required plant habit.

    1. Prune where required.

    2. Terminal pruned.

    3. Laterals pruned.

    4. Terminal and Laterals pruned.

COLUMN No. 7   **CANING**

COLUMN No. 8   **NORMAL METHOD OF RAISING**

    B – BUDDING

    C – STEM CUTTINGS

    D – DIVISION

    G – GRAFTS

    L – LAYERS

    R/C – ROOT CUTTINGS

    R – RUNNER

    S – SEED

COLUMN No. 9   **EXAMPLE** – provides a representative specific plant of the Genera, to which the specification applies.

    C.V.'s – Cultivars.

Fig. 7.3 (contd)

Specification of Standards for the Production of
Hardy Container Grown Plants

PLANT	Minimum Standards Vol. in Litres Hgt. in Cms.	Recommended Standards Vol. in Litres Hgt. in Cms.	Plant Habit	No. of breaks in lower ⅓	Pruning Code	Caning	Normal Method of Raising	EXAMPLE
1	2	3	4	5	6	7	8	9
SHRUBS								
Abelia	1/20	2/25	Bushy	3	2	–	C.	A. grandiflora
Acacia	2/30	4/40	Single leader	–	1	–	S.	A. dealbata
Acer Medium	3/30	4/40	Branched	2	1	–	C.S.L.G.	A. palmatum atropurpureum
,, Small	2/20	3/25	Branched	2	1	–	C.S.L.G.	A. jap. 'Aureum' A. palmatum Dissectum CVS.
Aesculus Small	4/20	6/30	Branched	2	1	–	S.G.	A. parvifolia
Amelanchier	3/30	4/40	Branched	3	1	–	S.L.G.	A. lamarkii (canadensis) A. canadensis
Aralia	3/30	4/40	Single leader	–	1	–	S.R/C.G.	A. chinensis
Arbutus	2/20	3/30	Branched	2	1	–	S.	A. unedo
Aronia	2/30	3/40	Branched	3	1	–	C.S.	A. melanocarpa
Arundinaria	3/40	4/60	Several shoots	3	1	–	D.	A. mureliae
,, Dwarf	1/15	2/25	Several shoots	3	1	–	D.	A. humilis
Artemisia	1/15	2/20	Bushy	3	1	–	C.	A. abrotanum
Atriplex	1/20	2/30	Bushy	3	2	–	C.S.	A. halimus
Aucuba	2/20	3/30	Bushy	3	2	–	C.	A. japonica
Azalea see Rhododendron section								
Azara	1/20	2/30	Leader and Laterals	3	1	1	C.	A. microphylla
Berberis Evergreen Vigorous	3/30	4/40	Bushy	3	4	–	C.S.	B. stenophylla
,, ,, Medium	2/20	3/30	Bushy	3	4	–	C.S.	B. darwinii
,, ,, Dwarf	2/15D	3/20D	Bushy	3	1	–	C.S.	B. candidula
Berberis Deciduous Vigorous	3/30	4/40	Branched	3	4	–	S.C.	B. Ottowensis C.V.S.
,, ,, Medium	2/20	3/30	Branched	3	4	–	S.C.	B. thunbergii CVS.
,, ,, Dwarf	1/10	2/15	Bushy	3	4	–	C.	B. thunbergii atro. Nana
Buddleia	2/30	3/40	Branched	3	4	–	C.	B. Davidii & CVS.
Buxus Medium	2/20	3/25	Bushy	3	1	–	C.	B. sempervirens CVS.
,, Dwarf	1/10	2/15	Bushy	3	1	–	C.	B.s. suffruticosa
Callicarpa	2/30	3/40	Branched	3	2	–	C.	C. giraldiana Profusion
Calluna see Erica								
Camellia	1.5/30	3/40	Leader with Laterals	–	1	-	C.G.	C. japonica CVS.
Caryopteris	1/15	2/20	Branched	3	2	–	C.	C. clandonensis
Ceanothus	1.5/45	3/60	Leader with Laterals	–	1	C.	C.	C. burkwoodii
(Also climbing and wall plants)								
Ceratostigma	1/15	2/20	Bushy	3	1	–	C.	C. willmottianum
Cercis	3/30	4/40	Branched	3	1	–	C.S.	C. siliquastrum
Chaenomeles	2/30	3/40	Branched	2	1	Cane C.V.'s	C.	C. japonica CVS.
Chimonanthus	2/30	3/40	Branched	3	2	–	S.C.G.	C. fragrans
Choisya	2/20	3/30	Bushy	2	2	–	C.	C. ternata
Cistus	1/20	2/30	Bushy	3	1	–	C.	C. Silver Pink
Clerodendron	3/30	4/40	Branched	2	1	–	R/C.S.	C. trichotumum
Clethra	2/20	3/30	Branched	3	1	–	C.S.	C. alnifolia
Convolvulus	0.5/10D	1/15D	Bushy	3	1	–	C.	C. cneorum
Colutea	3/30	4/40	Branched	3	2	–	S.C.	C. arborescens
Cornus Vigorous	3/30	4/40	Branched	3	2	–	C.	C. alba & CVS.
,, Medium	2/30	3/40	Branched	3	2	–	L.C.S.	C. florida 'Rubra'
,, Dwarf	0.5/10D	1/15D	Several shoots	3	1	–	D.	C. canadensis

Fig. 7.3 (contd)

firms appreciate this and take great care in ensuring that their plants are properly protected in transit. There are unfortunately others who buy in plants from wherever the cheapest can be found irrespective of their condition and take little interest or care in their delivery to site.

Severe competition today requires landscape contractors to seek keener and keener markets to reduce their costs. In the landscape industry more than any other you get what you pay for. Good quality plants cost more than inferior ones and it is essential that landscape architects ensure that their plants come from reputable sources at realistic prices if they are to get the quality they are looking for.

7.2 JLCPS/CPSE STANDARD FORM OF TENDER

The CPSE (previously JLCPS) Standard Form of Tender for the Supply and Delivery of Plants (see Appendix E) lays down a standard format for the specification of plants and for tenders for the supply of all trees, shrubs and herbaceous plants, whether container gown or not. It contains standard details, conditions, specification, schedules and a form of tender for the supply of all types of plants to statutory authorities and local authorities in the public sector, and landscape architects and managers acting on behalf or all types of client in the private sector alike.

The form is primarily intended for all types of enquiry for the supply of plants including those for contracts under the JCLI Form. When the form is used to obtain prices for a range of plants only certain species of which are to be selected, it is essential that this is clearly stated in the enquiry with the minimum quantity of any one species anticipated, if the prices quoted are not to be valueless.

Several points should be noted, as detailed below.

It is appreciated that the purchaser needs to retain the right to accept orders in whole or in part, but in the case of the latter (partial orders) it is accepted that the supplier has the right to re-negotiate rates where (1) the quantity or variety ordered differs significantly from the quantity specified, or (2) the value of the order placed differs significantly from the total tender.

Specifiers are reminded that some bushy plants are only available in small sizes and conifers are rarely available as standards.

The origin of plants other than those grown in the British Isles should be identified by the supplier against the names of relevant plants in the schedules.

Root systems are not specified in detail other than that they must be adequate in relation to the size of the plant, conducive to successful transplanting, and that trees are to be bottom-worked unless otherwise stated.

Any container-grown plants required must be so indicated with the minimum size of container stated, the roots to properly permeate the whole of the container without being pot-bound or rooted through.

Quantities (contrary to BS 1192) must be priced, monied-out, and totalled, with large quantities rounded off (transplants usually being in units of 25). Trees, shrubs, roses and herbaceous plants should be listed separately in alphabetical order to assist the estimator, leaving space below each plant for substitutes to be entered when these are allowed by the specifier. When plants are no longer available at the time of delivery, substitutes may only be made by mutual agreement. It is helpful if two copies of each schedule are sent with the enquiry so that the estimator can return the original and retain a copy for his file.

No plants are to be supplied until the acceptance of the tender has been confirmed in writing.

A minimum of two clear working weeks, with three weeks wherever possible, is the recommended time for tendering, with the closing date for receipt of tenders clearly shown on the reply envelope where these are provided.

Although not stated on the form it is suggested that tenders should remain open for acceptance for 28 days during which time prices will remain firm and stocks be guaranteed but beyond which prices may be subject to increase and stock of plants in the quantities specified may no longer be available.

The use of this form of tender ensures comparability of tenders so that like can be compared with like and all the plants supplied comply with the minimum standards laid down (see Fig. 7.4, for example). Although not always practicable it is strongly recommended that wherever possible the plants of the lowest tenderer are inspected in the nursery by prior appointment before the order is placed.

Delivery dates (the dates by which, or on which, deliveries are required) must be stated in the enquiry and are to be adhered to, save only delays on account of exceptionally adverse weather conditions or other reasons beyond the supplier's control. The supplier is required to advise the purchaser in advance of the week during which deliveries are intended, and, where sites are identified on the Form of Tender by the specified as not being continually manned, the supplier is required to give 48 hours notice of the date and anticipated time of arrival on site so that adequate labour for unloading and checking can be provided by the purchaser. Deliveries are to be made during normal working hours and, except where stated otherwise, to one location.

Complaints regarding quantity, quality and condition should always be made within seven days of delivery, which may be signed for as 'unexamined', the purchaser having the right to return at the suppliers' expense any plants the quality of which is below that which was specified.

Payment should always be made by the end of the month during which deliveries are made notwithstanding that separate invoices may be rendered in the event of deliveries being made in separate consignments. Prices are usually inclusive of delivery and are strictly net with no discount for prompt payment, exclusive of value added tax which will be charged at the rates ruling at the time of delivery.

Dimensions of Trees

Designation	Circumference of stem measured 1.0m from ground level	Minimum Height from ground level	Clear stem Ht. (m) from ground level to lowest branch
YOUNGER NURSERY STOCK			
Seedlings (1+0)			
(2+0)		max. 0.90 m	—
(etc.)			
Undercut (1+1)			
Seedling/(1+2)	not specified	max. 0.90 m	not specified
Transplant (etc.)			
Whip		0.90 – 1.20 m	not specified
		1.20 – 1.50 m	
		1.50 – 1.80 m	
		1.80 – 2.10 m	
		2.10 – 2.50 m	
STANDARD NURSERY STOCK Standard/feathered/weeping			
short	not specified	not specified	1.00 – 1.20 m
half	not specified	1.80 – 2.10 m	1.20 – 1.50 m
. . . .	4 – 6 cm	2.10 – 2.50 m	1.50 – 1.80 m
Light	6 – 8 cm	2.50 – 2.75 m	1.50 – 1.80 m
Standard	8 – 10 cm	2.75 – 3.00 m	1.80 minimum
Tall	8 – 10 cm	3.00 – 3.60 m	1.80 minimum
Selected	10 – 12 cm	3.00 – 3.60 m	1.80 minimum

Note: Minimum heights do not apply to weeping trees nor clear stem heights to feathered trees.

Designation	Circumference	Minimum Height	Clear stem Ht.
ADVANCED NURSERY STOCK (BS 5236)			
Heavy	12 – 14 cm	3.60 – 4.25 m	1.80 minimum
Extra heavy	14 – 16 cm	4.25 – 6.00 m	1.80 minimum
. . . .	16 – 18 cm	. . . .	1.80 minimum
. . . .	18 – 20 cm	. . . .	1.80 minimum

Note: Minimum height of conifers 2.0 – 3.5 m

Designation	Circumference	Minimum Height	Clear stem Ht.
SEMI MATURE (BS 4043)	20 – 75 cm	6.00 – 15.00	not specified

Fig. 7.4 Dimensions of trees – some standards quoted.

Postponement of deliveries until the following planting season after 31 March by the purchaser entitles the supplier to the reimbursement of the direct loss and expenses to which he has been put by the postponement.

Should it not be possible to resolve any dispute regarding an order based on the JLPSE/CPSE conditions either party has the right to refer the matter to an arbitrator appointed by the President of the Institute of Arbitrators on the request of any of the organizations named on the front of the form.

The Form of Tender requires the specifier to complete at the head of the form, in addition to his own name and address, the name and address of the project, the address to which delivery is to be made, and to state the date and time when deliveries are to be made especially for those sites which will not be continuously manned, together with the latest date and time for the receipt of the tender. The form also provides for the option of deleting the obligation to deliver the plants to site for these specifiers who prefer to collect them themselves.

Space then follows on the form for the supplier to summarize his tender, adding the cost of any non-standard special conditions imposed by the specifier, his delivery charges, and the total amount of his tender (exclusive of the value added tax to be added at the rates ruling at the date of delivery) in figures and in words.

The supplier also undertakes (subject to their being unsold on receipt of order) to supply the plants at the price quoted during the current bare-root planting season subject to the order being placed within four weeks of the date for submission of tenders.

The specifier does not bind himself to accept the lowest (or any) tender, and the supplier retains the right to withdraw his offer if the plants are to be supplied through a contractor whose identify is not known to him at the time of his tender, within 14 days of the identity of the contractor becoming known

7.3 JCT FORM OF TENDER FOR NOMINATED SUPPLIERS

Just as landscape subcontractors on building contracts have to comply with obligatory subcontract provisions and procedures to ensure compliance with the conditions of the main contract, landscape suppliers on building contracts have similar special conditions.

In this instance, however, the requirements are in some respects far less onerous: not only is there no restriction on naming a single supplier in the tender and contract documents (provided that the work is described in sufficient detail for it to be priced by the main contractor) but neither is the form of tender and employer subcontractor agreement obligatory.

Should, however, the work not be fully described and a prime cost or provisional sum be provided instead, then the supplier is considered to have been nominated and the detailed provisions then come into force. Since, under these circumstances, the main contractor can automatically obtain an extension to the contract period and the employer lose the right to liquidated and ascertained damages if the main contractor is delayed by the nominated supplier, it is essential that a contractual situation is created between the employer and nominated supplier by the use of a standard JCT Employer/Supplier Agreement similar to that available for subcontractors.

7.3.1 Form of Tender and Agreement (TNS/1)

Although this does not contain the detailed provisions (with regard to the specification, packaging and delivery of plants to site) set out in the CPSE Form, the JCT Form of Tender imposes different if equally onerous obligations. The Form of Tender (see Appendix F) reprints in full the voluminous provisions of JCT clause 36.4 which requires the architect only to nominate a supplier who will agree to enter into a contract to supply the goods required on the same terms as the main contract (unless the main contractor agrees otherwise). In practice this does not create any problems with two exceptions.

1. Clause 36.4.7 requires that 'The ownership of materials or goods shall pass to the main contractor upon delivery ... whether or not payment has been made in full'. This in effect precludes the architect from nominating, without the consent of the contractor, any supplier who operates a retention-of-title clause of any kind.
2. In addition, the Employer/Supplier Agreement incorporated into the Form of Tender obliges the supplier under clause 1.2 to '... commence and complete delivery in accordance with the arrangement of our contract of sale ... so that the contractor shall not be entitled to an extension of time'. In default of which, should it arise, the employer is entitled to recover from the nominated supplier the full liquidated damages to which he is entitled under the main contract – which may well be, on a multi-million-pound contract, a sum vastly in excess of the value of the goods to be supplied. The only proviso is that if delivery by the supplier has been delayed by (a) force majeure, (b) civil commotion, strike or lock out, (c) architect's instructions, or (d) failure of the architect to supply necessary instructions in time – situations unlikely to be of much relevance in connection with the supply of plants.

The JCT Form TNS/1 also deals with the obligation to exercise 'reasonable skill and care in the design of any of the goods to be supplied' – this is of little relevance to plants, particularly those whose ultimate destination and location is unknown to the supplier at the time of tender.

Under any form of contract or tender, the supply of plants is also subject to the full provisions of the Sale of Goods Act 1979 whereby Section 14 requires:

1. The goods will comply with the description detailed (specified).
2. The goods are of merchantable quality except
   (a) where attention is drawn to the fault at the time of sale, or
   (b) the buyer examines the goods before the contract is made*.
3. The buyer expressly or by implication states that the goods specified are reasonably fit for the purpose intended.

*This means that under the Act inspection in the nursery relieves the supplier of his obligations to provide that which was specified.

8

Plant handling

8.1 INTRODUCTION

Having obtained comparable tenders for the provision of plants of adequate minimum standards of quality, there remains the problem of ensuring their survival when lifted, packaged and transported to site by the nursery, and their subsequent handling and establishment on site where the efforts of the landscape contractor, subcontractor or purchaser are equally of crucial importance.

The survival and establishment of the plants specified should be the primary aim of every landscape architect, contractor, subcontractor and supplier. The efforts of the nurseryman to produce healthy and vigorous plants are worthless if the plants are put needlessly at risk during the period in which they are lifted and transported from the nursery to their intended new location, and while awaiting planting on site.

Meticulous care and attention to detail is essential during this period and involves:

1. The highest standards of plant handling within the nursery. This is almost entirely dependent on the standards set by the growers themselves since plant purchasers are rarely able to be present and inspect this work while it is being carried out.
2. A stringent specification for packaging while in transit, to be set out in tender documents and rigidly enforced by the purchaser; any plants not packaged in accordance with the minimum standards laid down to be rejected on delivery from the nursery.
3. A code of good practice for the handling of plants on site which, if followed, should ensure the successful establishment of healthy plants and which, if it were found by the supplier not to have been adhered to, would relieve him of further responsibility should the plants subsequently die.

Poor plant handling between the nursery bed and the final planting position, however healthy and carefully looked after the plant may be, must inevitably contribute to the majority of plant losses. The JLCPS/CPSE Code of Practice for Plant Handling (see Appendix E) was first published in 1980, but early editions failed to make compliance with its requirements obligatory and, concentrating on minimizing losses from desiccation, omitted detailed provisions for the protection of roots, and failed to differentiate between those items such as packaging and bundling which could be enforced by rejection on delivery and those items which were dependent on the concern of the nurseryman for his plants before they left his premises.

8.2 HANDLING WITHIN THE NURSERY

Once out of the ground, plants are highly susceptible to damage especially of their roots, which must therefore be exposed to damage for as short a time as possible. This applies to all plants – trees, shrubs or herbaceous – and every effort must be made to protect the roots and prevent them drying out, heating up, freezing, becoming water-logged or broken. These risks apply equally to container-grown and bare-root plants lifted and despatched during the dormant season, although the risks of damage to container-grown plants, while they still exist, are clearly less.

8.2.1 Time of lifting

Bare-root and root-balled plants must only be lifted when the ground is moist and the plant is dormant, usually between October and March for deciduous plants, and September to May for evergreens, dependent on local and seasonal weather conditions. Particular attention must always be paid to the protection of the roots on lifting when there is a strong drying wind or sun; it should never take place when there is a severe ground frost. If plants are to be delivered with the roots balled (which includes all evergreen plants over three years old) these must be adequately supported to prevent collapse.

Container grown plants can be moved at any time of the year provided that the root system is well established and the plants are fully hardened off.

8.2.2 Bundling

This must only take place when the foliage of evergreen plants is reasonably surface dry if heating up, with consequent damage to the plant, is not to occur. Bundles of bare root plants should be of a manageable size. Root-balled and container-grown plants must never be bundled.

8.2.3 Labelling

If plants are not labelled prior to lifting care must be taken to ensure that all species are kept separate and identifiable until such time as the labels can be provided.

Similar species such as *Alnus* whips (*A. cordata, A. glutinosa, A. incana*) or varieties of *Potentilla* must always be kept separately identifiable, in each and every bundle.

8.2.4 Protection

Care must be taken to ensure that bare roots are protected from physical damage and desiccation at all times, and that, when in an open vehicle, they are securely sheeted-over. All bare roots must be covered within two hours of lifting if irreparable damage to the plant is to be avoided. Ball-rooted and container-grown plants may be transported within the nursery without additional protection unless they are likely to be exposed to extreme or sudden changes of temperature for more than a short period of time.

8.2.5 Temporary storage within the nursery

(a) Bare-root plants

(i) Externally Plants may be kept outside in a moist, cool, sheltered and shaded location for several weeks in the nursery, provided that the roots are surrounded with a freely draining moisture-retentive material, moistened regularly as and when necessary. It is essential that good contact is ensured between the material and the roots, and that protection against damage from small rodents is provided.

(ii) Internally Exposure for a relatively short period even in an unheated packing shed (let alone a garden centre) can result in serious drying out and can result in the loss of the plant. The roots of plants exposed to such risks for more than a few hours must be frequently watered. If they are likely to be exposed for longer periods, they must be protected and maintained in a similar way to that laid down for temporary storage externally.

(iii) In cold stores Plants must be wrapped entirely in polythene unless they are packed or humidified in which case no further protection is necessary.

(b) Root-balled plants

Where roots are protected in this way, they can be kept for short periods provided permeable wrappings are kept moist by watering, and polythene wrappings are kept from direct sunlight. For longer periods, permeable wrappings must be placed on a concrete or well-drained surface and covered with the same freely draining moisture- retentative material, moistened as necessary and protected from small rodents in the same way as bare-root plants.

(c) Container-grown plants

These have only to be kept upright, watered as necessary and protected from strong winds and extremes of temperature.

(d) Transport

Moving plants around the nursery requires the same precautions and protection from damage as are laid down for plants in transit to the purchaser.

8.3 PLANTS IN TRANSIT FROM THE NURSERY TO SITE

While the preceeding recommendations for the lifting, handling, packaging and transportation of plants within the nursery are dependent on the standards set and the self-policing of the nurseryman, which can rarely be supervised by the purchaser, the following requirements can be laid down by the purchaser in his tender documents, and any shortfall from the standards of packaging specified can be immediately seen at the time of delivery to site. Any plants whose subsequent survival has been needlessly placed at risk as a result can be instantly identified and such plants be rejected and returned to the supplier at his own cost without argument.

8.3.1 Lifting

Large plants should have their original orientation clearly marked on the stem.

8.3.2 Bundling

Plants must be in bundles of the same species and size, all shoots must face in the same direction so that roots and shoots are not in contact, and must be of equal numbers. Plants must be loosely tied in bundles of a size manageable by one person (unless written agreement has been obtained in advance that mechanical handling equipment will be available at the place and time of delivery). Bundles are to be securely tied with string, twine, plastic strip or other supple material which will not, by its nature or tension, cause damage to the plants.

8.3.3 Labelling

Each individual plant, bundle, bag or lot of one species of plant shall be labelled with a securely attached pruning label, clearly indicating the plant name, grade and quantity in the bundle or bag with the total quantity clearly displayed together with the supplier's name. In a large consignment of plants of the same species, a secondary label, easily related to the primary label may also be necessary.

8.3.4 Protection in transit

(a) Bare-root plants

Plants up to 45 cm tall shall be entirely but loosely enclosed in plastic film bags (250 grams, 65 micron) securely tied at the top. Thorny or very bushy plants need only have their roots enclosed, provided the plastic bag is securely tied around the stem.

Plants between 45 cm and 60 cm tall shall have the roots totally enclosed in a plastic film bag of suitable size and thickness.

Plants between 60 cm and 90 cm tall may be supplied bare root but the roots shall at all times by kept moist and protected from drying out. Layers of plants in transit must be sheeted over.

92

Transplants from 90 cm to 120 cm tall should have their roots totally enclosed in plastic except when supplied for large-scale planting when exceptions may be acceptable to the purchaser, provided that this is clearly specified in the tender invitation.

Whips and trees between 120 cm and 350 cm tall (whips and BS 3936 standard nursery stock) may be supplied bare root, provided that the roots are kept moist at all times and protected from drying out. Layers in transit should be sheeted over.

Trees in excess of 350 cm tall (BS 5236 advanced nursery stock) may be supplied bare root provided that the roots are packed with pre-wetted moisture-retentive granular or fibrous material and enclosed in either a permeable material such as hessian which must be regularly watered or 500 gram/ 130 micron (minimum) plastic film.

(b) Root-balled plants (including BS 4043 semi-mature trees)

They must have the root balls kept moist, adequately supported with bands to prevent collapse, and protected against drying out by wrapping firmly with plastic film or moisture-retentive material firmly secured over the top of the root ball.

(c) Container-grown plants

These will not normally require additional packing but degradable pots shall be enclosed and firmly secured in 350 gram/65 micron polythene film.

Table 8.1 summarizes these requirements.

8.4 TRANSPORT OF PLANTS

8.4.1 In open/closed lorries and containers

All plants are to be loaded, stacked and unloaded in such a way that breakage or crushing – by the weight of plants above, by the securing ropes or by personnel responsible for loading/unloading – will not occur. The plants shall be completely and firmly covered with opaque sheeting (laid with due regard to the direction of travel). Plants in polythene bags should be sheeted to be shaded from direct sunlight.

All plants to be loaded in such a way that breakage or crushing by the weight of plants above is avoided during loading, transit and unloading. Plants should not be kept in the dark for more than four days.

8.4.2 Transit by third parties

Where transit is entrusted to others (neither the purchaser nor supplier), not only should consignments be in manageable units, but they should be securely crated and packaged to withstand physical damage and desiccation during a possibly prolonged journey.

It is equally essential that the need for care in handling, separating multiple

93

Table 8.1 Protection of plants and trees in transit

Description	Girth (metres)	Height (metres)	Max number in bundle	Protection
BS 3936: younger nursery stock				
Part 4 seedlings		0.15–0.30		totally enclosed in plastic
		0.30–0.45		
		0.45–0.60	unspecified	roots enclosed in plastic
		0.60–0.90		bare roots kept moist
		0.90–1.20		
Transplants		1.20–1.50		
Part 1 whips		1.50–1.80		
BS 3936: standard nursery stock				
Part 1 Short	—	—	(25)	
Half	—	1.80–2.10	(20)	
	4–6	2.10–2.50	15	bare roots kept moist
Lt/Stand	6–8	2.50–2.75	10	
Full	8–10	2.75–3.00	5	
Tall	8–10	3.00–3.50	5	
Selected	10–12	3.00–3.50	3	
BS 5236: advanced nursery stock				
Heavy	12–14	3.50–4.25		
Extra heavy	14–16	4.25–6.00		
	16–18		individual	root ball
	18–20			
Semi-mature	20–75	6.00–15.00		

loads and the effects of weather and time of delivery, is impressed on non-specialist hauliers when they have to be used.

8.4.3 Reception

It is essential that appropriate staff and facilities are available for unloading on delivery without delay, to minimize damage on arrival. Where sites are only manned at certain specific times these (or the date and times of delivery) should be clearly stated in the tender documents. Alternatively the purchaser should arrange for collection himself.

8.4.4 Additional precautions

Variations to the above requirements may be appropriate in certain special circumstances which should be identified and clearly set out in the tender documents so that any additional costs will be allowed for by the tenderers.

8.5 PLANT HANDLING AFTER DELIVERY TO SITE

Transplanting and re-establishment, notwithstanding the relatively benign British climate and soil conditions, involve a plant in considerable stress. If it is to be successful, it must be planned to satisfy the plant's basic biological requirements, irrespective of those of the client, the landscape architect and the contractor. Provided the nurseryman has complied with the foregoing requirements for lifting, packaging and transport, one more hurdle remains before the successful re-establishment of the plant can be ensured. This involves the caring, handling, temporary storage, transporting and planting of the nursery stock by the contractor or purchaser. Even if this is specified in detail it will be to no avail if blanket or standard specifications are issued irrespective of the particular requirements of the project (which is not to say, standard clauses should be incorporated in the interests of an instant appreciation of the specific requirements and good practice). A relatively short lifting and planting season, the logistics of lifting and supplying large numbers of different species and the financial pressures to complete a project within a given contract period or financial year irrespective of unpredictable or unsuitable weather conditions all add conflicting pressures on the ideal planting time. To ensure the certain survival of plants it is essential that:

1. Planting is planned and material is ordered as far as possible in advance.
2. Planting specifications are prepared in detail to suit the particular requirements of the site.
3. Planting is carried out only by skilled operatives under adequate supervision.
4. Aftercare is properly arranged and, where necessary, adequate finance is allocated for its provision.

8.6 PLANTING SEASONS

Irrespective of the time of delivery, bare-root plants will only survive if planted in their final location during their dormant period (usually between the beginning of October and the end of March). Early plantings before the end of the calendar year are always more successful than those carried out in the new year from January to the end of March. Planting in January or February is particularly dangerous in 'hostile sites'. Late planting of bare-root and root-balled stock is always vulnerable to desiccation from spring droughts and is to be avoided unless regular watering has been allowed for. Evergreens are best planted in early autumn or late spring. Container-grown plants, on the other hand, can be planted at any time of the year provided weather conditions are appropriate and they are regularly watered.

95

8.7 TEMPORARY STORAGE

8.7.1 Bare-root stock

If the ground or weather at the time of delivery are not suitable bare-root plants should always be stored temporarily on or off site in more appropriate conditions. For short periods of up to seven days plants can be kept at low temperatures of up to 5 °C in the packaging in which they have been delivered provided the roots are kept moist. For longer periods bare-root stock has to be heeled-in. Bare roots must be kept moist and kept in contact with a moisture-retentive medium such as a 50/50 mixture of coarse sand and peat or sawdust. Bundled plants must be cut open and spread out to ensure that such contact is achieved. Heeling-in sites must be well drained and sheltered, stout rails being provided to support trees of standard, advanced and semi mature size. Hose watering points are always essential. Under such circumstances plants can remain heeled-in for up to five months between November and March, but the shorter the period the better. It is essential to prevent the roots drying out when the plants are eventually lifted and transplanted to their final positions.

8.7.2 Root-balled trees

These must be equally well supported with the ball immersed in a deep layer of moist straw, hay, sand, peat, pulverized bark or other suitable material. Regular watering to prevent the root ball drying out is essential.

8.7.3 Container-grown stock

This must be stood on well-drained, level, weed-free ground and should be daily watered from April to October. Tall plants should be properly supported to prevent their being blown over.

8.8 TRANSPORTING TO FINAL LOCATION

The bare roots of plants in transit to their final location must at all times be protected from frost or drying out with wet sacks or planting bags.

8.9 GROUND PREPARATION

Plants must be planted into a medium that has:

1. A texture that retains and releases moisture and nutrients to the plant.
2. A crumb structure that promotes root growth and drainage which prevents waterlogging around the roots.

Ground preparation over an area of at least three times the diameter of the root spread and to a depth of one-and-a-half times the root depth is essential. Heavy clay soils must be made free draining and friable. Light sandy soils need their water-retaining capacity increased. Ground preparation must take place in advance of the planting season when the weather is more reliable, less soil structure damage is caused, and more time is available for planting operations.

8.10   PLANTING

Final planting can only be carried out when the soil is most friable and not frozen, dry or waterlogged. Before planting, all containers and wrapping must be removed, root-balled plants are to be placed in the pit before the hessian, plastic or other protection to the roots is removed. Damaged and torn roots or stems must be cut back cleanly with a sharp knife or secateurs. Any coiled roots, such as those found in container-grown plants, must be spread out to overcome any future stability problems. Stock should be planted at the same depth as it was grown in the nursery and staked in accordance with one or other of the provisions of BS 4043 and BS 5236 to ensure its stability until established.

Backfilling must be lightly firmed to ensure intimate contact of the soil with the roots. With large plants and trees successive layers of soil will have to be firmed as the backfilling proceeds, to ensure that the plant is securely held but such that the penetration of moisture is not restricted.

8.11   AFTERCARE

8.11.1   Frost

Frost may loosen the soil around a new plant's roots and this must be remedied as soon as possible by heeling to exclude any consequential air pockets around the roots.

8.11.2   Pruning

Pruning after planting and before leafing out is almost always advantageous to reduce leaf area and the consequent demand on the roots. This may also prevent any die-back that may otherwise occur, and in the long term promotes more vigorous growth.

8.11.3   Weed control

Weed control is essential to provide sufficient moisture and nutrients to the plants until they are well established. This usually takes a minimum of three years and cannot be achieved simply by cutting or mowing surrounding weeds. The application of pre-planting herbicides may help initially but a minimum of one metre (or three times the root spread) diameter area must be maintained weed-free around each tree or shrub until it is fully established. This is usually achieved by mulches, tree spats or herbicides.

8.11.4   Watering

Most plants in south-east and central Britain suffer from a moisture deficiency during the summer months, and all will benefit from irrigation on planting and during their early lives. Any newly planted tree or shrub requires watering after four weeks without an appreciable quantity of rain (less than 30 mm) from mid-May to mid-September. It is therefore prudent to allow on all planting specifications at least 20 litres of water to be provided once every two weeks for standard trees and 10 litres for smaller shrubs. Any smaller quantity will ensure no more than the bare survival of the plant without growth, any larger quantity could be wasteful and leach away the nutrients present in the soil. The overriding principle is to ensure that sufficient water is provided to saturate the full depth of the top soil whether based on clay or sand, and that sufficient waterings are allowed for in tender documents (see NBS clause 6401 in Fig. 3.1).

8.11.5 Mulching

This can not only assist in conserving soil moisture but also controls weeds which would otherwise rapidly transpire moisture and evaporation from the soil.

8.11.6 Vermin

Plants can be damaged by vermin such as voles, mice, hares, rabbits, deer and farm stock. Regular inspection, at least once a month, is essential if appropriate action is to be taken in time. In certain circumstances it is best to fence in the whole area; in others, individual plant guards or poison will suffice. (Care must be taken to ensure that when poison is used there is not the slightest risk of harm to livestock, domestic pets or wildlife, for which the contractor will become liable in law.)

8.11.7 Stakes

Stakes and ties must be provided and adjusted regularly to ensure the survival of new planting. It is no longer thought to be always necessary to stake new trees to the underside of the lowest branch. All stakes should be removed as soon as the plant is stable so that the tree may develop its own appropriate stem and root system.

8.11.8 Protective fencing and tree guards

The protection of trees and shrubs must always be measured in detail, and specified accordingly. Such phrases as 'allow for such protection as is thought necessary' are no longer considered adequate. It is incumbent on the specifier in the interest of compatability of tenders to state precisely where he considers protection to be necessary, and for the tenderer to price accordingly. Suitable clauses are such as those set out in NBS W21 1151–1251 and W31 6051–6651 (part of which we quoted in Figs 3.1 and 3.2).

8.11.9 Vandalism

More trees have died as a result of vandalism than those planted in unsuitable soil conditions. It is essential that those so damaged are replaced immediately and securely protected, trees should be well staked with adequate tree guards for the full height of the stem.

98

9

Landscape contract administration

9.1 THE LANDSCAPE ARCHITECT'S ADMINISTRATIVE DUTIES

The administrative duties of the landscape architect* on a landscape contract are

1. The invitation and receipt of tenders, reporting and advising thereon.
2. Giving general supervision in order to advise the employer on the progress and quality of the work.
3. Valuing work in progress, issuing interim certificates for payment of work on account.
4. Listing work outstanding at practical completion and defective items at the end of the Defects Liability Period.
5. Issuing instructions and valuing variations to the contract on the client's behalf, extending the contract period and condemning work not in accordance with the contract.

The Landscape architect is paid one fifth of his total fee for post contract services and the first three occur on every project. The last two items may and often do arise but only when certain events happen, which are usually unforeseen or outside the landscape architect's control.

9.1.1 Tendering procedures

The invitation of tenders is the most important activity in which the landscape architect has a responsibility to act fairly to landscape contractors in accordance with certain accepted codes and conventions. Those for

*The duties attributable to the 'landscape architect' in this chapter apply equally to landscape managers, supervising officers, and leisure and amenity managers in local authorities. As explained in Chapter 5 the name 'landscape architect' is not protected as is that of 'architect' by the Architects Registration Act. All that is necessary therefore is for the title of the person to whom these duties are delegated to be inserted in the appropriate place in the Recitals of the JCLI Form of Contract for Landscape Works.

the building industry are set out in the NJCC Code of Procedure for Single-stage Selective Tendering (see Appendix G), and most, if not all, the principles apply equally to the landscape industry; of the most important are the following:

1. 'Open' tendering, when tender documents are sent to any contractor in response to a notification in local or technical press is rarely in the best interest of client or contractor and is no longer a practice recommended by DoE to local authorities. Where this is still a requirement of standing orders it can best be complied with by investigating the suitability of all applicants and then inviting tenders from the six considered most appropriate. In this context it is only fair to invite tenders from firms of the same size and of the same standards of competence.

    The Code of Procedure for Selective Tendering, agreed with the contractors, the local authorities and DoE, lays down precise requirements for the numbers of contractors invited, the correction of errors and the notification of the results of tenders submitted.

    It is essential to choose the right-sized firms for the particular project. Rolls Royce will not quote a cheap price for repairing a Ford nor will Ford provide the quality to be expected of Messrs Rolls Royce, i.e. the two quotations will be comparable in neither quality nor price.

2. Writing or telephoning those selected to inform them of the scope of the project, consultants involved, content of tender documents (i.e. with or without quantities), form of contract and dates for the invitation and submission of tenders, to confirm that they are willing and able to submit a tender by the date and time stated.

3. In the tender documents it is essential, if all tenders are to be submitted on a comparable basis, to state the contract period and whenever possible the anticipated contract commencement and completion dates. If tenders on any other basis are to be considered, i.e. shorter or longer periods, fixed price or fluctuations then they should be submitted as additional and supplementary tenders. It is then possible, having chosen the lowest tender, to consider and if necessary negotiate alternative offers. It is also essential to state in tender documents the period during which tenders remain open for acceptance (usually 28 days), and which of the two alternatives is to be used for the adjustment of any errors found in the tender prior to the signing of the contract: NJCC alternative 2 (bona fide errors to be adjusted in the contract sum prior to signing the contract) or alternative 1 (contractors to stand by their tender and absorb any extra costs as a result, or withdraw – commonly known as stick or bust). The former is usually adopted for private clients, and the latter in local authority or public sectors. (An example of a Form of Tender is given in Fig. 9.1).

Tender for *Landscape Improvements*
Church Street Old Peoples Home

To .... *1 B Fair ALI*
Chief Landscape Architect
Barchester District Council
The Close, Barchester

Sir(s)

I/We having read the conditions of contract specification
and schedules of quantity delivered to me/us and having
examined the drawings attached thereto do hereby offer to
execute and complete in accordance with the conditions of
contract the whole of the works described within the period
specified from the date of possession for the sum of *£13,564*

Thirteen thousand, five hundred and sixty four pounds only

I/We agreed that should obvious pricing or errors in
arithmetic be discovered before acceptance of this offer in
the priced schedules of quantity submitted by me/~~us these~~
~~errors will be dealt with and adjusted (Alternative 1)~~ will
not be adjusted and we will stand by our tender (Alternative
2) in accordance with Section 6 of the current NJCC for
Building Code of Procedure for Single Stage Selective
Tendering.

This tender remains open for consideration for 28/~~56~~ days
(2.) from the date fixed for the submission for lodgement of
tenders.

Date this *Twenty fifth day of December.* 19*85*

Name .... *J. T. RAMITIN LTD*

Address .... *Cold Comfort Nurseries*
Barchester Road
Candleford CA5 1XT

Signature .... *B.S.T.G.*
B.S.T. Guest. Chief Estimator

References: 1. Delete as appropriate before issuing.
2. The period specified should not normally
exceed 28 days and only in exceptional
circumstances should be extended to 56
days.

SUMMARY OF TENDER

Preliminaries	£1500 · 00
Hard Landscape	5,564 · 00
Top soil	1180 · 00
Grassed areas	820 · 00
Shrubs and Herbaceous Plants	2951 · 00
Trees	1549 · 00
TOTAL	13,564 · 00

Fig. 9.1 An example of a Form of Tender for use with the JCLI Form of
Contract.

Askham Bryan College
of Agriculture and Horticulture
LIBRARY BOOK

The following considerations are common to all projects.

Dates for the commencement of work on site are of crucial importance and, if not stated in the tender documents, should be ascertained and confirmed prior to its submission. In addition a period of four weeks' notice prior to starting on site is normally essential for the efficient mobilization of the necessary labour by the contractor, and for the procurement of hard landscape and plant materials, particularly those not readily available ex-stock. Should specific items be unavailable it is always recommended that the approval of any substitutes are obtained prior to the submission of tenders. It is always essential to resist the temptation to indulge in or co-operate in 'Dutch' auctions after tenders have been submitted.

If the consultants are not engaged on a full service basis, and post-contract services have been excluded from their responsibility, this should be made clear at the time of tender.

If the period for the execution of the work on site is not included in the tender documents this should be ascertained prior to the submission of tenders so that all tenders are submitted on the same basis, regardless of considerations of time for completion of the work. Should any changes subsequently arise these can always be negotiated with the lowest tenderer.

It is also essential to know the date for commencement of the work at the time of tender, since the date for completion of the works has financial consequences if subsequent upkeep or maintenance is required; six months' upkeep during the summer costs considerably more than six winter months.

The code in respect of the period recommended for the preparation of tenders, the length of time for their acceptance, the adjustment of errors, and the notification of the results, should be strictly adhered to. Tenders should never be opened as they come in nor left lying around before the deadline for their submission.

When the date and time for the submission for tenders has passed – noon on Monday being commonly used, now that postal deliveries are so uncertain, and many tenders are being delivered by hand – it is only fair on those tendering in time to return unopened all those received after the due date marked 'returned – received out of time'. (Proof of date and time of posting are not acceptable. All tenders should be stamped with the date and time of receipt.)

When the tenders have been opened, the landscape architect must list those received to the employer, with his recommendations. This should be followed as soon as possible in a letter or a formal report which in either case should cover the following.

1. The full list of names and tender sums of those received, including those others invited to tender but who did not do so (with the reasons

where known). At this stage it is usual to notify all but the lowest two or three that their tender is unlikely to be recommended for acceptance but without any indication of the other tenders received.

2. A financial analysis and arithmetic check on the lowest tender should follow to establish that the tender is fairly, accurately and consistently priced, and free from any major arithmetic errors. Should any errors be found, the tenderer should be given the opportunity to correct or stand by his tender (dependent on which option is stated in the tender document).

3. A recommendation to accept the lowest tender (adjusted where necessary) should follow as soon as possible, with confirmation of his ability to undertake the work within the time laid down and to the standard required. This should be based on the previous experience of the tenderer by the landscape architect, or by references taken up prior to the invitation of tenders, or as a result of having worked for the employer before. Under these conditions only rarely will a recommendation for acceptance of a tender other than the lowest be justified.

Only when acceptance of the recommendation has been received should the amounts and names of the other tenders received be notified to the other tenderers (in separate lists, with the amounts in ascending order, followed by the names listed alphabetically, including the lowest. (Fig. 9.2 shows an example of a 'standard' letter which can be used for this purpose.) This ensures that, while disclosing the names of the other tenderers and the amounts of the tenders, they cannot be identified with any particular one of them.

9.1.2 Pre-contract meeting

Upon confirmation of the acceptance of the landscape architect's recommendation for the acceptance of a tender a pre-contract meeting should be arranged with the lowest tenderer, at which the following should be confirmed:

1. The names, addresses and telephone numbers of consultants and contractors' staff.
2. Dates for possession and completion.
3. Distribution and number of copies of contract documents.
4. Procedure for issuing instructions, variations and certificates.
5. Site access, services, signs, security, noise restrictions, etc.
6. Site personnel, working hours, accommodation, safety and welfare requirements.
7. Quality control, testing and samples, site works orders, clerk of works, labour returns and weekly reports.
8. Dates of regular progress meetings, site inspections and valuations.
9. Any other business.

Unsuccessful Tenders
_____

Dear Sir,

Job Reference

....

We acknowledge the receipt of your tender dated ....
but wish to inform you that a more acceptable quotation has been received.

We shall, however, be glad to approach you again for future inquiries.

A list of firms who tendered and a list of the tender prices are
attached for your information.

Tenderers (in alphabetical order)

....

....

....

....

Prices

....

....

....

....

Yours faithfully,

Fig. 9.2 An example of a 'standard' letter informing unsuccessful tenderers about other tenders submitted.

When the contract has been signed and the preparations for a start on site have been completed the following are the most important duties and obligations of the various parties in the administration of the contract.

9.2 THE CONTRACTOR'S OBLIGATIONS (JCLI CLAUSE 1.1)

The contractor *must always* carry out and complete the works in accordance with the contract documents diligently and in a good and workmanlike manner. *If* the progress of the work is delayed he *must* inform the landscape architect, stating the reasons and estimating the delay in completion (clause 2.2).

104

9.3 THE EMPLOYER'S OBLIGATIONS

If the employer fails to honour certificates by the due date the contractor may determine his employment (not the contract however).

9.4 THE LANDSCAPE ARCHITECT'S DUTIES (JCLI CLAUSE 1.2)

The landscape architect's duties are no less onerous but more numerous, and include the following.

The landscape architect *must* always supply any further information necessary for the satisfactory completion of the work, issue any instructions necessary, issue interim certificates, certificates of practical completion, making good defects and the final certificate (clauses 3.5, 1.2, 2.4, 2.5, 2.7 and 4.4).

If he is notified that completion of the works is delayed for reasons beyond the control of the contractor, he *must* extend the contract period by a reasonable amount or recommend the deduction of liquidated or ascertained damages. *If* the works are varied he *must* issue instructions in writing and value the variations in accordance with the contract documents. *If* any errors are found in or between the contract documents he *must* issue the necessary instructions for their correction (clauses 2.2, 2.3, 3.5, 3.6, and 4.1).

If the contractor does not proceed with the work diligently or he goes into liquidation the landscape architect may recommend to the employer that the employment of the contractor be determined. He may equally: instruct that one or any of the contractor's employees is excluded from the works; issue instructions for the expenditure of Prime Cost or provisional sums; inspect evidence of insurance; or give instructions for tests and the removal of defective work (clauses 7.1, 3.4, 3.5, 3.7, and 6.4).

9.5 OBLIGATORY DUTIES (ALWAYS NECESSARY)

9.5.1 Landscape architect's instructions (clause 1.2)

A relatively simple requirement provided that they are always in writing in a readily identifiable form such as that issued by the Landscape Institute (Fig. 9.3). Any which involve a material alteration to the authorized expenditure are to be notified to the employer and preferably, wherever possible, the value agreed with the contractor before it is carried out.

9.5.2 Progress payments (clause 4.3)

These must be certified at the intervals of not less than four weeks for the value of work properly executed and any unfixed materials properly but not prematurely brought and stored on site. The value of any work not properly executed and retention must be deducted from the valuation and

				Landscape Architects Instruction

Landscape Architect's name and address
MANNING CLAMP + PARTNERS
31-32 The Green
RICHMOND
Surrey

Works
Elderly Person Housing
Dukes Road,

situate at
Richmond

To contractor
Town & Country Landscapes Ltd.
Dukes Meadows, Mortlake SW 14

Under the terms of the Contract

Instruction no. 16

Date

dated 3rd January 1985

I/We issue the following instructions. Where applicable the contract sum will be adjusted in accordance with the terms of the relevant Condition.

	Instructions	For office use: Approx costs £ omit	£ add
16.01	**PLANTING**		

OMIT: The provisional sum of £500.00 and in lieu thereof place your order with Messrs Meadows Nurseries in accordance with their attached quotation dated 9th January 1985 in the sum of £978.46 subject to the following

i)	Substitute Taxus hibernica in lieu Malus	£26. 20.
ii)	Reduce climbers to one of each	41.90
iii)	Substitute Forsythia for Hamemelis	70.00
		£138.10
iv)	33% reduction in fertiliser and planting 33% x £220	70.00
		£208.10
v)	Omit watering and replanting	195.86
		403.96

Less VOP adjustment to contract base date 574.50
128.04

To AMOUNT OF REVISED TENDER   £446.46

Office reference

Signed_____ Landscape Architect

Notes

Amount of contract sum £
± Approximate value of previous instructions £ _____
£
± Approximate value of this instruction £ _____
Approximate adjusted total £

Distribution: Client ☐   Contractor ☐ Quantity surveyor ☐   Clerk of works ☐   File ☐

Fig. 9.3 Landscape architects instruction. (Reproduced with permission of the Landscape Institute.)

excluded from the Certificate. (At the same time the client should be notified of any forthcoming variations and increased costs of labour and materials to which the contractor is entitled and which might cause the authorized expenditure to be exceeded.) The Landscape Institute (LI) standard form for Interim/Final Certificates covers these points (see Fig. 9.4).

9.5.3 Practical completion (clause 2.4)

A matter solely for the opinion of the landscape architect and usually when the works are sufficiently (*not* 'almost') complete to be put to the use intended without risk or inconvenience to the user. No standard form for this has been produced by the LI or JCLI, a letter incorporating the following form of words will usually suffice.

'I/We certify that in accordance with the conditions of contract, subject to the completion of any outstanding items and/or making good any defects, shortages or other faults which appear during the Defects Liability Period, the Works had achieved, in my/our opinion, practical completion on . . . , the Defects Liability Period will expire on . . . , and that one-half of any retention monies deducted from past previous Certificates are now to be certified for payment.'

If only part of the works are to be handed over, these should be identified accordingly together with their approximate value. The effect of this will be to signify the stopping of any further liquidated ascertained damages which might be deducted, and to notify the employer of his subsequent responsibility for insurance for any subsequent injury to persons or damage to other property and the works.

9.5.4 Making good any defects (clause 2.5)

Similar wording should be used when the Defects Liability Period has expired, all defective work has been made good, and the balance of retention monies can be released.

9.5.5 Final valuation (clause 4.4)

The landscape contractor is responsible under clause 4.4 of the JCT and JCLI contracts to forward within three months (or other such period as has been stated in the tender documents) of practical completion to the landscape architect or quantity surveyor all the financial evidence he needs to complete his final valuation. As soon as these details have been received, the Defects Liability Period has expired and all defects have been made good, the landscape architect must, within 28 days, issue his Final Certificate releasing the balance of money due to the landscape contractor. Although the final valuation is a matter entirely for the landscape architect or quantity surveyor it is usual good practice (to avoid future disputes,

Valuation and Current Financial Statement for Landscape
Interim/Final Certificate

No.

Employer's name and address: E.O. Burlington Esq. Chiswick House, London W4.

Contractor's name and address: Town and Country Landscapes Ltd. Dukes Meadows Mortlake SW14

Contract _ _ _ _ _ _ _ Improvements to Garden _ _ _ _ _ _ _ _ _ _ _ _ _ _ _ _ _ _ Office reference _ 17/36 _ _ _

AUTHORISED EXPENDITURE		ESTIMATED FINAL COST	
To amount of Contract	£ 7,500	To amount of Contract	£ 7,500 _ _ _ _
Additional authorised expenditure	£ 1,250 _ _ _	*Less* contingencies	£ 1,000 _ _ _ _ _
			£ 6,500 _ _ _ _
		Estimated value of Variations to date	+ £ 1,950 _ _ _ _
			£ 8,450 _ _ _ _
		Estimated value of Variations yet to be issued	± £ _ _ 150 _ _ _ _
			£ 8,600 _ _ _ _
Estimated increased costs (if allowable)	£ _ _ 750 _ _ _ _	Estimated increased costs (if allowable) ± £ _ _ 750 _ _ _ _	
TOTAL AUTHORISED EXPENDITURE	£ 9,500	**ESTIMATED TOTAL COST**	£ 9,350

Signed _____ William W. Kent FLI _____ Landscape architect. Date _____ 3.2.85 _____

Distribution: Client ☑   Quantity surveyor ☑   File ☑

Landscape architects name and address:
William W. Kent
12 Carlton House Terrace
London SW1Y 5AH

Landscape Architects Interim/Final

Certificate

Employer's name and address:
E. O.Burlington Esq
CHISWICK HOUSE
London W4

Certificate No.	FIVE
Date of Valuation	3.2.80
Date of Certificate	7.2.80

Contractor's name and address:
Town & Country Landscapes Ltd.
Dukes Meadows
Mortlake SW14

Valuation of work executed £	7,250.00
Value of materials on site £	1,250.00
	£ 8,500.00
Less retention £	425.00

Contract: Improvements to Garden

Reference: 17/36

I/We hereby certify that under the terms of the Contract

Total to date £	7,075.00
Less amount previously certified £	5,000.00
	2,075.00

dated: _____

the sum of (words) 3rd February 1980

Two thousand and seventy five pounds

(Exclusive of any Value Added Tax)

is due from the Employer to the Contractor

Signed _____ William W. Kent FLI _____ Landscape architect   Date: _____ 3.2.85 _____

Distribution: Client ☐   Contractor ☐   Quantity surveyor ☐   File ☐

Fig. 9.4   Interim/Final Certificate. (Reproduced with permission of the Landscape Institute.)

possibly leading to arbitration) to obtain the landscape contractor's written agreement beforehand and to advise the employer of the details prior to the issue of the Certificate.

A brief statement and summary (such as shown in Tables 9.1 and 9.2) will usually suffice.

9.6 OBLIGATORY DUTIES (IF THEY ARISE)

9.6.1 Approvals (clause 1.1)

It is important to ensure that any 'approvals' of the landscape work – particularly as to the quality of workmanship and materials – are used sparingly if the landscape contractor is not to be relieved of his responsibility to comply with the contract documents in all respects. The same applies to shop drawings which should always be returned with or without 'comment', drawing attention to the need to 'check all setting-out dimensions, tolerances, sections and junctions with adjacent work on site'.

The landscape architect must, however, always bring to the landscape contractor's attention information of which he is aware (including the route of public service cables) or at least draw his attention to the need to find out!

9.6.2 Extensions to contract period (clause 2.2)

The contract requires that the landscape contractor must notify the landscape architect if completion will be delayed for reasons beyond his control when the landscape architect must extend the contract period for completion of the works by such a period of time as may be reasonable. This calls for a considerable exercise of judgement on the part of the landscape architect, bearing in mind that there must be delays to completion (not progress); many delays will be concurrent and not consecutive, some being within and some outside the control of the contractor. The landscape architect must notify the contractor of the extension granted as soon as he is able but is under no obligation to notify him of the reasons or amounts of individual delays reached in coming to his decision.

Only the following are normally considered to be reasons 'beyond the control of the contractor':

1. Force majeure.
2. Loss or damage occasioned by any one or more of the points referred to in clause 6.3 (loss or damage by fire, storm, flood, etc).
3. Civil commotion or strikes affecting the works.
4. Compliance with the landscape architect's instructions.
5. Delay in the receipt of landscape architect's instructions.
6. Delay by persons employed or engaged by the employer not forming part of the contract.

Table 9.1 Example of a Statement for Final Valuation.

Job...

Contractor...

Statement of final cost

Amount of contract:	£
Less contingencies:	£ _____

Additional works:
1.
2.
3.
4.
5.
6.
7.
8.
9.
10. _____
£   £ _____

Less omissions: £
1.
2.
3.
4.
5.
6. _____
£   £ _____

Net adjustment from adjustment of provisional sums and
sundry items: £ _____

                                                         £ _____

9.6.3 Liquidated and ascertained damages

Should the contract completion be delayed for reasons *not* beyond the control
of the contractor and for which the landscape architect is therefore unable to
grant an extension he must notify the employer in writing accordingly before
the contract date for completion so that the employer deducts the necessary

Table 9.2 Example of Summary of Account and Final Valuation (for use when no Q.S. is employed).

Job:

Client:

Contractor:

To amount of contract	£
Adjustment of variations prime cost and provisional sums:	£
To total amount of additions:	£
To total amount of omissions:	£ _____
Net deduction/extra	£ _____
Total cost of work executed	£ _____

We hereby certify that this Final Valuation properly prepared in accordance with the Terms and Conditions of the Contract is agreed in the above total of
£   (write out in words)
representing the total claim under this Contract.

Signed:

Contractor..

Date...

Architect..

Date..

(Note: this form has to be sent to the contractor in duplicate with a request that he sign and return one copy to the landscape architect.)

amount of liquidated and ascertained damages from the next Interim Certificate.

9.6.4 Variations

All variations which the landscape architect makes must be confirmed in writing and valued by the landscape architect on a fair and reasonable basis, using where relevant the prices in the priced specification/schedules/schedule of rates.

To ensure that these are 'fair and reasonable' the following rules should be followed.

1. Similar work executed under similar conditions and quantity shall be valued in accordance with the rates of the priced specification/schedules/schedule of rates.
2. Similar work executed under dissimilar conditions or quantity shall be in accordance with rates based on those in the priced specification/schedules/schedule of rates/Bills of Quantity.
3. Work not of similar character shall be valued at fair rates and prices with an appropriate adjustment for the cost of preliminary items.
4. Work which cannot be properly valued by measurement shall be valued on the basis of the rules for prime cost of daywork as defined by the RICS and BEC at the date of tender subject to the provision of the necessary supporting evidence having been delivered to the landscape architect not later than the end of the week following that in which the work has been executed.

Dayworks can only be used therefore when the variation cannot be 'measured' and if, when acknowledging their receipt, the following words are used, the situation is made clear to all concerned, ensuring that dayworks are only used in the appropriate circumstances.

'Thank you for daywork sheets no. . . . Where necessary an Instruction for the variation will follow. This acknowledgement does not, however, indicate our agreement that the Works are variations to the Contract, that if so they wil be valued on a dayworks basis, nor that the labour, materials and plant stated are correct.'

This is particularly important since the listing of labour and materials used does not necessarily imply that they were necessary for the proper execution of the work. The contractor is only entitled to reimbursement for a reasonable quantity of labour and material. The valuation of work on a daywork basis does not relieve him of his obligation to carry out the work as expeditiously and economically as possible.

9.7 OPTIONAL DUTIES (IF THE LANDSCAPE ARCHITECT SO DECIDES)

9.7.1 Notice to proceed with the works (clause 7.1)

If it appears to the landscape architect that the landscape contractor is neglecting his primary responsibility to proceed diligently with the works he may, if he thinks fit, suggest to the employer that he, the employer, should exercise his right to determine the contract. If the employer agrees, then a letter should be sent to the contractor by recorded delivery using the following words.

'Owing to your neglect and failure to proceed with the above work in accordance with Clause 7.1 of your contract dated . . . WE HEREBY GIVE YOU NOTICE to proceed with the above in a reasonable manner and with due diligence employing the necessary labour and materials for the due performance thereof.

In the event of your neglect to comply with this notice during a period of . . . days from the date hereof, we are instructed by the employer to inform you that he will excercise his powers under Clause 7.1 of the said Contract and determine the Contract'.

This usually has the desired effect and either the work is speeded up or the contractor writes setting out the reasons for the delay and the course of action he intends to take to remedy the situation.

9.7.2 Determination of the contractor's employment (clause 7.1)

Should the contractor ignore the foregoing notice then the employer may wish to exercise his right to determine the employment of the contractor. Before so doing, legal advice is essential, with rigid adherance to the proper procedures if, however clear-cut the rights and wrongs of the case may seem to be, the case is not to fail because of such legal technicalities as the service of notice or the contractor being able to establish that he has only 'postponed or suspended' the work.

9.7.3 Exclusion from the works (clause 3.4)

Although this option of the landscape architect to exclude employees of the contractor from the works (no longer dismissed) is clearly set out in the Contract, its formal implementation is rarely necessary. On the infrequent occasions when the need arises, the problem can usually be resolved by a discrete discussion with the landscape contractor without recourse to the legality of the Contract clause.

9.7.4 Expenditure of prime cost and provisional sums, inspection of evidence of insurance, test and/or removal of defective work (clauses 3.5, 3.7 and 6.4)

Should the need for any of these arise, then the necessary provisions of the Contract should be used empowering the landscape architect to issue such instructions as he considers necessary.

9.7.5 Oral instructions (clause 3.5)

Messages must unambiguously indicate to whom they are meant, whose action is required and if confirmation is necessary. They must be in a form readily understood by the individual concerned, e.g. no Latin tags to foremen.

1. The telephone can be used for simple question-and-answer problems, but not for complicated, difficult or delicate problems. Important points should always be subsequently confirmed in writing.

2.   Personal visits are required for all difficult and delicate matters and discussions particularly when personal relationships are involved, and also should be confirmed in writing.

3.   Letters and memos must essentially be clear, orderly and concise, and have the advantage that they can be dealt with at the convenience of the receiver.

9.7.6   Supervision

Apart from his duties under the contract, the landscape architect's obligations with his client or employer require him to inspect the work to ensure the progress and quality is generally in accordance with the contract documents.

This is part of a separate agreement between the two, and in no way relieves the contractor of his own separate obligation to complete the work in accordance with contract documents.

There is however an implied right of access for the landscape architect to the site in order for him to carry out his other contractual duties under the landscape contract; it is usual for the landscape architect to carry out the necessary inspections in order to discharge his duties to his client at the same time.

9.7.7   Meetings

'Committee' meetings involve a number of people reaching a decision on the basis of a majority vote of its members. This is also binding on the minority who cannot disassociate themselves from it without resigning. A chairman conducts the meeting but is not individually responsible for the decisions reached. Other than a few client committee meetings, landscape architects rarely come into contact with this category of meeting.

'Consultants' meetings when someone meets subordinates (to advise him within their individual sphere of responsibility) so that he can come to a decision within the wider implication of the whole project, are clearly different.

Site and progress meetings are partly 'information' meetings, exchanging and recording information about activities and operations, and partly 'problem-solving' meetings.

Neither consultants' nor site meetings involve a chairman, voting or a corporate responsibility. Matters to be discussed at such meetings should be promulgated beforehand and 'matters arising' kept to a minimum. Minutes should always record decisions without attempting to précis or record discussion, and should clearly indicate what action is required and (in a separate column) by whom. For this reason it is helpful for all concerned if weekly/fortnightly/monthly progress meetings are held at regular intervals in suitable accommodation on site, and a memorandum (not minutes) sets out the decisions in summary form on a format similar to that in Table 9.3.

9.8   CLERKS OF WORKS

There is no specific provision for a clerk of works in the JCLI Contract although there is no reason why the employer should not employ one.

While the landscape architect is not expected to be on site permanently, but merely to appear at intervals to inspect and check the work, if a clerk of works is employed on the site full-time, he can be expected to ensure conformity with the design although still 'solely as inspector on behalf of the employer' with no power to issue instructions to the contractor. His presence in no way relieves the contractor of his obligations to complete the work in accordance with the contract documents.

A recent case however — following the judgment of *East Ham v. Bernard Sunley* in 1966, before responsibilities for supervision under the 1977 revision to the JCT Form of Building Contract was changed — established that in the event of negligence of the clerk of works his employer was vicariously responsible and the agreed damages were reduced accordingly.

The contractor is responsible under his contract with the employer to carry out and complete the works in accordance with the contract documents. In practice, if he is to submit the lowest tender in competition, this means the lowest standard of workmanship and materials he considers the landscape architect will accept.

The employer is responsible to the contractor for honouring certificates which he has agreed (probably without realizing it) that the landscape architect should issue. The landscape architect also has to issue such instructions as are necessary for the completion of the works, and has to grant such extensions to the contract period as are justified. These are matters which the employer puts very low in priority in the list of duties he requires of the landscape architect. Some duties the landscape architect has to do on every contract, some he has to do only if they arise, some he may do if he considers them to be justified.

In addition the landscape architect is responsible to the employer under the landscape architect's appointment for:

1.   Contract administration.
2.   Inspecting the progress and quality of work on site.
3.   Making periodic financial reports.

A Building Research Establishment study (BRE Current Paper 7/81 — Quality Control on Building Sites) found that of 500 events relating to quality on building projects, 98 were of a serious nature, of these 36 related to faults in workmanship arising from carelessness and not ignorance, and no less than 57 arose from inadequate design project information. In both cases 41% were never satisfactorily resolved. (See Table 9.4.)

Table 9.3 Example of a memorandum of a progress meeting

Date:

Job title:

Present:	Name	Representing
	....	....
	....	....
	....	....
	....	....
	....	....

Contract sum: £ . . . Certified value to date £ . . .

Contract commencement date ../../.. Contract completion date ../../..

Contract period . . . Weeks contract No . . .

Overall progress . . . % . . .weeks ahead/behind

Total days inclement weather this month . . . Total to date . . .

1.0 Progress review

    Item   % Scheduled   % Achieved   Weeks +/− schedule

    Progress generally   %...

2.0 Matters arising from last meeting.

3.0 Construction Problems: Building and civil engineering
                                      Structural engineering
                                      Services engineering
                                      Planting.

4.0 Outstanding information required.

5.0 Quality control/samples.

6.0 Any other business.

7.0 Date of next meeting.

Table 9.4 Some causes of observed 'quality-related events' (Crown copyright. Reproduced by permission of the Controller, HMSO.)

Lack of skill	Skill has been used in the sense of manual dexterity.
Lack of care	When past work has shown that tradesmen possessed sufficient skill, but had performed poorly on current work, lack of care was deemed to be the cause.
Lack of knowledge	Lack of the knowledge that competent tradesmen could be expected to possess in connection with their trade, to be used, for example, in the interpretation of drawings and in making minor detail design decisions.
Poor planning by tradesman	Tradesmen failing to plan the order of their work correctly sometimes resulted in their having to carry out a detailed and difficult re-design which was of a lower standard than the original.
Poor contractor's organization	For example, removal of rubble and debris, stacking of materials and management of concreting work.
No protection of completed work	Lack of or inadequate protection had resulted in work being spoilt.
No co-ordination of design	For example, differences between architects' and engineers' drawings were causing confusion on site.
Difficult to build	Very high levels of skill and near-perfect materials were needed to build the design correctly.
Design will not work	Faithful implementation of design would not achieve intended performance, e.g. a damp-proof course would not function properly as detailed.
Unclear/missing project information	On drawings, Bills of Quantities or specifications.
Low quality design	When the design detail, or material specification, was well below the standard of the rest of the building.
Designer not understanding materials	When a material had been specified that was inadequate for the purpose.

It is not surprising therefore that it has been suggested that while the project architects and landscape architects are best qualified and experienced for the task, because of their other commitments (including those of resolving the problems arising from inadequate design/project information), they are least able to carry out properly their site inspectorate obligations to the employer. One solution therefore is for them to decline to accept inspection duties on the grounds that they are unable to carry them out adequately, but few would wish to sacrifice the control of the operation this would entail.

While retaining a general supervisory role they have therefore to delegate inspection duties to separate, suitably qualified people on site whose sole duty is to inspect the work to ensure that it is being executed in accordance with the contract documents. These people must never, under any circumstances, be given authority to order or permit any variations or departures from the contract documents. Any inadequacies, discrepancies, errors or divergencies in design/project information always being referred to the landscape architect to issue the necessary instructions. Nor do they 'approve' the work any more than building inspectors and district surveyors do who now confine themselves to the negative task of not objecting to the subsequent stages being put in hand.

Inspection of work in progress is particularly important when it will be concealed by subsequent stages, the most crucial being the five listed on page 119, the project landscape architect having added those others which he predicts will be necessary on each individual project and which the contractor should be told, in the contract documents, that he should not put in hand until the previous stage has been inspected. If the contractor is not to be held up, it will be rarely possible for the project landscape architect to be able to do this at the short notice that in practice will inevitably occur.

If the landscape architect is not to undertake these duties, there are three choices open to him.

1. For the duties to be delegated to a firm specializing in such work.
2. To other consultants or 'clerks of works' engaged by the employer direct (this will not relieve him of his responsibility – see the judgement in *Moresk Cleaners v. Hicks* (1966)).
3. By the landscape architect employing the site inspectorate on his own staff, with or without additional fee, dependent on the individual circumstances and size of the job.

Inspections carried out on a regular basis will not suffice to reduce their incidence. It is for this reason that inspectors should have the flexibility to be on site at crucial stages of the construction. The most crucial stages are where work will be covered up by subseqent operations. On each project, the landscape architect should stipulate the crucial stages, so that inspections can be carried out on a *predictive* rather than a haphazard basis. Examples of such crucial stages of general construction which should be positively inspected are:

(a) Formations prior to casting of foundations.
(b) Drains when laid, and after backfilling.
(c) Excavations to remove topsoil and/or to reduced levels.
(d) Hardcore beds prior to laying of pavings or casting of sub-floors.
(e) Damp-proof membranes, damp-proof courses, cavity closures, and cavity trays.

The implementation of site inspections on a *predictive* basis, should start on the drawing board. As the detailed design proceeds, the landscape architect should be compiling a check list of all aspects of the construction which will require to receive the special attention of the site inspectorate. This in addition to general check lists.

Site inspectors should be required to submit detailed reports to the landscape architect following each inspection. These reports, in addition to recording general matters such as progress by comparison with programme, information or instructions required, queries raised by the contractor and/or clerk of works, etc., should also record the crucial works positively inspected and whether or not these were satisfactory.

10

Indoor planting

10.1 INTRODUCTION

While all the preceeding requirements for plants grown externally, with regard to specification, handling and planting, apply equally for indoor plants, there are in addition certain other basic needs which it is essential to comply with if the establishment and survival of indoor plants are to be also ensured.

Plants are no different to people and are unlikely to survive if kept for more than a short while in low light and low temperatures.

10.2 LIGHT REQUIREMENTS

It does not matter if the source is natural or artificial, but no plant can survive in conditions of less than 250 lux, and internal artificial illumination levels greater than 2000 lux, are seldom possible. Some indoor plants may have originated in the tropics or sub-tropics growing under full sun with light intensities of 100 000 lux and others in deep shade of less than 100 lux. However, with gentle acclimatization and a reduction in energy usage many plants when grown indoors will still replace their leaves at 3000 lux or less. Table 10.1 details the light requirements of some common plants and trees.

Supplementary lighting can seldom be achieved from fluorescent 'warm white' lamps, nor with incandescent lighting without a compensating blue filter. High-intensity discharge lamps with a high output in both blue and red wavelengths are available, with an acceptable colour rendering, provided that this is supplied for between 8 and 18 hours per day, 7 days per week but no more and no less. Under these circumstances indoor plants will thrive and enhance the interior space for which they are provided.

The various types of lamp available include the following:

1. 'Planting lights': PAR38 shaped 150-watt colour-corrected incandescent lamps. If fixed 1.0 m above the plant canopy, they will provide 600 lux as flood lights, and 2000 lux as spot lamps.
2. 'Tungsten ballast discharge lamps': provided as fluomeric or blended, they do not require additional control gear. 160-watt lamps will give 300 lux at 1.0 m for floods, and 2000 lux at 2.0 m for spots, having a much longer life than basic 'planting lights'.
3. 'High-intensity discharge lamps': require special control gear to be built in with 250-watt lamps, providing over 3000 lux at 2.0 m.
4. 'Full-spectrum fluorescent': the most effective 2 × 1800 mm tubes; at 1.5 m they provide about 1200 lux.

10.3 ACCLIMATIZATION

Many indoor plants used in Britain are grown near Amsterdam and Ghent, but most larger trees used internally are grown in full sun in Florida or Southern Spain and if they are transported or shipped in total darkness for more than five days can lose 90% of their leaves. While these may be replaced under nursery conditions, they are unlikely to do so if delivered straight to site, since they need time to develop the thinner leaf skin and chlorphyllous structure necessary to take into account their exposure to the reduced light and to develop the necessary greener leaves. The stomata in the underside of the leaves also have to reduce in size in order to take account of the reduced rate of photosynthesis.

The food reserves of the plant will also have been reduced during its transportation to overcome the increased stress to which it has been subjected and to renew at least the foliage lost during the process.

The roots of large trees and shrubs taken from open ground will be immediately subjected to a root/shoot ratio imbalance when placed in the container, which will also take time to readjust.

In general all plants not grown in a glass house or other such controlled environment must have been grown with 55% shade for three months or preferably 70% shade for a minimum of six months prior to having been transferred to the nursery.

10.4 TEMPERATURE REQUIREMENTS

Most interior plants thrive in the same temperate temperature conditions as people, i.e. 18–25 °C during the day and 13–18 °C at night with an absolute minimum of 10 °C (50°F) for tropical plants and 5 °C for house plants generally (which is normally achieved in totally enclosed unheated internal spaces) and a maximum of 43 °C above which photosynthesis stops. Temperatures above or below these limits will inevitably cause damage especially to

Table 10.1 Light levels for interior landscape plants. The requirement for individual species is shown as a band on a lux scale meant to represent light available at the foliage canopy. This lux amount is required for 12 to 14 hours a day, 365 days a year.

Key ——— Light level for healthy growth
     – – – Minimum level for survival

	250 lux	500 lux	750 lux	1250 lux	2000 lux
Trees and large plants (1.5 m to 10 m)					
Araucaria excelsa					
Cordyline australis					
Dracaena fragrans massangeana					
Dracaena Marginata					
Ficus benjamina. P. Elastica					
Ficus lyrate					
Ficus nitida					
Kentia forsteriana					
Pandanus utilis					
Phoenix dactylifera. P. canariensis. P. roebelenii					
Schefflera actinophylla					
Medium plants (0.5 m to 1.5 m)					
Chamaedora elegans					
Chamaerops humilis					
Codiaeum					
Cordyline stricta					
Cordyline terminalis					
Dieffenbachia amoena Tropic Snow					
Dizygotheca elegantissima					
Dracaena deremensis					
Heptapleurum arboricola					
Monstera deliciosa					
Pandanus veitchii					
Philodendron Red Emerald. Green Emerald. etc					

Philodendron pertusum. P. erubescens. P. selloum. etc.
Rhapis excelsa
Yucca elephantipes

Low growing (to 1.0 m) and ground cover

Bromeliads (*Aechmea. Nidularium Vriesia. etc*)
Aglaonema
Ananas bracteatus
Asplenium nidus
Chlorophytum variagatum
Ficus pumila
Maranta tricolor
Nephrolepis exaltata
Philodendron tuxla
Sansevieria laurentii
Scindapsus aurea

Climbing plants
Cissus antaratica
Philodendron scandens. P. pumila
Rhoicissus Ellen Danica

Plants for cool areas
Aspidistra elatior
Cordyline australis
Fatsia Japonica
Fatshedera lizei
Ferns–hardy
Medera, green varieties
(climbing and trailing)
Laurus nobilis (bay)
Ligustrum lucidum
Pittosporum, various

indoor plants if they are exposed to them for more than a very short time. The effect of placing a plant directly in the path of an air stream from air-conditioning grilles is particularly dangerous.

Plants such as *Ficus benjamina*, *Dracaena marginata* and *Howea fosteriana* underplanted with *Spathiphyllum*, *Mauna loa* and *Philodendum scandens* subjected to temperatures of 20—25 °C will recover when heating is reduced to 12-14 °C.

Relative humidity may cause greater problems than those of the temperature. Many plants, initially grown in humidities of 60-80%, need time to acclimatize themselves to the 45-55% relative humidity that people normally prefer. Equally, few indoor plants will tolerate a relative humidity below 35%.

It has been suggested that 50% of plant losses are due to incorrect lighting, 40% due to incorrect watering, with only 10% attributable to pests, diseases and other causes. Concentration of effort on the first two will therefore pay dividends.

10.5   IRRIGATION

Most indoor plants are still dependant on a soil culture with a variety of irrigation systems, although hydro culture is growing in popularity and increased knowledge of the technicalities of its application can often provide markedly better results.

10.5.1   Manual watering

This must be carried out at least once, and sometime twice, per week. This can, however, over-compact the surface of the soil restrict the passage of air to the roots and prevent the leaching into them of the nutrients necessary for the plants' survival. Regular trowelling of the surface and proper drainage at the base to dispose of any surplus in manual watering systems is therefore essential. Manual watering is best carried out in heavy doses at well-spaced intervals to allow fluctuation between field capacity and moist state.

10.5.2   Automatic systems

These are available from specialist suppliers to provide soft water on either a drip or a sprinkler basis, but under these circumstances corresponding drainage facilities for the water surplus to the plants' requirements are also essential.

10.5.3   Reservoir-based systems

To overcome the risks of irregular maintenance or to reduce labour costs, indoor plant containers are now often provided with water being fed in from a filler pipe and transferred to the growing medium by capilliary action. Such containers, therefore, must be of only such a depth that the water will rise to plants with roots balls of a limited size. Such systems, however, can fail if the plants are over-watered.

10.5.4 Hydroculture

The system of growing indoor plants on a container with a clay granule inert supporting medium has been available for many years. The plants (which should be grown specifically for this method for no less than ten weeks after transplanting from compost) then derive their water and food direct from the solution – carefully balanced to provide for the plant's complete needs – in the bottom of the container.

10.6 SOIL

All indoor plants should be rooted in an uncompacted substrata with at least 20% cavities, and should be salt-free. Root balls must be moist at the time of planting and should be set in a compost such as 6 parts loam, 2 of peat, 2 of bark and 1 part sand without foreign matter or stones over 50 mm diameter. This has been found by experience to suit the majority of plants, provided it contains only a small trace of fertilizer and salt of less than 1000 p.p.m., the plants having been established in their growing container for at least six months prior to delivery

The sand must be non-calcareous, coarse-grained river-washed, and free from all extraneous matter. Peat should be coarse-textured, baled, horticultural sphagnum peat to BS 4156.

All compost mixes must completely surround the plant and be measured and blended accurately, thoroughly moistened to between 30–40% with a pH between 5.5 and 6.5. It should be placed in layers no more than 300 mm thick, lightly trodden down and levels made up as and when any settlement occurs.

Soils should be separated from the drainage layer with a synthetic fibre separator to keep the soil fines from entering the drainage layer, which must, itself, be formed of pre-washed leca placed to a minimum thickness of 100 mm level to within ±25 mm over any given planter.

10.7 FEEDING

Most soil composts contain sufficient fertilizer for at least six months' growth after which time small amounts of liquid feed every 4–6 weeks during the winter, should suffice. Organic fertilizers are not advisable nor are controlled-release fertilizers, unless provided by experts.

With hydroculture, ion exchange resin should be applied every six months with a little liquid fed in soft water areas. Foliar feeds are available but are not generally advisable.

BALI MAINTENANCE CONTRACT

An Agreement made this _____ day of _____ One thousand nine hundred and _____ between _____ whose office is situate at _____
_____ (hereinafter called "the Company" which expression includes its agents or servants) of the one part and _____
_____ (hereinafter called "the Owners") of the other part.

Whereby it is agreed as follows:

1)   The Company shall from the _____ day of _____ One thousand nine hundred and _____ until the _____ day of _____ One thousand nine hundred and _____ keep the displays of plants described in the Schedule hereto (hereafter referred to as "the plants") full and the plants clean and cared for and will replace dead or dying plants with others of a like nature. For this purpose the Company shall send a representative once every _____ weeks to inspect and attend to the plantings in accordance with the terms hereof.

2)   This contract shall remain in force for twelve months from the above date and thereafter be renewed annually until cancelled by either party in the manner set forth in paragraph 5 hereof.

3)   In consideration of the above service performed or about to be performed the Owners will pay to the Company the sum of £_____ per calendar month plus VAT to be invoiced on a three monthly basis in advance. This sum to be subject to an annual revision equal to the inflation rate notified within the Retail Price Index in existence during the last month prior to renewal date.

4)   This contract does not include accident or misuse of plants by the Owners, their employees or third parties and is made on the understanding that the Owners will continue to supply the environmental conditions in existence when the contract is first signed. In the event of plant loss being caused by temperatures falling below 10 degrees centigrade/50 degrees fahrenheit replacement plants will be charged for unless a colder temperature regime has been agreed in writing. This also applies to displays being moved to unsuitable positions without the Company's consent and in such cases any untoward plant replacement will be covered by an additional charge. Water will also be provided to the Company free of charge by the Owners.

5)   Beyond the primary period of contract, i.e. twelve months, the agreement shall continue on the same terms and conditions on an annual basis subject to the consent of the Owners and subject to the right of the Owners to cancel the agreement subject to three months' notice in writing prior to the end of the second or subsequent years.

Schedule of items covered by this Contract

The Owners_____   The Company_____
_____   _____

Signed by _____   Signed by _____
Title _____   Title _____
Date _____   Date _____

Fig. 10.1   BALI maintenance contract form, for interior plant displays.

10.8 MAINTENANCE

It is essential that all plants are seen to be in a healthy and vigourous condition when planted, any not fulfilling this requirement being removed from site and immediately replaced by others of the same type and size. A proper maintenance plan – setting out the programme for regular watering, clearing dead plant material and rubbish from containers, feeding, dusting and spraying with pesticides – should then be immediately put in hand and continued for a period of at least 12 months and preferably 3 years.

Dust can be initially removed by wiping with a damp cloth or feather duster; heavier deposits require the use of a mild detergent, applied with a fine spray using soft water. One of two monthly treatments of white spirit or 'leaf shine' can sometimes be used for some dicotolydens to reduce dust but is not advisable except in special circumstances and then only under close supervision.

A suitable maintenance contract is given in Fig. 10.1 which is based on the standard BALI maintenance contract for interior plant displays. (Plant losses of 10% per annum must be expected and allowed for.)

10.9 PESTS AND DISEASES

Although indoor plants are usually supplied relatively free from pests, they rapidly lose their resistance, due to the low light levels.

Tree cuts should be treated with a fungicidal sealant such as Arbrex 805 and the indoor plant maintenance contractor must allow for all necessary spraying or dusting against pests and diseases. Fungicides, herbicides and insecticides must be non-toxic to normal use by people, birds and animals, and be included in the Agricultural Chemical Approval Scheme's list of products. It is essential that they are always applied strictly in accordance with the manufacture's printed instructions, whether as contact or systemic compounds. Pyrethrum, resmethrin, melathin, kelthane and methylated spirits are most effective and most popular contact herbicides for aerial pest and diazinon for subterranean ones.

127

11

Landscape maintenance

11.1 INTRODUCTION

Although building owners are usually aware that they are responsible for the regular daily/weekly/monthly/annual cleaning/repair/maintenance/servicing of new buildings as soon as they have taken possession and occupied them, e.g. emptying waste paper bins, cleaning floors, windows and lavatories, replacing light bulbs, etc., they rarely, if ever, remember that they are responsible for the same care and attention of the spaces between and around their buildings.

Shrub borders need the almost daily clearing of litter in urban areas, grass needs weekly mowing and watering during the summer months, and even trees need an annual pruning and sometimes tree surgery.

It is clearly inequitable to expect the landscape contractor to include the cost of this work in his initial tender for supply and planting, unless it is specified in detail and separately identified, any more than it is to expect him to provide blanket cover for the cost of replacing any trees and shrubs damaged by vandalism. Where this work is required, therefore, it should be clearly identified in the bills, schedules or tender summary for the landscape contractor to price. Equally, problems will inevitably arise if another subcontractor is employed, or if the employer himself adequately or inadequately accepts the responsibility for such maintenance. In the event of plants being found to be dead at the end of the Defects Liability Period as a result of sub-standard stock, inadequate plant handling in transit or negligent planting by the landscape contractor, it is always difficult, if not impossible, to provide sufficient evidence to refute the counter-claim that their death arose from some act or lack of care or inadequate watering on the part of those responsible for their subsequent care during the Defects Liability Period.

It is always essential, therefore, to obtain from the landscape contractor at the time of tender, a separate tender for the regular upkeep of trees, shrubs and grassed areas after practical completion of the work if it is intended that he should be responsible for making good all defects at the end of the Defects Liability Period. In such circumstances, where the landscape contractor is to be held responsible for replacing dead and defective plants and for the upkeep of the landscape works after practical completion and during the Defects Liability Period, this separate agreement should set out in detail the maintenance work to be included in each individual item, for trees, shrubs, herbaceous planting and grassed areas within the site for each season of the year.

Such regular maintenance must be laid down to be executed with the minimum inconvenience and obstruction of access to the user and occupiers of the site. Any work necessary must be carried out as discreetly and inconspicuously as possible since no work can be tolerated which prohibits the normal access or use of the site. In this connection all sites should provide for a gardener's store in a convenient central location with hose points at approximately 50–metres centres, so that equipment and materials do not always have to be specially brought each time they are needed on site. Landscape areas must be designed to permit the maximum use of labour-saving equipment, with ramps provided to enable all parts of the site to be accessible (not only to the physically handicapped but also for mechanical equipment) irrespective of the existence of steps elsewhere on site. It is also essential for provision to be made for all machinery, plant and equipment to be returned to the store, all rubbish, weeds and superfluous material to be removed, and the site to be left clean and tidy on completion.

Any plants damaged during maintenance operations should be reported to the employer immediately so that remedial measures can be initiated without delay, all other defects being accepted as the responsibility of the initial landscape contractor.

All maintenance work should be performed at appropriate intervals and suitable weather conditions for the total number of times stated in the bills, specification or schedules, including any measures specified as being necessary for the application of herbicides and pesticides for the control of disease, weeds and pests.

Most landscape contracts, therefore, provide for the regular maintenance of planted areas for the first year after practical completion by the contractor who has supplied and planted them. At the same time the firm then also accepts responsibility for the replacement of all trees, shrubs and grassed areas which may have failed during the same period for any reason other than theft or vandalism Only in the most rare instances is it advisable for an employer to use his own staff or pay another contractor to carry out this work during the first 12 months after practical completion. The risks of dispute arising from such divided responsibility are self evident. If the subsequent maintenance is entrusted to the initial contractor problems arising from lack of communication between the parties and resulting in the second contractor being blamed for the death of the initial contractor's plants, can be avoided. The work must, however, be clearly described and set out for pricing for the landscape contractor to include an accurate price in his tender.

11.2 TREE MAINTENANCE

Mature trees require the least frequent regular maintenance of all plants at a negligible cost provided they are inspected at least twice each year to ensure that they remain in a satisfactory and healthy condition. Every May and October, however, roots must be watered with an approved liquid manure (such as 10% nitrogen, 15% phosphoric acid and 10% potash) at the rate 60 grams per square metre. Weeds and grass must on no account be allowed within 500 mm of the stem until such time as the tree is properly established. No evidence as yet exists of the relative advantages of tree spats, mulch, or herbicides. Periodically stakes must be checked, tightened or replaced to ensure that no chaffing of tree bark has been allowed to arise, and any protective vermin spats adjusted. All dead, diseased and broken branches – such as those arising from wind or malicious damage – must be cleanly removed and the scar treated with a compound such as Arbrex 805. After a severe frost, the soil around all roots must be firmly trodden down. An experienced arboriculturalist should always be used for pruning so that the natural shape and habit of the tree is preserved. Trees irreparably damaged or destroyed by vandalism must always be replaced as soon as seasonal weather conditions permit.

11.3 SHRUB MAINTENANCE

Shrubs must be maintained in spring and autumn in the same way as trees. Additionally, at least once each month, during the growing season, unless herbicides have been previously applied, shrub borders must be lightly forked over and any weeds removed, keeping the soil open and pliable without disturbing the roots of the plants and the soil around them then re-firmed.

Live and dead weeds must be cleared away or buried, perennial weeds must be removed with their roots and destroyed. Informal flowering hedges are to be lightly pruned after flowering, to remove dead heads, straggling side and upright shoots but not, under any circumstances, clipped back, nor pruned back to a rigid line unless specifically so instructed.

By planting shrubs at comparatively close centres, i.e. 750 mm or less, this should ensure comparatively weed-free borders are established relatively quickly with subsequent low maintenance costs arising from the minimization of labour expenditure.

11.4 GRASS MAINTENANCE

Short mown grass is the most demanding of all planted areas in terms of maintenance, requiring to be cut at least once in April, twice in May, three times in June, weekly in July and August, and twice in September – at least sixteen cuts each year apart from the inevitable trimming of grass edges and mowing margins. Allowance must be made for grass to be rolled at least once in April, June and August.

Long grass, on the other hand, particularly that including bulbs or meadow flowers, must never be cut until late in the summer and that in heavy shade never closer than 75 mm. Fallen leaves must be swept up each October and thereafter as necessary during the winter.

All grass areas must be dressed in spring and autumn with an approved turf fertilizer, selective weed-killer and moss retardant if necessary. Between May and August short-grass cuttings may be collected and spread as mulch over shrub borders and under the ground-cover foliage and forked into the soil in the winter.

11.5   IRRIGATION

Regular watering must be provided for all newly planted and seeded areas during the first months of the summer if healthy growth of trees, shrubs, herbaceous plants and grassed areas is to be ensured. This must be carried out with a fine rose or sprinkler until the full depth of topsoil is saturated. This is usually necessary once every two weeks in June and September, and weekly in July and August, usually a minimum of twelve waterings a year.

11.6   PLANNED MAINTENANCE

Sometimes planning authorities in granting a consent include a condition laying down a time limit during which an agreed landscape scheme must be planted and maintained. The DoE has suggested that maintenance for long periods is unenforceable, implying a continuing obligation on future (unknown) owners. Notwithstanding the requirements of a planning authority, a regular maintenance plan for the building owner to put in hand following the practical completion of a project, is clearly essential.

The various tasks to be carried out on any particular project throughout the year must therefore be scheduled, preferably with guidance as to the estimated time required to carry out each task, so that the actual maintenance costs for each site can be accurately established and quoted for.

The various seasons' requirements for different planted areas throughout the year make the efficient deployment of labour and machinery throughout the year extremely difficult. Trees require sucker growth and formative pruning only once a year, between June and October. Shrub borders require forking over and spraying with herbicides once a year in April or March. The same border will probably require weeding and hoeing at least six times during the following May-to-September period, and the grass will need to be cut no less than sixteen times during the same period. Table 11.1 summarizes these maintenance requirements.

Table 11.1 Landscape planned maintenance

Week No.	Trees Fertilize	Trees Prune	Trees Water	Shrubs Fertilize/Weed	Shrubs Prune	Shrubs Water	Herbaceous Fertilize/Weed	Herbaceous Dig	Herbaceous Water	Meadow grass Fertilize/Weed	Meadow grass Cut	Meadow grass Water	Short grass Fertilize/Weed	Short grass Cut	Short grass Water
January 1															
2															
3															
4															
February 1															
2															
3															
4															
March 1															
2	✓	✓		✓	✓		✓	✓		✓			✓		
3															
4															
April 1															
2				✓			✓						✓	✓	
3															
4															
May 1														✓	
2				✓			✓							✓	
3														✓	
4															
June 1						✓			✓					✓	✓
2		✓		✓			✓							✓	✓
3						✓			✓					✓	✓
4															
July 1						✓			✓					✓	✓
2				✓		✓	✓		✓					✓	✓
3						✓			✓					✓	✓
4						✓			✓						✓
August 1						✓			✓		✓			✓	✓
2				✓		✓	✓		✓					✓	✓
3						✓			✓					✓	✓
4						✓			✓						✓
September 1						✓			✓					✓	✓
2		✓		✓			✓								
3						✓			✓					✓	✓
4															
October 1				✓			✓	✓			✓			✓	
2															
3															
4															
November 1															
2															
3															
4															
December 1															
2															
3															
4															

Table 11.2 Time required to complete some landscape maintenance operations

Operation	Minutes
Turf	
Mowing (and catching clippings)	
Small area (100 sq m) with hand-manoeuvred 20-inch mower	15
Large area (0.5 ha) with rider-operated 60-inch rotary mower	30
Edging (30 m)	
By hand	45
By mechanical edger	
Curbs	20
Other edges	20
Fertilizing	
Small area (100 sq m) with rotary spreader	5
Large area (0.5 ha) with rotary spreader	30
Spraying	
Small area (100 sq m) with a back-carried tank	10
Large area (0.5 ha) with 300-gallon tank	
Spray gun operated by two men for one hour	120
Spray hawk with boom on sprayer, in open area	105
Trees	
Spraying (not included are times for filling, mixing and travel)	
Small (three-inch caliper)	25
Large (eight-inch caliper)	10
Pruning (heavy)	
Small (three-inch caliper)	15
Large (eight-inch caliper)	60
Watering	(variable)
Shrubs	
Spraying	
Small (910–1200 mm)	1
Large (2150–2500 mm)	2
Pruning	
Small (910–1200 mm)	5
Large (2150–2500 mm, for rejuvenation)	30
Watering	(variable)
Ground cover	
Spraying 100 sq m	10

From *Plants in the Landscape* by P. L. Carpenter, T. D. Walker and F. O. Lanphear., W. H. Freeman and Company, New York. Copyright © 1975.

11.7 MAINTENANCE COSTS

As can be seen from Table 11.1, a site which may need 10 man-days each month to maintain during the summer may therefore only require less than 3 man-days each month during the winter. Alternative tasks for the surplus 7 man-days each month are therefore essential if the care of the plants is not to be entrusted to casual labour taken on solely for the summer months. This is clearly not fair either to the plants or to the supervisory staff. Activities such as repair and maintenance of hard landscape areas, mechanical plant and grass-cutting equipment are therefore best left to the autumn and winter months when they can be carried out under cover, leaving the replacement of dead and diseased plants to the spring, and keeping the summer free for weeding, watering and grass cutting.

11.8 TIME

It must be evident therefore that while the cost of maintaining trees is less than that of shrub borders, and shrubs less than long or short grass, the overriding consideration in the cost of maintaining soft landscape is the economic deployment of the labour involved. If due cognisance is given to the time taken to achieve the various tasks (see Table 11.2) an economic maintenance plan can be established to keep the landscape works in the condition the landscape architect intended.

11.9 CONCLUSIONS

It is essential therefore to consider, at the outset of each project, the funds available for subsequent maintenance. High, medium or low maintenance costs are inversely proportional to the initial capital outlay. As a general rule inner urban areas suggest a maintenance-free hard landscape combined with high-maintenance planting, suburban areas an intermediate solution, and for the more rural areas a natural semi-wild low-maintenance solution.

When this has been established a suitable solution can be designed accordingly and the necessary budget for its subsequent upkeep set aside.

Tailpiece

The foregoing pages have attempted to do no more than highlight a few of the most important aspects of good practice and procedure in the management of landscape contracts – covering the more significant aspects of contract documentation, tendering, forms of contract, plant handling and contract administration.

A good contract can only be achieved by the requisite experience and expertise of the parties in the exercise of their various responsibilities, and always with the mutual respect and cooperation of all concerned. It requires a meticulous attention to detail and it is hoped that those who have persevered to the end will find that the various procedures suggested will make their tasks more tolerable, even enjoyable, in the future.

References

BS 1192 : Part 4 : 1984. Construction drawing practice. Recommendations for landscape drawings.

Clamp, H. (1984) *The Shorter Forms of Building Contract*. Granada Publishing, London.

Parris, J. (1982) *The Standard Form of Building Contract*. Granada Publishing, London.

Turner, D. F. (1985) *Building Subcontract Forms*. Granada Publishing, London.

Appendices

Appendix A Summaries of landscape British Standards

BS 3936 :—
Specification for nursery stock

BS 3936 : Part 1 : 1980
Specification for trees and shrubs.
Trees and shrubs including conifers and woody climbing plants, suitable to be transplanted and grown for amenity. Covers origin, root system, condition, dimensions, packaging and labelling and forms and sizes to be supplied for a wide range of species.

Brief summary (A7-1981) of BS 3936 : Part 1 : 1980

CI/SfB   /   /   W   /

Part 1. Specification for trees and shrubs

1. Scope
. . . trees and shrubs, including woody climbing plants and conifers, that are suitable to be transplanted and grown for amenity.

BS 3936 : Part 2 : 1978

Roses
Definitions and requirements for rootstocks, age, condition, trimming and dimensions of bush and shrub, climbing, rambler and pillar, standards, half-standards and weeping standards, dwarf and miniature roses, packaging and labelling.

Brief summary (A3-1979) of BS 3936 : Part 2 : 1978

CI/SfB   /   /   W   /

1. Scope
1.1 . . . . rose plants that are grafted or budded on to root-stocks and are suitable for transplantation and growth for amenity purposes. Miniature roses on their own roots are outside the scope of this standard.
1.2 The following types of rose plants are specified:
  (a) bush and shrub roses;

Part 2. Roses

  (b) climbing, rambler and pillar roses;
  (c) standards, half-standards and weeping standards;
  (d) dwarf roses;
  (e) miniature roses.

NOTE. Because of the natural variability of the plants and because the list of available varieties is constantly changing, this British Standard cannot include a list of varieties corresponding to each type. Only the grower or supplier can decide which type of plant is to be offered for sale.

. . . .

140

BS 3936 : Part 3 : 1978
Fruit

Origin, root system and rootstock, form of trees (illustrated), condition, packaging, certification and plant health. Labelling requirements of apples, pears, cherries, plums, peaches, nectarines and apricots, blackcurrants, redcurrants and whitecurrants, gooseberries, raspberries, blackberries and loganberries, and strawberries.

Brief summary (A9–1981) of BS 3936 : Part 3 : 1978

1. Scope

. . . requirements for the following fruit trees, bushes, canes and plants suitable to be transplanted and grown to produce food:

(a) apples and pears;
(b) cherries;
(c) plums;

Part 3. Fruit

(d) peaches, nectarines and apricots;
(e) blackcurrants;
(f) red currants and white currants;
(g) gooseberries;
(h) raspberries;
(i) blackberries and loganberries;
(j) strawberries.

BS 3936 : Part 4 : 1984

Specification for forest trees. Requirements for origin, dimensions, root and shoot, description, condition and packaging of forest trees for timber production.

Brief summary of BS 3936 : Part 4 : 1984

1. Scope

. . . . requirements for forest tree stock, to be grown for timber production, of the species specified in table 1. It deals with bare root nursery stock grown in open ground as well as stock raised in containers.

It includes requirements as to origin, dimensions, root and shoot, description, condition and packaging.

Table 1. Species

Preferred common name

Grand Fir	Sycamore
Noble Fir	Italian Alder
Common Alder	Grey Alder
Norway Maple	Common Silver Birch

Part 4. Specification for forest trees

Sweet Chestnut	Lodgepole Pine (inland)*
Lawson Cypress	Bishop Pine
Beech	Corsican Pine
Ash	Scots Pine
European Larch	Gean
Japanese Larch	Douglas Fir
Hybrid Larch	Sessile Oak
Southern Beech – Roble	Pedunculate Oak
Southern Beech – Rauli	Western Red Cedar
Norway Spruce	Small-leaved Lime
Sitka Spruce	Large-leaved Lime
Shore Pine	Western Hemlock

*Shore Pine and Lodgepole Pine (inland) are sometimes referred to respectively as Lodgepole Pine (coastal) and Lodgepole Pine.

141

BS 3936 : Part 5 : 1985
Specification for poplars and tree willows. Definitions of terms for the parts of the plants and the scientific and common names; requirements as to origin, dimensions, description of age, quality of shoot, condition and marking.

Brief summary of BS 3936 : Part 5 : 1985

Part 5. Specification for poplars and tree willows

1. Scope
.... some requirements for poplar and willow rooted plants and sets to be grown for timber production or amenity trees of the species and cultivars specified in Table 1.
It includes requirements as to dimensions, shoots description, condition and packaging.

CI/SfB / / W /

Table 1. Species and hybrids

Common name	
White poplar	Black cottonwood
Grey poplar	White willow
Black poplar	Cricket bat willow
Black poplar hybrids	Crack willow and other spp.

BS 3936 : Part 7 : 1968
Bedding plants grown in boxes or trays. Origin; growing medium; number of plants in a box; gaps; condition; planting dates; labelling.

Brief summary (1972) of BS 3936 : Part 7 : 1968

Part 7. Bedding plants grown in boxes or trays

1. Scope
.... the most common ranges of bedding plants .... which are grown and sold in the United Kingdom in boxes of trays .... for planting out direct into open ground for display.
....

CI/SfB / / W /

BS 3936 : Part 9 : 1968
Bulbs, corms and tubers
Description; quality and labelling requirements; minimum dimensions and size classes for the more common bulbs, corms and tubers which are bought and sold in the United Kingdom.

Brief summary (1972) of BS 3936 : Part 9 : 1968

Part 9. Bulbs, corms and tubers

1. Scope
.... dimensional, quality and marking requirements for .... ranges of dormant bulbs, corms and tubers.
....

CI/SfB / / W /

BS 3936 : Part 10 : 1981
Specification for ground cover plants
Definitions and requirements for origin, root system, condition, dimensions, packaging, designation and labelling. Appendix gives information about minimum spread of 101 types of plant and indication of whether they are deciduous, evergreen or herbaceous.

Brief summary (A9-1981) of BS 3936 : Part 10 : 1981

Part 10. Ground cover plants

1. Scope
.... requirements for ground cover plants of the following types: shrubs (including conifers) and herbaceous perennials (including grasses).

CI/SfB	/	/	W	/

Included for information only in Appendix A is an indication of whether the plants are deciduous, evergreen or herbaceous.

BS 3998 : 1966
Recommendations for tree work
Safety, season and equipment; workmanship; inspection. Individual operations; cuts; pruning; lifting of crown; cleaning out; crown thinning; reducing and reshaping; restoration; repair work; bracing; feeding; tree removal. Appendices cover safety precautions, season, method for protecting a large tree to be used as an anchor, three methods for feeding trees after tree work, examples of methods for treatment of roots with ammonium sulphamate or sodium chlorate.

Summary (1972) of BS 3998 : 1966

1. Scope
.... general recommendations for tree work.

....

The recommendations include cuts; pruning; lifting of crown; cleaning out; crown thinning; reducing and shaping; restoration; repair work; bracing; feeding; and tree removal.

....

CI/SfB	/	(90.42)	/	W	/

CI/SfB | / | (90.42) | / | W | /

BS 4043 : 1966 (1978)
Recommendations for transplanting semi-mature trees

Selection of trees for transplanting, season for transplanting, preparation by root pruning. Tree pits, drainage, tree lifting operations. Lifting, loading and transporting; planting: backfilling and mulching; operational damage. Guying and securing the tree, wrapping, watering and spraying. Appendices classifying trees suitable for transplanting, giving guidance as to the size of prepared root systems, and with examples of guying and securing techniques. (Confirmed 1978.)

Summary (1972) of BS 4043 : 1966

1. Scope
. . . . transplanting semi-mature trees. *An Appendix* . . . . lists trees which are suitable for transplanting in this way.

. . . .

2. Definition

. . . .

Semi-mature tree. A tree or shrub at an advanced stage of growth which is to be transplanted with an earth root-ball, or in certain cases bare roots, and is of such combined size and weight that special equipment will be needed to carry out the operation.

Such trees will generally be between 20 ft and 50 ft (6 m and 15 m) in height and will weigh between 5 cwt (250 kg) and 10 ton (10 tonne); they also include certain shorter trees and shrubs, which weigh more than 5 cwt (250 kg) and need special lifting techniques or equipment because of their spread and weight.

. . . .

CI/SfB | / | (90.42) | / | / |

BS 4428 : 1969 (1979)
Recommendations for general landscape operations (excluding hard surfaces)

Deals with the following general landscape operations: preparatory operations, including earthwork, land shaping and drainage; seeding of grass areas; turfing; planting of shrubs, hedges, climbers, herbaceous plants and bulbs; individual tree planting; forestry planting for amenity purposes. (Confirmed 1979.)
AMD 938, April 1972 (Gr 0)®

Summary (1972) of BS 4428 : 1969
incorporating Amendment Slip No. 1

1.1 Scope
(1) Preparatory operations, including earthwork, land shaping and drainage.
(2) Seeding of grass areas.
(3) Turfing.
(4) Planting of shrubs, hedges, climbers herbaceous plants and bulbs.
(5) Individual tree planting.
(6) Forestry planting for amenity purposes.

BS 5236 : 1975
Recommendations for the cultivation and planting of trees in the extra large nursery stock category

Recommendations for description, production, preparation for sale, packaging, labelling, planting, mulching and staking.

Recommendations on dimensions for trees sold in the form of standards.

Brief summary (1977) of BS 5236 : 1975

1. Scope
.... cultivation and planting of trees intermediate in size and mass between ordinary nursery stock (as specified by BS 3936 : Part 1) and semi-mature trees (as defined in BS 4043) and suitable to be transplanted and grown for amenity purposes.

3. Definition
advanced nursery stock (of trees). Trees transplanted from their original and grown-on for transplanting to their final site at an advanced stage of growth.

CI/SfB / **(90.42)** / **W** /

Their height is normally between 3.6 m and 6 m .... in the case of deciduous trees and between 2 m and 3.5 m in the case of conifers.

Publications referred to

BS 3936　Specification for nursery stock Part 1 Specification for trees and shrubs

BS 4043　Recommendations for transplanting semi-mature trees

BS 5837 : 1980
Code of practice for trees in relation to construction

Principles to follow to achieve satisfactory juxtaposition of trees and construction. Recommends types of trees for planting near buildings, structures, plant and services. Advice on planting and maintenance of trees in urban locations and paved areas.

Brief summary (A6–1980) of BS 5837 : 1980

Foreword
Trees fulfil certain functions in improving the environment and they require reasonable conditions in which to thrive. Underground services and building foundations also make demands on the ground. Space in built-up areas is at a premium and this can contribute to the intimate quality of cities, towns and villages. Trees and buildings are not incompatible, but it is essential to create conditions that can enable buildings to be seen in a setting of trees and function satisfactorily. Time is important when considering matters relating to trees; a large tree lost through negligence or misunderstanding cannot be replaced for decades. Employers should ensure that the contractor, who rarely sees a tree deteriorate seriously while he is on site, takes precautions from the planning stage

CI/SfB / **(90.1)** / **W** /

onwards to ensure the safety of valuable mature trees. It is essential that those concerned with development are educated in the need to take the necessary precautions to protect trees from damage during construction, in order to retain the maximum number of suitable trees in development areas.

1. Scope
.... principles to be followed in order to achieve the satisfactory juxtaposition of trees and construction.

The code recommends types of trees for planting near buildings, structures, plant and services and gives advice on *reduction of damage to existing trees,* on planting trees in urban locations and paved areas and also on maintenance.

145

BS 3882 : 1965 (1978)
Recommendations and classification for top soil

Description of top soil; classification by texture; classification by soil reaction (pH); classification by stone content; size of stones. Notes on method of test for top soil; designation of top soil. (Confirmed 1978.)
AMD 3089, May 1979®

Brief summary (A5–1980) of BS 3882 : 1965 incorporating Amendment No. 1

CI/SfB / / **W** /

1. Scope

. . . top soil for general landscape work purposes. *The standard* also classifies top soil in relation to three particular characteristics–texture, reaction (lime content) and stone content which it may sometimes be desirable to specify fairly closely. It is primarily concerned with top soil as dug which is to be imported on to a site.

An Appendix . . . . gives notes on some relevant methods of test for top soil. *Another Appendix . . . .* lists the information to be given for the purpose of an order or an enquiry.

BS 3969 : 1965 (1978)
Recommendations for turf for general landscape purposes

Common and botanical names of grasses and perennial weeds. Constituent desirable grasses; undesirable grasses and weeds; soil; condition; dimensions of turves; delivery. (Confirmed 1978.)

Brief summary (1972) of BS 3969 : 1965

Foreword

A coarser turf, not complying with the requirements of this standard, may be entirely satisfactory for areas where quality is less important, such as for children's playing areas or for the prevention of erosion on banks.

CI/SfB / / **W** /

1. Scope

. . . turf for general landscape purposes, such as lawns. *The standard* does not specify all the requirements of turfs specially grown or specially selected for purposes such as bowling greens or golf greens.

BS 4156 : 1967 (1979)
Peat

Peat produced for general horticulture and landscape purposes. Requirements as to pH, moisture content, ash, particle size, yield (volume out) and marking. (Confirmed 1979.)

Summary (1972) of BS 4156 : 1967

CI/SfB / / **W** /

1. Scope

. . . pH, moisture content, ash, particle size and marking requirements for peat produced for general horticultural and landscape purposes.

146

BS 5551 : — —
Fertilizers

BS 5551: Part 2
Sampling

**BS 5551 : Part 2 : Section 2.3
1978**
ISO 3963
Sampling from a conveyor by stopping the belt (reference method)

BS 5551 : Part 3
Physical properties

**BS 5551 : Part 3 : Section 3.1 :
1981**
ISO 3944
Method for the determination of bulk density (loose).
Applicable to dry fertilizers, other than powdered materials or products containing a large proportion of particles exceeding 5 mm in diameter.

**BS 5551 : Part 3 : Section 3.2 :
1983**
ISO 5311
Method for determination of bulk density (tapped)

BS 5551 : Part 4
Chemical analysis

**BS 5551 : Part 4 : Section 4.1 :
Subsection 4.1.1 : 1981**
ISO 4176
Nitrogen gravimetric method for determination of nitrate nitrogen.
Reference method applicable to all fertilizers.

**BS 5551 : Part 4 : Section 4.1 :
Subsection 4.1.2 : 1982**
ISO 5314
Determination of ammoniacal nitrogen, titrimetric method after distillation.

BS 5551 : Part 4 : Section 4.2 :
Determination phosphorus.

**BS 5551 : Part 4 : Section 4.2 :
Subsection 4.2.1 : 1978**
ISO 5316
Extraction of water-soluble phosphates.

BS 881, 589 : 1974
Nomenclature of commercial timbers including sources of supply.
Comprises BS 881 'Nomenclature of hardwoods' which tabulates recognized hardwoods and includes botanical species standard names, alternative commercial names, sources of supply and average densities in kg/m³. Also BS 589 'Nomenclature of softwoods' which tabulates recognized softwoods and includes botanical species standard

names, alternative commercial names, sources of supply and average densities in kg/m³.

BS 1831 : 1969
± ISO/R 257, ISO 765, ISO/R 1750
Recommended common names for pesticides.
Coined common names for 278 pesticides.
Chemical names, structural formulae, classification according to use (acaricide, avicide, bactericide, fungicide, herbicide, insecticide, molluscicide, nematicide, plant growth regulator, rodenticide) and other non-proprietary names. Common names for pesticides of uncertain composition, common names considered by ISO but not recommended, organic pesticides not requiring common names. Index of common names, chemical names, other names listed.
AMD 3097, July 1979 (Gr 0)

**Supplement No. 1 (1970) to
BS 1831 : 1969**
Provides a further thirty recommended common names for pesticides.
AMD 1774, June 1975 (Gr 0)

147

**Supplement No. 2 (1970) to
BS 1831 : 1969**
Provides a further thirty-two
recommended common names.
AMD 4175, February 1983 (Gr 0) ®

**Supplement No. 3 (1974) to
BS 1831 : 1969**
A further 119 recommended common
names.
AMD 1774, June 1975 (GR 0)

BS 2468 : 1963
Glossary of terms relating to agricultural
machinery and implements.
Contains terms and definitions relating to
agricultural machinery, implements, parts
and accessories, covering a wide range of
agricultural work. Terms are grouped
under appropriate classes and sections and
a comprehensive alphabetical index is
provided.
Numerous ilustrations are also included in
the glossary.

BS 3975 : — —
Glossary for landscape work

BS 3975 : Part 4 : 1966
Plant description.
Plant types; plant parts; plant forms;
general character; particular
character; commercial classes.

BS 3975 : Part 5 : 1969
Horticultural, arboricultural and forestry
practice.
Provides working definitions for terms
commonly used in nursery practice,
horticultural upkeep and ground
maintenance, tree work and forestry.

BS 1192 : — —
Construction drawing practice.

BS 1192 : Part 1 : 1984
Recommendations for general principles.
Sets out general principles for the
preparation of all drawings for the
construction industry, including schedules
prepared on drawing sheets and
numbered as one of a drawing set.
Applicable to drawings produced by
computer techniques, and to drawings that
will be reproduced by microfilming in
accordance with BS 5536.

BS 1192 : Part 4 : 1984
Recommendations for landscape drawings.
Recommendations for the preparation of
landscape drawings and schedules.
Includes symbols and abbreviations which
are used in a series of typical drawings.
Appendices include summaries of
information commonly used when
landscape drawings are being prepared.

CI/SfB / / W / (Agh)

Brief summary (1972) of BS 3975 :
Part 4 : 1965

Part 4. Plant Description
The section headings are
41. Type
42. Plant parts
43. Form
44. Character — general
45. Character — particular
46. Commercial class.

CISfB / (90.42) / / (Agh)

Brief summary (1972) of BS 3975 :
Part 5 : 1969

Part 5. Horticultural
Arboricultural and Forestry
Practice

The section headings are
51. Nursery practice
52. Horticulture upkeep and grounds
maintenance
53. Tree work
54. Forestry.

149

Form of Tender and Conditions of Subcontract

For use with the JCLI Agreement for Landscape Works.

Information for Tenderers

1. Contract name and location: ....

2. Employer: ....

3. Contractor: ....

4. Landscape Architect: ....

5. The Form of Contract is the JCLI Agreement for Landscape Works, completed as follows:

   Clause 2·1: The Works may be commenced on .... and shall be completed by ....

   Clause 2·3: Liquidated damages: £ .... per week or part of a week.

   Clause 2·5: Defects Liability Period: .... months

   Clause 2·7: Plant Failures grass .... months after Practical Completion

           shrubs and trees .... months after Practical Completion

           semi mature and ELNS trees .... months after Practical Completion

   Clause 4·4   Documents for Final Valuation ....

   Clause 4·5   Contributions levy and tax changes ....

   Clause 6·3 A/B Insurance against fire .... clause A/B deleted.

   Clause 6·3A   Percentage to cover professional fees ....

   Clause 6·5B   Provisional sum for malicious damage ....

   *Clause 6·3A will be deleted.
   *Clause 6·3B will be deleted, the insurance under clause 6·3A being the full value plus .... %

6. The Subcontractor shall, before tendering, visit the Site or otherwise make himself familiar with the extent of the Subcontract Works, the Site Conditions, and all local conditions and restrictions likely to affect the execution of the work. The Subcontractor may have access to any available drawings or work programmes relative to the preparation of his tender on request and by appointment.

7. Two copies of this Form are provided — One copy to be priced, signed by the Subcontractor and

   returned to .... the other is for his retention.

1

Form of Tender

1. Tender price for ....
   (The Enquirer should enter trade or brief description of Works)

   .... Total tender price

   The Tenderer should enter the amount of his tender in words and figures.

   2a The tender is to be adjusted for price fluctuations of labour only/materials only*/labour and materials* as set out in Subcontract Condition 4·4, a list of relevant basic prices being enclosed.

   2b The tender is to be adjusted for price fluctuations by use of the NEDO Price Adjustment Formula Indices (Category ....)/the Specialist Engineering Installation Indices (Category ....)*.

   *2c The tender is to be on a firm price basis.

3. **Schedule of Daywork Charges**
   The Subcontractor is requested to insert his hourly daywork rates in the space provided in the Schedule below. His rates for labour shall be deemed to include overheads and profit and all payments in connection with Holidays with Pay, Bonus and Pension Schemes, Subsistence Allowances, Fares and Travelling Time, Imported Labour Costs, Non-Productive Overtime Costs, and any other payments made under the Working Rule Agreement, any Regulation, Bye-law or Act of Parliament. The Subcontractor is also invited to insert in the space provided the percentage addition he will require for his overheads and profits on the nett cost of materials and on plant charges.

   (i) **Labour**

   Craftsmen @ ....£ .... per hour

   Labourers/Mates @ .... £ .... per hour

   (ii) **Materials and Plant**
   Materials invoice cost plus .... %

   Plant Charges plus .... %

4. Period of notice required before commencing the Subcontract Works: ....
   Time required to complete the Subcontract Works (the Subcontract Period unless agreed

   otherwise): ....

5. We, the undersigned, agree that this quotation will be open for acceptance within .... week(s) and that we have read and understand the terms and conditions printed overleaf and that should our quotation be accepted we will enter into a Subcontract in accordance with the said terms and conditions.

For and on behalf of ....

   ....

Signed .... Date ....

*Delete if not required.

2

151

Askham Bryan College
of Agriculture and Horticulture
LIBRARY BOOK

Conditions of Subcontract

1·0 Intentions

Subcontractor's Obligation
1·1 The Subcontractor shall with due diligence and in a good and workmanlike manner carry out and complete the Works in accordance with the Subcontract Documents using materials and workmanship of the quality and standards therein specified provided that where and to the extent that approval of the quality of materials or of the standards of workmanship is a matter for the opinion of the Landscape Architect such quality and standards shall be to the reasonable satisfaction of the Landscape Architect.
No approval expressed or implied by the Contractor and/or the Landscape Architect shall in any way relieve the Subcontractor of his responsibility for complying with the requirements of this Subcontract.

Principal Contract and Special Conditions
1·2 The Subcontractor is deemed to have full knowledge of, and so far as they are applicable to the Works agrees to comply with, the provisions of the Principal Contract as though the same were incorporated herein and the Main Contractor were the Employer and the Subcontractor were the Contractor. Any conditions contained in the Subcontractor's Tender shall be excluded.

Information provided by others
1·3 The Subcontractor must make written application to the Contractor for instructions, drawings, levels or other information at a date which is not unreasonably distant from nor unreasonably close to the date on which it is necessary for the Subcontractor to receive the same.

Information provided for others
1·4 Any instructions, drawings, levels or other information relating to the Works which is requested from the Subcontractor must be provided in due time and so as not to cause disruption or delay to the works to be performed under the Principal Contract.

2·0 Commencement and Completion

Progress and Completion
2·1 The Works are to be commenced within the period of notice stated on the Form of Tender and are to be completed within the Subcontract period subject only to such fair and reasonable extension of time as the Contractor shall allow. The Works are to be carried out diligently and in such order, manner and time as the Contractor may reasonably direct so as to ensure completion of the Principal Contract Works or any portion thereof by the completion date or such extended date as may be allowed under the Principal Contract. If the Subcontractor is in breach of the foregoing he shall pay or allow to the Contractor the amount of loss or damage suffered by the Contractor in consequence thereof.

Overtime
2·2 No overtime is to be worked without the Subcontractor first obtaining the consent in writing of the Contractor. No additional payment for overtime will be made unless the Subcontractor is so advised in writing by the Contractor and, if the Subcontractor is so advised, he will be reimbursed the net additional non-productive rate incurred, including any net additional cost of Employers' Liability and Third Party Insurances. The Subcontractor will be required to obtain any necessary overtime permit from the appropriate authority.

Annual Holidays
2·3 Under the Annual Holiday Agreement, the Site will be closed down for certain periods which may be whilst the Subcontractor's work is in progress. The Subcontractor will be deemed to have included in his Tender for any additional costs and time resulting from such closure.

Maintenance and Defects Liability
2·4 The Subcontractor will (1) maintain the Works at his own expense to the Contractor's and the Landscape Architect satisfaction both during the progress of the Works and until the Landscape Architect has issued a Certificate of Practical Completion including the Works and (2) make good at his own expense, and at a time to be decided by the Contractor, any defects or damage to the Works.

3·0 Control of the Works

Assignment
3·1 Neither the Contractor nor the Subcontractor shall, without the written consent of the other, assign this Contract.

Use of Site
3·2 The Site shall not be used for any purpose other than for the carrying out of the Works. Works to be executed outside the Main Contractor's Site boundary shall be carried out to suit the convenience of adjacent occupiers or Local Authorities at times to be agreed by the Contractor in writing.

Variations
3·3 No variation shall vitiate this Subcontract. The Subcontractor shall advise the Contractor in writing of all work involving a variation or extra work within 14 days of such variation or extra work becoming apparent, at the same time submiting detailed and priced calculations based upon this Subcontract showing such price adjustment, if any. Variations or extra work shall not be undertaken by the Subcontractor nor shall he receive payment for such variation or extra works without written authority from the Contractor.
Where variations or extra works cannot be valued by reference to this Subcontract then the value of such variations or extra works shall be subject to agreement between the Contractor and/or the Landscape Architect and the Subcontractor.

Dayworks

3·4 No daywork will be permitted except where in the opinion of the Contractor and/or the Landscape Architect, it would be unfair to value such work at other than daywork rates. Where the Subcontractor considers he has claim to daywork due notice must be given and valuation by daywork approved by the Contractor in writing prior to the execution of the work in question in order to facilitate checking the time and materials expended thereon. All daywork sheets shall be rendered by the end of the week during which the work is executed. All daywork will be paid for at the rates stated on the Form of Tender.

Adjustment for Provisional Sums

3·5 Instructions will be issued in respect of Provisional Sums. No loss of profit will be allowed in respect of such instructions.

4·0 Payments

Discount to the Contractor

4·1 The Subcontractor will allow for all payments to be made in full within 17 days of the date of the Landscape Architect's Certificate to the Employer without any cash discount for prompt payment. Any such discount included on the Form of Tender will be deducted from the tender sum before the order for the subcontract works is placed.

Progress Payments

4·2 Payment will, subject always to these terms and conditions, be made to the Subcontractor as and when the value of such Works under the terms of the Principal Contract is included in a Certificate to the Contractor and the Contractor receives the monies due thereunder. Applications for payment are to be rendered to the Contractor in duplicate by the Subcontractor.
Payment shall be by instalments of the rate of:
95% of the value executed as the Works proceed.
2½% upon practical complete of the Works.
2½% on satisfactory completion of making good defects under the Principal Contract or as soon as the final account for all Works executed under this Subcontract shall have been agreed, whichever may last happen.
Progress payments shall be on account only and shall not be held to signify approval by the Contractor and/or the Landscape Architect of the whole or any part of the Works executed nor shall any final payment prejudice any claim the Contractor may have in respect of any defects in the Works whenever such defects may appear.

Estimates of Loss, etc.

4·3 In addition to the Contractor' Common Law rights of set off, if the Subcontractor shall cause the Contractor loss by reason of any breach of this Contract or by any tortious act or by any breach of statutory duty giving rise to a claim for damages or indemnity or contribution by the Contractor against the Subcontractor, or the Contractor shall become entitled to payment from the Subcontractor under this Contract, then without prejudice to and pending the final determination or agreement between the parties, the Contractor shall bona fide estimate the amount of such loss, indemnity or contribution or payment, such estimate to be binding and conclusive upon the Subcontractor until such final determination or agreement.

Fluctuations (to apply only if item 2a of the Form of Tender is completed).

4·4 The sum or sums referred to in this Subcontract shall be based upon the rates of wages and such other emoluments, allowances and expenses (including the cost of Employers' Liability and Third Party Insurances) as are properly payable by the Subcontractor to work-people engaged upon or in connection with the Works in acccordance with the rules or decisions of the wage fixing body of the trade or trades concerned applicable to the Works. Such rates of wages and the prices of materials shall be as detailed in the Basic Price List as provided by the Subcontractor and attached hereto.
Should any fluctuations from the Basic Price List occur during the currency of this Subcontract, the net additional cost actually and properly incurred or saving that ought to have been made, by such fluctuations shall be added to or be deducted from the total amount payable under the terms and conditions of this Subcontract. Fluctuations in the cost of materials will be adjusted net.
Provided always that immediate notice in writing shall be given of such fluctuations, and an approved weekly return submitted to the Contractor showing the total number of men and hours and the deliveries of materials effected for detailed checking by the Contractor and Landscape Architect.

5·0 Statutory Obligations:

Safety, Health and Welfare

5·1 The Subcontractor shall comply with the Contractor's requirements on matters affecting the safe conduct of work on the Site and all statutes, bye laws and regulations affecting the Works and the carrying out thereof.

Statutory Payments

5·2 The Subcontractor shall include in his quotation for any payments to be made under the Working Rule Agreement, all payments in connection with holidays with Pay, Bonus and Pension Schemes, National Insurance, Subsistence Allowances, Fares and Travelling Time, Imported Labour Costs or any payments required by Regulations, Bye-law or Act of Parliament.

6·0 Injury, Damage and Insurance

Responsibilities of the Subcontractor

6·1 The Subcontractor shall indemnify the Contractor against all claims, causes of action, costs, loss and expense whatsoever in respect of:

153 **4**

1. Personal injury or death of any person or injury or damage to any property real or personal arising out of or in the course of or caused by any works executed by the Subcontractor and/or the execution of such works (including but not restricted to the use of any plant, equipment or facilities whether in connection with such execution or otherwise) and/or any design undertaken by the Subcontractor and

2. Any negligence or breach of duty on the part of the Subcontractor, his Subcontractors, his or their servants or agents and

· 3. Any breach or non-performance or non-observance by the Subcontractor, his Subcontractors, his or their servants or agents of the provisions of the Principal Contract in so far as they relate or apply to the Works and are not inconsistent with the provisions of this Subcontract.

4. Any act, omission, default or neglect of the Subcontractor, his Subcontractors, his or their servants or agents which involves the Contractor in any liability under the Principal Contract.

5. Any damage, claim loss or expense to or involving any plant (whether of the type aforesaid or otherwise) hired or loaned or otherwise made available to the Subcontractor or operating for the Subcontractor's benefit.

Responsibilities of Others

6·2 The Subcontractor shall not be responsible for loss or damage caused by fire, storm, tempest, lightning, flood, bursting and overflowing of water tanks, apparatus or pipes, earthquake, aircraft or anything dropped therefrom, aerial objects, riot and civil commotion, to the Works or to any materials (other than temporary buildings, plant, tools, scaffolding and machinery provided by the Subcontractor, or any scaffolding or other plant which is loaned to him by the Contractor), properly upon the Site and in connection with and for the purpose of the Subcontract. In the event of any such loss or damage, the Subcontractor shall, if and when directed by the Contractor in writing, proceed immediately with the rectification or replacement of the damaged work and materials and the erection and completion of the Works in full accordance with the terms, provisions and conditions hereof, and expenses in respect of any of the matters referred to in sub-clause 6.1.1 and 6.1.2 above and shall on demand produce to the Contractor adequate evidence of such insurance.

Subcontractor's Work, Materials and Plant

6·3 The Works, materials, tools, plant, scaffolding, machinery and buildings of the Subcontractor, the subject of or used in connection with this Subcontract whether on Site or not, shall in every respect be at the Subcontractor's risk (except those risks for which the Subcontractor is not responsible under Clause 6·2).

Subcontractor's Insurance

6·4 The Subcontractor shall adequately insure:
1 His and the Contractor's liability in respect of any claims, causes of action, costs, losses and expenses in respect of any of the matters referred to in sub-clauses 6·1·1 and 6·1·2.

2 Against all Employers' Liability and Third Party (including Third Party Fire) risks arising out of the execution of the Works.

The Subcontractor shall produce on demand policies of such insurances, together with receipts for premiums, or other adequate evidence of such insurance.

In case of neglect by the Subcontractor to effect the insurances, the Contractor shall be at liberty to insure on behalf of the Subcontractor and to deduct the premium so paid from any monies due or becoming due to the Subcontractor.

7·0 Determination

Determination by the Contractor

7·1 The Contractor may without prejudice to any other of his rights or remedies determine the Subcontractor's employment under this Subcontract if the Subcontractor:-

1. fails forthwith upon notice from the Contractor to commence remedial work to any defective workmanship and/or materials or fails to proceed with the same with due diligence or to complete such remedial work to the satisfaction of the Contractor or the Landscape Architect within a set period as the Contractor may specify in the said notice or if none is so specified within a reasonable time.

2. fails to withdraw immediately, at the request of the Contractor, any one or more of his employees to whom the Contractor objects or whose presence on the Works may contravene the conditions of this or the Principal Contract, or may cause labour disputes in the Subcontractor's or any other trade, and to replace such employees within a reasonable time by others against whom there is no such objection.

3. makes any arrangements with his creditors, has a Receiving Order made against him, executes a Bill of Sale, or commits an act of bankruptcy or, being a limited company, goes into liquidation, or has a Receiver appointed.

4. fails within seven days' notice in writing from the Contractor to comply with any of the obligations on the part of the Subcontractor herein contained.

Upon determination by the Contractor the Subcontractor shall not remove any of his equipment, materials or property from the Site and, notwithstanding anything contained in these conditions, shall be entitled to no further payment until completion of the Works by the Contractor or by others whereupon the Subcontractor shall become entitled to payment for Works executed and materials provided by the Subcontractor subject always to the right of the Contractor to set off all losses expense and damages suffered or which may be suffered by the Contractor by reason of such determination and subject further to any other right of set off which the Contractor may have. For the purposes of such completion the Contractor shall have the right to use the Subcontractor's equipment, materials and property on the Site and to any materials or fabricated work lying at the Subcontractor's works or workshop which have been bought or fabricated for the purpose of this Subcontract.

Determination by the Subcontractor

2 The Subcontractor may without prejudice to any other of his rights or remedies determine the Subcontractor's employment under this Subcontract if the Contractor:

1. fails to make any payments in accordance with this subcontract.

2. unreasonably attempts or obstructs the carrying out of the Subcontractor's Works

3. makes any arrangements with his creditors, has a Receiving Order made against him, executes a Bill of Sale, or commits an act of bankruptcy or, being a limited company, goes into liquidation, or has a Receiver appointed.

Upon determination by the Subcontractor the Contractor shall pay to the Subcontractor, after taking into account amounts previously paid, such sum as shall be fair and reasonable for the value of work begun and executed, materials on site and the removal of all temporary buildings, plant tools and equipment. Provided always that the right of determination shall be without prejudice to any other rights or remedies which the Subcontractor may possess.

8·0 Temporary Works and Services, Attendance, Related Works

Temporary Accommodation

8·1 The Subcontractor shall provide to the approval of the Contractor and at his own expense, any requisite temporary site office, workshop accommodation, together with the necessary equipment, lighting, power, fuel etc.

Welfare facilities

8·2 The Subcontractor shall, at his own risk have reasonable and free use of the temporary welfare accommodation and/or services (including First Aid facilities and treatment) which the Contractor or the Employer may provide on the Site in connection with the Works.

Temporary services

8·3 The Subcontractor shall, at his own risk, have reasonable and free use, in common with others engaged upon the Site, of the water supply, temporary plumbing, temporary lighting and temporary electric power. Electric power supply for small tools and equipment used on the Site shall not exceed 110V A.C. single phase. Any electrical equipment used to carry out the Works must be in good mechanical condition and suitable for the electric power supply and fittings made available and fitted with suitable plugs, sockets and connectors to BS4343 (CEE 17) or any other standard that the Contractor may direct.

Use of Scaffolding

8·4 The Subcontractor shall at his own risk and at such time(s) and for such period(s) as the Contractor may direct have free use of the Contractor's scaffolding, ladders and mechanical hoisting facilities which may be available on the Site or already in position.

Delivery and Storage of Materials

8·5 The Subcontractor shall provide all materials, package and carriage to and from the Site. He will be responsible for unloading during the progress of his Works, storing in the areas provided and moving his own materials at the Site. Any materials delivered prior to commencement on Site shall be off-loaded by the Contractor at the sole risk and cost of the Subcontractor.

Removal of Rubbish etc.

8·6 All rubbish and/or surplus materials and plant of the Subcontractor must be removed forthwith from the vicinity of the Works, paths, roads etc., to an approved position on the Site.

Cutting Away

8·7 In no circumstances whatsoever shall any cutting away be done without the prior written authority of the Contractor.

Sub-surfaces

8·8 The Subcontractor shall satisfy himself before commencing work, as to the suitability of any surfaces to which the Subcontractor is to fix, apply or lay his work.

JCLI

This Form is issued by the
Joint Council for Landscape Industries
comprising:-

Landscape Institute
Horticultural Trades Association
British Association Landscape Industries
National Farmers Unions
Institute of Leisure and Amenity Management.

Published for the Joint Council for Landscape Industries by the Landscape Institute
12 Carlton House Terrace, London SW1Y 5AH and available from RIBA Publications Limited
66 Portland Place, London W1N 4AD.
© JCLI January 1986

Printed by Duolith Ltd.
Welwyn Garden City, Herts.

Issued January 1986

6

155

This Agreement is made the _____ day of _____ 19___

between _____

of_____
(hereinafter called 'the Employer')

of the one part AND _____

of (or whose registered office is at)_____

_____

(hereinafter called 'the Contractor') of the other part.

Whereas

Recitals   1st   the Employer wishes the following work_____

_____

_____

(hereinafter called "the Works") to be carried out under the direction of

_____

(hereinafter called "Landscape Architect") and has caused drawings numbered
(hereinafter called "the Contract Drawings") [a] and/or a Specification (hereinafter called "the Contract Specification") [a] and/or schedules [a] and/or schedules of rates [a] and/or Bills of Quantities [a] which documents are together with the Conditions annexed hereto (hereinafter called "the Contract Documents") showing and describing the works to be prepared and which are attached to this Agreement.

The law of England/Scotland shall be the proper law of this Agreement [a].

2nd   The Contractor has priced the Specification [a] or the schedules [a] or Bills of Quantities [a] or provided a schedule of rates [a];

3rd   the Contract Documents have been signed by or on behalf of the parties hereto;

4th   [a] the quantity surveyor appointed in connection with this contract shall mean

_____

or in the event of his death or ceasing to be the quantity surveyor for this purpose such other person as the Employer nominates for that purpose;

[a]   Delete as appropriate

156

Now it is hereby agreed as follows

Article 1
For the consideration hereinafter mentioned the Contractor will in accordance with the Contract Documents carry out and complete the Works.

Article 2
The Employer will pay to the Contractor the sum of _____

_____

_____ (£ _____)

exclusive of VAT or such other sum as shall become payable hereunder at the times and in the manner specified in the Contract Documents.

Article 3
The term "Landscape Architect" in the said Conditions shall mean

_____

or in the event of his death or ceasing to be the Landscape Architect for the purpose of this Contract such other person as the Employer shall within 14 days of the death or cessation as aforesaid nominate for that purpose, provided that no person subsequently appointed to be the Landscape Architect under this Contract shall be entitled to disregard or overrule any certificate or instruction given by the Landscape Architect for the time being.

Article 4
If any dispute or difference concerning this Contract shall arise between the Employer or the Landscape Architect on his behalf and the Contractor such dispute or difference shall be and is hereby referred to the arbitration and final decision of a person to be agreed between the parties or, failing agreement within 14 days after either party has given to the other a written request to concur in the appointment of an arbitrator, a person to be appointed on the request of either party by the President or a Vice-President for the time being of the Landscape Institute.

As witness the hands of the parties hereto

Signed for and on behalf of the Employer _____
(For the Employer)

in the presence of _____
(Witness)

Signed for and on behalf of the Contractor _____
(For the Contractor)

in the presence of _____
(Witness)

157

Contents

Note:
Clauses marked * should be completed/deleted
as appropriate
†see note on page 8

158

Conditions hereinbefore referred to

1.0 Intentions of the parties

Contractor's obligation

1·1 The Contractor shall with due diligence and in a good and workmanlike manner carry out and complete the Works in accordance with the Contract Documents using materials and workmanship of the quality and standards therein specified provided that where and to the extent that approval of the quality of materials or of the standards of workmanship is a matter for the opinion of the Landscape Architect such quality and standards shall be to the reasonable satisfaction of the Landscape Architect.

Landscape Architect's duties

1·2 The Landscape Architect shall issue any further information necessary for the proper carrying out of the Works, issue all certificates and confirm all instructions in writing in accordance with these Conditions.

Contract Bills and SMM

1·3 Where the Contract Documents include Contract Bills, the Contract Bills unless otherwise expressly stated therein in respect of any specified item or items are to have been prepared in accordance with the Standard Method of Measurement of Building Works, 6th Edition, published by the Royal Institution of Chartered Surveyors and the Building Employers Confederation (formerly National Federation of Building Trades Employers) and the Joint Council for Landscape Industries Rules for the Measurement of Landscape Works.

2·0 Commencement and completion

Commencement and completion

2·1 The Works may be commenced on

. . . .

and shall be completed by

. . . .

Extension of contract period

2·2 If it becomes apparent that the Works will not be completed by the date for completion inserted in clause 2·1 hereof (or any later date fixed in accordance with the provisions of this clause 2·2) for reasons beyond the control of the Contractor, then the Contractor shall so notify the Landscape Architect who shall make, in writing, such extension of the time for completion as may be reasonable.

Damages for non-completion

2·3 If the Works are not completed by the completion date inserted in clause 2·1 hereof or by any later completion date fixed under clause 2·2 hereof then the Contractor shall pay or allow to the Employer liquidated damages at the rate of £ . . . . .per week for every week or part of a week during which the Works remain uncompleted.

Completion date

2·4 The Landscape Architect shall certify the date when in his opinion the Works have reached practical completion.

Defects liability

2·5 Any defects, excessive shrinkages or other faults, other than tree, shrub, grass and other plant failures, which appear within three months [b] . . . . of the date of practical completion and are due to materials or workmanship not in accordance with the Contract or frost occurring before practical completion shall be made good by the Contractor entirely at his own cost unless the Landscape Architect shall otherwise instruct.
The Landscape Architect shall certify the date when in his opinion the Contractor's obligations under this clause 2·5 have been discharged.

Partial Possession by Employer

†2·6 If before practical completion of the Works the Employer with the consent of the Contractor shall take possession of any part then:
The date for possession of the part shall be the date of practical completion of the part and clause 4·3 shall apply to the part.
In lieu of the sum to be paid by the Contractor under clause 2·3 for any period during which the Works remain uncompleted after the Employers possession of any part the sum paid shall bear the same ratio to the sum stated in clause 2·3 as does the Contract Sum less the value of the part to the Contract Sum.

Failures of Plants (Pre-Practical Completion)

†2·7 Any trees, shrubs, grass or other plants, other than those found to be missing or defective as a result of theft or malicious damage and which shall be replaced as set out in clause 6·5 of these conditions, which are found to be defective at practical completion of the works shall be replaced by the Contractor entirely at his own cost unless the Landscape Architect shall otherwise instruct. The Landscape Architect shall certify the dates when in his opinion the Contractor's obligations under this clause have been discharged.

(Post-Practical Completion)

*A The maintenance of trees, shrubs, grass and other plants after the date of the said certificate will be carried out by the Contractor for the duration of the periods stated in accordance with the programme and in the manner specified in the Contract to be defective within . . . . months, any shrubs, ordinary nursery stock trees or other plants found to be defective within . . . . months and any trees, semi-mature advanced or extra large nursery stock found to be defective within . . . . months of the date of Practical Completion and are due to materials or workmanship not in accordance with the contract shall be replaced by the Contractor entirely at his own cost unless the Landscape Architect shall otherwise instruct. The Landscape Architect shall certify the dates when in his opinion the Contractor's obligations under this clause have been discharged.

*B The maintenance of the trees, shrubs, grass and other plants after the date of the said certificate will be undertaken by the Employer who will be responsible for the replacement of any trees, shrubs, grass or other plants which are subsequently defective.

3·0 Control of the Works

Assignment

3·1 Neither the Employer nor the Contractor shall, without the written consent of the other, assign this Contract.

---

[b] If a different period is required delete 'three months' and insert the appropriate period.

* Delete (A) or (B) as appropriate.

Sub-contracting

3·2 The Contractor shall not sub-contract the Works or any part thereof without the written consent of the Landscape Architect whose consent shall not unreasonably be withheld.

Contractor's representative

3·3 The Contractor shall at all reasonable times keep upon the Works a competent person in charge and any instructions given to him by the Landscape Architect shall be deemed to have been issued to the Contractor.

Exclusion from the Works

3·4 The Landscape Architect may (but not unreasonably or vexatiously) issue instructions requiring the exclusion from the Works of any person employed thereon.

Landscape Architect's instructions

3·5 The Landscape Architect may issue written instructions which the Contractor shall forthwith carry out. If instructions are given orally they shall, in two days, be confirmed in writing by the Landscape Architect.

If within 7 days after receipt of a written notice from the Landscape Architect requiring compliance with an instruction the Contractor does not comply therewith then the Employer may employ and pay other persons to carry out the work and all costs incurred thereby may be deducted by him from any monies due or to become due to the Contractor under this Contract or shall be recoverable from the Contractor by the Employer as a debt.

Variations

†3·6 The Landscape Architect may, without invalidating the contract, order an addition to or omission from or other change in the Works or the order or period in which they are to be carried out and any such instruction shall be valued by the Landscape Architect on a fair and reasonable basis, using where relevant prices in the priced specification/schedules/Bills of Quantity/schedule of rates [c].

If any omission substantially varies the scope of the work such valuations shall take due account of the effect on any remaining items of work.

† Instead of the valuation referred to above, the price may be agreed between the Landscape Architect and the Contractor prior to the Contractor carrying out any such instruction.

P.C. and Provisional sums

3·7 The Landscape Architect shall issue instructions as to the expenditure of any P.C. and provisional sums and such instructions shall be valued in accordance with clause 3·6 hereof.

Objections to a Nomination

†3·8 The Landscape Architect shall not nominate any person as a nominated sub-contractor against whom the Contractor shall make reasonable objection or who will not enter into a sub-contract that applies the appropriate provisions of these conditions.

Disturbance of Regular Progress

†3·9 If upon written application being made to him by the Contractor within a reasonable time of it becoming apparent, the Landscape Architect is of the opinion that the Contractor has been involved in direct loss and/or expense for which he would not be reimbursed by a payment under any other provisions of this contract by reason of the regular progress of the Works or part of the Works having been materially affected by reasons within the control of the Employer, his agents or servants, then the Landscape Architect shall ascertain such loss and expense and include it in any payments due under clause 4·2.

4.0 Payment

Correction of inconsistencies

4·1 Any inconsistency in or between the Contract Drawings [c] and the Contract Specification [c] and the schedules [c] shall be corrected and any such correction which results in an addition, omission or other change shall be treated as a variation under clause 3·6 hereof. Nothing contained in the Contract Drawings [c] or the Contract Specification [c] or the schedules or the Bills of Quantity [c] or the Schedule of Rates [c] shall override, modify or affect in any way whatsoever the application or interpretation of that which is contained in these Conditions.

Progress payments and retention

4·2* The Landscape Architect shall if requested by the Contractor, at intervals of not less than four weeks calculated from the date for commencement subject to any agreement between the parties as to stage payments, certify progress payments to the Contractor, in respect of the value of the Works properly executed, including any amounts either ascertained or agreed under clauses 3·6 and 3·7 hereof, and the value of any materials and goods which have been reasonably and properly brought upon the site for the purpose of the Works and which are adequately stored and protected against the weather and other casualties less a retention of 5% (. . . . . %) [e] and less any sums previously certified, and the Employer shall pay to the Contractor the amount so certified within 14 days of the date of the certificate.

Penultimate certificate

†4·3 The Landscape Architect shall within 14 days after the date of practical completion certified under clause 2·4 hereof certify payment to the Contractor of 97½% of the total amount to be paid to the Contractor under this contract so far as that amount is ascertainable at the date of practical completion, including any amounts either ascertained or agreed under clauses 3·6 and 3·7 hereof less the amount of any progress payments previously certified to the Employer, and less the cost of any subsequent maintenance included in the contract in accordance with Clause 2·7A unless the failures of plants as set out in clause 2·7 are in excess of 10% in which case the amount retained shall be adjusted accordingly, and the Employer shall pay to the Contractor the amount so certified within 14 days of that certificate.

Final certificate

4·4 The Contractor shall supply within three months/ . . . . [d] from the date of practical completion all documentation reasonably required for the computation of the amount to be finally certified by the Landscape Architect and the Landscape Architect shall within 28 days of receipt of such documentation, provided that the Landscape Architect has issued the certificate under clause 2·5 and 2·7A hereof, issue a final certificate certifying the amount remaining due to the Contractor or due to the Employer as the case may be and such

[c] Delete as appropriate to follow any deletions in the recitals on page 1.

[d] If a different period is required delete 'three months' and insert the appropriate percentage period. Normally 10%.

[e] If a different percentage is required delete 5% and insert the appropriate retention %.

160

sum shall as from the fourteenth day after the date of the final certificate be a debt payable as the case may be by the Employer to the Contractor or by the Contractor to the Employer.

Contribution, levy and tax changes [f]
4·5 Contribution, levy and tax changes shall be dealt with by the application of Part A of the Supplementary Memorandum to the Agreement for Landscape Works. The percentage addition under Part A, clause A5 is . . . . %.

Fixed price [f]
4·6A No account shall be taken in any payment to the Contractor under this Contract of any change in the cost to the Contractor of the labour, materials, plant and other resources employed in carrying out the Works except as provided in clause 4·5 hereof, if applicable.

Fluctuations [f]
4·6B The Contract sum shall be adjusted in accordance with the provisions of Part D of the Supplementary Memorandum and the Formula Rules current at the date stated in the tender documents, and which shall be incorporated in all certificates except those relating to the release of retention and shall be exclusive of any Value Added Tax. These provisions shall also be incorporated as appropriate in any sub contract agreement.

5.0 Statutory obligations

Statutory obligations, notices, fees and charges
5·1 The Contractor shall comply with, and give all notices required by, any statute, any statutory instrument, rule or order or any regulation or byelaw applicable to the Works (hereinafter called 'the statutory requirements') and shall pay all fees and charges in respect of the Works legally recoverable from him. If the Contractor finds any divergence between the statutory requirements and the contract documents or between the statutory requirements and any instruction of the Landscape Architect he shall immediately give to the Landscape Architect, a written notice specifying the divergence. Subject to this latter obligation, the Contractor shall not be liable to the Employer under this Contract if the Works do not comply with the statutory requirements where and to the extent that such non-compliance of the Work results from the Contractor having carried out work in accordance with the Contract Documents or any instruction of the Landscape Architect.

Value Added Tax
5·2 The sum or sums due to the Contractor under Article 2 hereof this Agreement shall be exclusive of any Value Added Tax and the Employer shall pay to the Contractor any Value Added Tax properly chargeable by the Commissioners of Custom and Excise on the supply to the Employer of any goods and services by the Contractor under this Contract in the manner set out in Part B of the Supplementary Memorandum to the Agreement for Landscape Works.

Statutory tax deduction scheme
5·3 Where at the date of tender the Employer was a 'contractor', or where at any time up to the issue and payment of the final certificate the Employer becomes a 'contractor', for the purposes of the statutory tax deduction scheme referred to in Part C of the Supplementary Memorandum to the Agreement for Landscape Works, Part C of that Memorandum shall be operated.

Fair Wages Resolution
5·4 If the Employer is a local authority the contractor shall in respect of all persons employed by him (whether in the execution of this contract or otherwise) in every factory, workshop or place occupied or used by him for the executions of this contract comply with the conditions of Fair Wages Resolutions.

Prevention of corruption
5·5 If the Employer is a local authority he shall be entitled to cancel this contract and to recover from the Contractor the amount of any loss resulting from such cancellation, if the Contractor shall have offered or given or agreed to give to any person any gift or consideration of any kind or if the Contractor shall have committed any offence under the Prevention of Corruption Acts 1889 to 1916 or shall have given any fee or reward the receipt of which is an offence under sub-section (2) of section 117 of the Local Government Act 1972 or any re-enactment thereof.

6.0 Injury, damage and insurance

Injury to or death of persons
6·1 The Contractor shall be liable for and shall indemnify the Employer against any expense, liability, loss, claim or proceedings whatsoever arising under any statute or at common law in respect of personal injury to or death of any person whomsoever arising out of or in the course of or caused by the carrying out of the Works, unless due to any act or neglect of the Employer or of any person for whom the Employer is responsible. Without prejudice to his liability to indemnify the Employer the Contractor shall maintain and shall cause any subcontractor to maintain such insurances as are necessary to cover the liability of the Contractor, or, as the case may be, of such sub-contractor, in respect of personal injury or death arising out of or in the course of or caused by the carrying out of the Works. Provided that nothing in this clause contained shall impose any liability on the sub-contractor in respect of negligence or breach of duty on the part of the Employer, the Contractor, his other sub-contractors or their respective servants or agents.

Damage to property
6·2 The Contractor shall, subject to clause 6·3A.B[g], be liable for and indemnify the Employer against and insure and cause any sub-contractor to insure against any expense, liability, loss, claim or proceedings in respect of any damage whatsoever to any property real or personal insofar as such damage arises out of or in the course of or by reason of the carrying out of the Works and is due to any negligence, omission or default of the Contractor or any person for whom the Contractor is responsible or of any sub-contractor or person for whom the sub-contractor is responsible.

Insurance of the Works − Fire etc. − New Works
6·3A The Contractor shall in the joint names of Employer and Contractor insure against loss and damage by fire, lightning, explosion, storm, tempest, flood, bursting or overflowing of water tanks, apparatus or pipes, earthquake, aircraft and other aerial devices or articles dropped therefrom, riot and civil commotion, for the full value of the Works thereof plus . . . . % [h] to

---

[f] Delete clause 4·5 if the contract period is of such limited duration as to make the provisions of part A of the Supplementary Memorandum to this agreement inapplicable.
[g] Delete 6·3A or 6·3B as appropriate.
[h] Percentage to be inserted.

cover professional fees all work executed and all unfixed materials and goods intended for, delivered to, placed on or adjacent to the Works and intended therefore (except temporary buildings, plant, tools and equipment owned or hired by the Contractor and his sub-contractors). Upon acceptance of any claim under the insurance mentioned in this clause 6·3A the Contractor shall with due diligence restore or replace work or materials or goods damaged and dispose of any debris and proceed with and complete the Works. The Contractor shall not be entitled to any payment in respect of work or materials or goods damaged other than the monies received under the said insurance (less the percentage to cover professional fees) and such monies shall be paid to the Contractor under certificates of the Landscape Architect at the periods stated in clause 4·0 hereof.

Insurance of the Works – Fire, etc. – Existing structure [j]

6·3B The Works (and the existing structures together with the contents thereof owned by him and for which he is responsible) and all unfixed materials and goods intended for, delivered to, placed on or adjacent to the Works and intended therefor (except temporary buildings, plant, tools and equipment owned or hired by the Contractor or any sub-contractor) shall be at the sole risk of the Employer as regards loss or damage by fire, lightning, explosion, storm, tempest, flood, burst or overflowing of water tanks, apparatus or pipes, earthquake, aircraft and other aerial devices or articles dropped therefrom, riot and civil commotion, and the Employer shall maintain adequate insurance against that risk.

If any loss or damage as referred to in this clause occurs then the Landscape Architect shall issue instructions for the reinstatement and making good of such loss or damage in accordance with clause 3·5 hereof.

Evidence of insurance

6·4 The Contractor shall produce, and shall cause any sub-contractor to produce, such evidence as the Employer may reasonably require that the insurances referred to in clauses 6·1 and 6·2 and, where applicable 6·3A, hereof have been taken out and are in force at all material times. Where clause 63B hereof is applicable the Employer shall produce such evidence as the Contractor may reasonably require that the insurance referred to therein has been taken out and is in force at all material times.

Malicious Damage or Theft (before Practical Complete)

†6·5A All loss or damage arising from any theft or malicious damage prior to practical completion shall be made good by the Contractor at his own expense.

B The Contract sum shall include the provisional sum of £...............* to be expended as instructed by the Landscape Architect in respect of the cost of all work arising from any theft or malicious damage to the works beyond the control of the Contractor prior to practical completion of the works.

7·0 Determination

Determination by Employer

7·1 The Employer may but not unreasonably or vexatiously by notice by registered post or recorded delivery to the Contractor forthwith determine the employment of the Contractor under this Contract if the Contractor shall make default in any one or more of the following respects:

1 if the Contractor without reasonable cause fails to proceed diligently with the Works or wholly suspends the carrying out of the Works before completion;

2 if the Contractor becomes bankrupt or makes any composition or arrangement with his creditors or has a winding up order made or (except for the purposes of reconstruction) a resolution for voluntary winding up passed or a receiver or manager of his business or undertaking is duly appointed or possession is taken by or on behalf of any creditor of any property the subject of a charge.

In the event of the Employer determining the employment of the Contractor as aforesaid the Contractor shall immediately give up possession of the site of the Works and the Employer shall not be bound to make any further payment to the Contractor until after completion of the Works. Provided always that the right determination shall be without prejudice to any other rights or remedies which the Employer may possess.

Determination by Contractor

7·2 The Contractor may but not unreasonably or vexatiously by notice by registered post or recorded delivery to the Employer forthwith determine the employment of the Contractor under this Contract if the Employer shall make default in any one or more of the following respects:

1 if the Employer fails to make any progress payment due under the provisions of Clause 4·2 hereof within 14 days of such payment being due;

2 if the Employer or any person for whom he is responsible interferes with or obstructs the carrying out of the Works or fails to make the site of the Works available for the Contractor in accordance with clause 2·1 hereof;

3 if the Employer suspends the carrying out of the Works for a continuous period of at least one month;

4 if the Employer becomes bankrupt or makes a composition or arrangement with his creditors, or has a winding up order made or a resolution for voluntary winding up passed on a receiver or manager of his business is appointed or possession is taken by or on behalf of any creditor of any property the subject of a charge.

Provided that the employment of the Contractor shall not be determined under clauses 7·2·1, 7·2·2 or 7·2·3 hereof unless the Employer has continued the default for seven days after receipt by registered post or recorded delivery of a notice from the Contractor specifying such default.

In the event of the Contractor determining the Employment of the Contractor as aforesaid the Employer shall pay to the Contractor, after taking into account amounts previously paid, such sum as shall be fair and reasonable for the value of work begun and executed, materials on site and the removal of all temporary buildings, plant, tools and equipment. Provided always that the right of determination shall be without prejudice to any other rights or remedies which the Contractor may possess.

8·0 Supplementary Memorandum

Meaning of references in 4·5, 4·6, 5·2 and 5·3

8·1 The references in clauses 4·5, 4·6, 5·2 and 5·3 to the Supplementary Memorandum to the Agreement for Landscape Works are to that issued for use with this Form by the Joint Council for Landscape Industries as endorsed hereon.

---

*   The amount to be inserted should take account of the Works and the place where they are carried out. Delete [A] or [B] as appropriate.

The Joint Council of Landscape Industries
has issued a Supplementary Memorandum
for use with this Form, where applicable,
as referred to in the list of Contents on
page 3 and in clause 8·1.

The Council has also issued Practice Note No. 1 and
Practice Note No. 2.

Practice Note No. 1 and 2 are now superseded by
Practice Note No. 3 which is attached.

The complete document now comprises 3 items:
Form of Agreement for Landscape Works.
Supplementary Memorandum.
JCLI Practice Note No. 3.
The Supplementary Memorandum and
Practice Note No. 3 may be torn off as convenient.

Dated _____ 19 __

Agreement for Landscape Works

(In Scotland when English Law is not to apply
supplementary clauses in respect of Building
Regulations and Arbitration may be required)

First issued April 1978, revised April 1981
reprinted with corrections April 1982 and
revised April 1985

Between _____

_____

and _____

_____

This Form is issued by the
Joint Council for Landscape Industries
comprising:-

Landscape Institute
Horticultural Trades Association
British Association Landscape Industries
National Farmers Unions
Institute of Leisure and Amenity Management.

†Note: All clauses other than those marked † are
similar to those in the Joint Contracts Tribunal
Agreement for Minor Building Works.

Published for the Joint Council for Landscape
Industries by the Landscape Institute
12 Carlton House Terrace, London SW1Y 5AH and
available from RIBA Publications Limited
66 Portland Place, London W1N 4AD.
© JCLI April 1985

Printed by Duolith Ltd.
Welwyn Garden City, Herts.

Issued October 1985

Agreement for Landscape Works: Supplementary Memorandum

This Memorandum is the Supplementary Memorandum referred to in the Joint Council for Landscape Industries "Agreement for Landscape Works", 1981 Edition, clauses 4·5, 4·6, 5·2 and 5·3.

Unless otherwise specifically stated, words and phrases in the Supplementary Memorandum have the same meaning as in the Agreement for Landscape Works.

PART A – CONTRIBUTION, LEVY AND TAX CHANGES

Deemed calculation of Contract Sum – rates of contribution etc.

A1   The sum referred to in Article 2 (in this clause called "the Contract Sum") shall be deemed to have been calculated in the manner set out below and shall be subject to adjustment in the events specified hereunder:

A1·1   The prices used or set out by the Contractor in the contract documents are based upon the types and rates of contribution, levy and tax payable by a person in his capacity as an employer and which at the date of the contract are payable by the Contractor. A type and rate so payable are in clause A1·2 referred to as a 'tender type' and a 'tender rate'.

Increases or decreases in rates of contribution etc. – payment or allowance

A1·2   If any of the tender rates other than a rate of levy payable by virtue of the Industrial Training Act 1964, is increased or decreased, or if a tender type ceases to be payable, or if a new type of contribution, levy or tax which is payable by a person in his capacity as an employer becomes payable after the date of tender, then in any such case the net amount of the difference between what the Contractor actually pays or will pay in respect of

·1   workpeople engaged upon or in connection with the Works either on or adjacent to the site of the Works, and

·2   workpeople directly employed by the Contractor who are engaged upon the production·of materials or goods for use in or in connection with the Works and who operate neither on nor adjacent to the site of the Works and to the extent that they are so engaged

or because of his employment of such workpeople and what he would have paid had the alteration, cessation or new type of contribution, levy or tax not become effective, shall, as the case may be, be paid to or allowed by the Contractor.

Persons employed on site other than 'workpeople'

A1·3   There shall be added to the net amount paid to or allowed by the Contractor under clause A1·2 in respect of each person employed on the site by the Contractor for the Works and who is not within the definition of 'workpeople' in clause A4·6·3 the same amount as is payable or allowable in respect of a craftsman under clause A1·2 or such proportion of that amount as reflects the time (measured in whole working days) that each such person is so employed.

A1·4   For the purposes of clause A1·3

no period less than 2 whole working days in any week shall be taken into account and periods less than a whole working day shall not be aggregated to amount to a whole working day;

the phrase "the same amount as is payable or allowable in respect of a craftsman" shall refer to the amount in respect of a craftsman employed by the Contractor (or by any sub-contractor under a sub-contract to which clause A3 refers) under the rules or decisions or agreements of the National Joint Council for the Building Industry or other wage-fixing body and, where the aforesaid rules or decisions or agreements provide for more than one rate of wage emolument or other expense for a craftsman, shall refer to the amount in respect of a craftsman employed as aforesaid to whom the highest rate is applicable; and

the phrase "employed . . . by the Contractor" shall mean an employment to which the Income Tax (Employment) Regulations 1973 (the PAYE Regulations) under section 204 of the Income and Corporation Taxes Act, 1970, apply.

Refunds and premiums

A1·5   The prices used or set out by the Contractor in the contract documents are based upon the types and rates of refund of the contributions, levies and taxes payable by a person in his capacity as an employer and upon the types and rates of premium receivable by a person in his capacity as an employer being in each case types and rates which at the date of tender are receivable by the Contractor. Such a type and such a rate are in clause A·6 referred to as a 'tender type' and a 'tender rate'.

A1·6   If any of the tender rates is increased or decreased or if a tender type ceases to be payable or if a new type of refund of any contribution levy or tax payable by a person in his capacity as an employer becomes receivable or if a new type of premium receivable by a person in his capacity as an employer becomes receivable after the date of tender, then in any such case the net amount of the difference between what the Contractor actually receives or will receive in respect of workpeople as referred to in clauses A1·2·1 and A1·2·2 or because of his employment of such workpeople and what he would have received had the alteration, cessation or new type of refund or premium not become effective, shall, as the case may be, be allowed by or paid to the Contractor.

A1·7   The references in clauses A1·5 and A1·6 to premiums shall be construed as meaning all payments howsoever they are described which are made under or by virtue of an Act of Parliament to a person in his capacity as an employer and which affect the cost to an employer of having persons in his employment.

Contracted-out employment

A1·8   Where employer's contributions are payable by the Contractor in respect of workpeople as referred to in clauses A1·2·1 and A1·2·2 whose employment is contracted-out employment within the meaning of the Social Security Pensions Act 1975 the Contractor shall for the purpose of recovery or allowance under this clause be deemed to pay employer's contributions as if that employment were not contracted-out employment.

Meaning of contribution etc.

A1·9   The references in clause A1 to contribution, levies and taxes shall be construed as meaning all impositions payable by a person in his capacity as an employer howsoever they are described and whoever the recipient which are imposed under or by virtue of an Act of Parliament and which affect the cost to an employer of having persons in his employment.

Materials – duties and taxes

A2·1   The prices used or set out by the Contractor in the contract documents are based upon the types and rates of duty if any and tax if any (other than any value added tax which is treated, or is capable of being treated, as input tax (as referred to in the Finance Act 1972) by the Contractor) by whomsoever payable which at the date of tender are payable on the import, purchase, sale, appropriation, processing or use of the materials, goods, electricity and, where so specifically stated in the Contract Documents, fuels specified in the list attached thereto under or by virtue of any Act of Parliament. A type and rate so payable are in clause A2·2 referred to as a 'tender type' and a 'tender rate'.

A2·2   If in relation to any materials or goods specified as aforesaid, or any electricity or fuels specified as aforesaid and consumed on site for the execution of the Works including temporary site installations for those Works, a tender rate is increased or decreased or a tender type ceases to be payable or a new type of duty or tax (other than value added tax which is treated, or is capable of being treated as input tax (as referred to in the Finance Act 1972) by the Contractor) becomes payable on the import, purchase, sale, appropriation, processing or use of those materials, goods, electricity or fuels, then in any such case the net amount of the difference between what the Contractor actually pays in respect of those materials, goods, electricity or fuels and what he would have paid in respect of them had the alteration, cessation or imposition not occurred, shall, as the case may be, be paid to or allowed by the Contractor. In clause A2 the expression 'a new type of duty or tax' includes an additional duty or tax and a duty or tax imposed in regard to specified materials, goods, electricity or fuels in respect of which no duty or tax whatever was previously payable (other than any value added tax which is treated, or is capable of being treated, as input tax (as referred to in the Finance Act 1972) by the Contractor).

164

Fluctuations — work sublet

A3·1   If the Contractor shall decide to sublet any portion of the Works he shall incorporate in the sub-contract provisions to the like effect as the provisions of

clauses A1, A4 and A5 including the percentage stated in clause 4·5 pursuant to clause A5

which are applicable for the purposes of this Contract.

A3·2   If the price payable under such a sub-contract as aforesaid is decreased below or increased above the price in such sub-contract by reason of the operation of the said incorporated provisions, then the net amount of such decrease or increase shall, as the case may be, be allowed by or paid to the Contractor under this Contract.

Provisions relating to clauses A1, A3 and A5

Written notice by Contractor

A4·1   The Contractor shall give a written notice to the Landscape Architect of the occurrence of any of the events referred to in such of the following provisions as are applicable for the purposes of this Contract:
· 1   clause A1·2
· 2   clause A1·6
· 3   clause A2·2
· 4   clause A3·2

Timing and effect of written notices

A4·2   Any notice required to be given by the preceding sub-clause shall be given within a reasonable time after the occurrence of the event to which the notice relates, and the giving of a written notice in that time shall be a condition precedent to any payment being made to the Contractor in respect of the event in question.

Agreement — Landscape Architect and Contractor

A4·3   The Landscape Architect and the Contractor may agree what shall be deemed for all the purposes of this Contract to be the net amount payable to or allowable by the Contractor in respect of the occurrence of any event such as is referred to in any of the provisions listed in clause A4·1.

Fluctuations added to or deducted from Contract Sum — provisions setting out conditions etc. to be fulfilled before such addition or deduction

A4·4   Any amount which from time to time becomes payable to or allowable by the Contractor by virtue of clause A1 or clause A3 shall, as the case may be, be added to or deducted from the Contract Sum:

Provided:

— evidence by Contractor —

· 1   As soon as is reasonably practicable the Contractor shall provide such evidence as the Landscape Architect may reasonably require to enable the amount payable to or allowable by the Contractor by virtue of clause A1 or clause A3 to be ascertained: and in the case of amounts payable to or allowable by the sub-contractor under clause A4·1·3 (or clause A3 for amounts payable to or allowable by the sub-contractor under provisions in the sub-contract to the like effect as clauses A1·3 and A1·4) — employees other than workpeople — such evidence shall include a certificate signed by or on behalf of the Contractor each week certifying the validity of the evidence reasonably required to ascertain such amounts.

— actual payment by Contractor —

· 2   No amount shall be included in or deducted from the amount which would otherwise be stated as due in progress payments by virtue of this clause unless on or before the date as at which the total value of work, materials and goods is ascertained for the purposes of any progress payment the Contractor shall have actually paid or received the sum which is payable by or to him in consequence of the event in respect of which the payment or allowance arises.

— no alteration to Contractor's profit —

· 3   No addition to or subtraction from the Contract Sum made by virtue of this clause shall alter in any way the amount of profit of the Contractor included in that Sum.

— position where Contractor is in default over completion —

· 4·1   No amount shall be included in or deducted from the amount which would otherwise be stated as due in progress payments or in the final certificate in respect of amounts otherwise payable to or allowable by the Contractor by virtue of clause A1 or clause A3 if the event (as referred to in the provisions listed in clause A4·1) in respect of which the payment or allowance would be made occurs after the completion date fixed under clause 2.

· 4·2   Clause A4·4·4·1 shall not operate unless:
· 1   the printed text of clause 2 is unamended; and
· 2   the Landscape Architect has, in respect of every written notification by the Contractor under clause 2 of the Agreement, fixed such Completion Date as he considered to be in accordance with that clause.

Work etc. to which clauses A1 and A3 are not applicable

A4·5   Clause A1 and clause A3 shall not apply in respect of:

· 1   work for which the Contractor is allowed daywork rates in accordance with any such rates included in the Contract Documents;

· 2   changes in the rate of value added tax charged on the supply of goods or services by the Contractor to the Employer under this Contract.

Definitions for use with clause A1

A4·6   In clause A1:

· 1   the expression 'the date of the contract' means the date 10 days before the date when the Agreement is executed by the parties;

· 2   the expressions 'materials' and 'goods' include timber used in formwork but do not include other consumable stores, plant and machinery except electricity and, where specifically so stated in the Contract Documents, fuels;

· 3   the expression 'workpeople' means persons whose rates of wages and other emoluments (including holiday credits) are governed by the rules or decisions or agreements of the National Joint Council for the Building Industry or some other wage-fixing body for trades associated with the building industry;

· 4   the expression 'wage-fixing body' means a body which lays down recognised terms and conditions of workers within the meaning of the Employment Protection Act 1975, Schedule II, paragraph 2(a).

Percentage addition to fluctuation payments or allowances

A5   There shall be added to the amount paid or allowed by the Contractor under
· 1   clause A1·2
· 2   clause A1·3
· 3   clause A1·6
· 4   clause A2·2
the percentage stated in clause 4·5.

PART B — VALUE ADDED TAX

B1   In this clause 'VAT' means the value added tax introduced by the Finance Act 1972 which is under the care and management of the Commissioners of Customs and Excise (hereinafter called 'the Commissioners').

B2·1   The Landscape Architect shall inform the Contractor of the amount certified under clause 4·2 and immediately the Contractor shall give to the Employer a written provisional assessment of the respective values of those supplies of goods and services for which the certificate is being issued and which will be chargeable at the relevant times of supply on the Contractor at any rate or rates of VAT (including zero). The Contractor shall also specify the rate or rates of VAT which are chargeable on those supplies.

B2·2   Upon receipt of the Contractor's written provisional assessment the Employer shall calculate the amount of VAT due by applying the rate or rates of VAT specified by the Contractor to the amount of the supplies included in his assessment, and shall remit the calculated amount of such VAT to the Contractor when making payment to him of the amount certified by the Landscape Architect under clause 4·2.

B3·1   After the issue by the Landscape Architect of his certificate of making good defects under clause 2·5 of the Agreement the Contractor shall, as soon as he can finally so ascertain, prepare and submit to the Employer a written final statement of the value of all supplies of goods and services for which certificates have been or will be issued which are chargeable on the Contractor at any rate or rates of VAT (including zero). The Contractor shall also specify the rate or rates of VAT which are chargeable on those supplies and shall state the grounds on which he considers such supplies are so chargeable. He shall also state the total amount of VAT already received by him.

165

B3·2 Upon receipt of the written final statement the Employer shall calculate the amount of VAT due by applying the rate or rates of VAT specified by the Contractor to the value of the supplies included in the statement and deducting therefrom the total amount of VAT already received by the Contractor and shall pay the balance of such VAT to the Contractor within 28 days from receipt of the statement.

B3·3 If the Employer finds that the total amount of VAT specified in the final statement as already paid by him exceeds the amount of VAT calculated under clause B3·2, he shall so notify the Contractor, who shall refund such excess to the Employer within 28 days of receipt of the notification together with a receipt under clause B4 hereof showing a correction of the amounts for which a receipt or receipts have previously been issued by the Contractor.

B4 Upon receipt of any VAT properly paid under the provisions of this clause the Contractor shall issue to the Employer an authenticated receipt.

B5·1 In calculating the amount of VAT to be paid to the Contractor under clauses B2 and B3 hereof, the Employer shall disregard any sums which the Contractor may be liable to pay to the Employer as liquidated damges under clause 2·3.

B5·2 The Contractor shall likewise disregard such liquidated damages when stating the value of supplies of goods or services in his written final statement under clause B3·1.

B6·1 If the Employer disagrees with the final statement issued by the Contractor under clause B3·1 he may request the Contractor to obtain the decision of the Commissioners on the VAT properly chargeable on the Contractor for all supplies of goods and services under this contract and the Contractor shall forthwith request the Commissioners for such decision.

B6·2 If the Employer disagrees with such decision, then, provided he secures the Contractor against all costs and other expenses, the Contractor shall in accordance with the instructions of the Employer make all such appeals against the decision of the Commissioners as the Employer may request.

B6·3 Within 28 days of the date of the decision of the Commissioners (or of the final adjudication of an appeal) the Employer or the Contractor as the case may be, shall pay or refund to the other any VAT underpaid or overpaid in accordance with such decisions or adjudication. The Contractor shall also account to the Employer for any costs awarded in his favour. The provisions of clause B3·3 shall apply in regard to the provision of authenticated receipts.

B7 The provisions of clause 8 shall not apply to any matters to be dealt with under clause B6.

B8 If any dispute or difference between the Employer and the Contractor is referred to an Arbitrator appointed under Article 4 or to a Court, then insofar as any payment awarded in such arbitration or court proceedings varies amounts certified for payment of goods or services supplied by the Contractor to the Employer under this Contract or is an amount which ought to have been but was not so certified, then the provisions of this Part B shall so far as relevant and applicable apply to any such payments.

B9 Notwithstanding any provisions to the contrary elsewhere in the Agreement the Employer shall not be obliged to make any further payment to the Contractor if the Contractor is in default in providing the receipt referred to in clause B4; provided that this clause B9 shall only apply where the Employer can show that he requires such receipt to validate any claim for credit for tax paid or payable under this Agreement which the Employer is entitled to make to the Commissioners.

PART C – STATUTORY TAX DEDUCTION SCHEME – FINANCE (No.2) ACT 1975 [a]

C1 In this clause 'the Act' means the Finance (No.2) Act 1975; "the Regulations" means the Income Tax (Sub-Contractors in the Construction Industry) Regulations 1975 S.I. No. 1960; "contractor" means a person who is a contractor for the purposes of the Act and the Regulations; 'evidence' means such evidence as is required by the Regulations to be produced to a 'contractor' for the verification of a 'sub-contractor's' tax certificate; 'statutory deduction' means the deduction referred to in section 69(4) of the Act or such other deduction as may be in force at the relevant time; "'sub-contractor'" means a person who is a sub-contractor for the purposes of the Act and the Regulations; 'tax certificate' is a certificate issuable under section 70 of the Act.

Provision of evidence – tax certificate
C2·1 Not later than 21 days before the first payment becomes due under clause 4 or after the Employer becomes a 'contractor' as referred to in clause 5·3 the Contractor shall:

either

·1 provide the Employer with the evidence that the Contractor is entitled to be paid without the statutory deduction;

or

·2 inform the Employer in writing, and send a duplicate copy to the Landscape Architect, that he is not entitled to be paid without the statutory deduction.

C2·2 If the Employer is not satisfied with the validity of the evidence submitted in accordance with clause C2·1·1 hereof, he shall within 14 days of the Contractor submitting such evidence notify the Contractor in writing that he intends to make the statutory deduction from payments due under this Contract to the Contractor who is 'a sub-contractor' and give his reasons for that decision. The Employer shall at the same time comply with clause C5·1.

Uncertificated Contractor obtains tax certificate
C3·1 Where clause C2·1·2 applies, the Contractor shall immediately inform the Employer if he obtains a tax certificate and thereupon clause C2·1·1 shall apply.

Expiry of tax certificate
C3·2 If the period for which the tax certificate has been issued to the Contractor expires before the final payment is made to the Contractor under this Contract the Contractor shall, not later than 28 days before the day of expiry:

either

·1 provide the Employer with evidence that the Contractor from the said date of expiry is entitled to be paid for a further period without the statutory deduction in which case the provisions of clause C2·2 hereof shall apply if the Employer is not satisfied with the evidence;

or

·2 inform the Employer in writing that he will not be entitled to be paid without the statutory deduction after the said date of expiry.

Cancellation of tax certificate
C3·3 The Contractor shall immediately inform the Employer in writing if his current tax certificate is cancelled and give the date of such cancellation.

Vouchers
C4 The Employer shall, as a 'contractor', in accordance with the Regulations, send promptly to the Inland Revenue any voucher which, in compliance with the Contractor's obligations as a 'sub-contractor' under the Regulations, the Contractor gives to the Employer.

Statutory deduction – direct cost of materials
C5·1 If at any time the Employer is of the opinion (whether because of the information given under clause C2·1·2 of this clause or of the expiry or cancellation of the Contractor's tax certificate or otherwise) that he will be required by the Act to make a statutory deduction from any payment due to be made the Employer shall immediately so notify the Contractor in writing and require the Contractor to state not later than 7 days before each future payment becomes due (or within 10 days of such notification if that is later) the amount to be included in such payment which represents the direct cost to the Contractor and any other person of materials used or to be used in carrying out the Works.

C5·2 Where the Contractor complies with clause C5·1 he shall indemnify the Employer against loss or expense caused to the Employer by any incorrect statement of the amount of direct cost referred to in that clause.

C5·3 Where the Contractor does not comply with clause C5·1 the Employer shall be entitled to make a fair estimate of the amount of direct cost referred to in that clause.

Correction of errors
C6 Where any error or omission has occured in calculating or making the statutory deduction the Employer shall correct that error or omission by repayment to, or by deduction from payments to, the Contractor as the case may be, subject only to any statutory obligation on the Employer not to make such correction.

---

[a] The application of the Tax Deduction scheme and these provisions is explained in JCT Practice Note No. 22.

Relation to other Clauses of Agreement
C7 If compliance with this clause involves the Employer or the Contractor in not complying with any other provisions of the Agreement, then the provisions of this clause shall prevail.

Application of Arbitration Agreement
C8 The provisions of Article 4 (arbitration) shall apply to any dispute or difference between the Employer or the Landscape Architect on his behalf and the Contractor as to the operation of this clause except where the Act or the Regulations or any other Act of Parliament or statutory instrument rule or order made under an Act of Parliament provide for some other method of resolving such dispute or difference.

PART D — FLUCTUATIONS
Procedure for the recovery from the Employer of any Fluctuations in the cost of labour and materials (*delete if not applicable*).

Adjustment of Contract Sum — NEDO Price Adjustment Formula for Landscape Contracts
D1·1 The Contract Sum shall be adjusted in accordance with the provisions of this clause and the Formula Rules current at the Date of Tender issued for use with this clause by the Joint Contracts Tribunal for the Standard Form of Building Contract hereinafter called 'the Formula Rules'.

D1·2 Any adjustment under this clause shall be to sums exclusive of value added tax and nothing in this clause shall affect in any way the operation of Clause 5·2 (value added tax) and Part B of this Memorandum.

D2 The Definitions in rule 3 of the Formula Rules shall apply to this clause.
The adjustment referred to in this clause shall be effected (after taking into account any Non-Adjustable Element) in all certificates for payment (other than those under Clause 4·2 of these Conditions (release of retention)) issued under the provisions of these Conditions.
If any correction of amounts of adjustment under this clause included in previous certificates is required following any operation of rule 5 of the Formula Rules such correction shall be given effect in the next certificate for payment to be issued.

Fluctuations — Articles manufactured outside the United Kingdom
D3 For any article to which rule 4·2 of the Formula Rules applies the Contractor shall insert in a list attached to the Contract Documents the market price of the article in sterling (that is the price delivered to the site) current at the Date of Tender. If after that Date the market price of the article inserted in the aforesaid list increases or decreases then the net amount of the difference between the cost of purchasing at the market price inserted in the aforesaid list and the market price payable by the Contractor and current when the article is bought shall, as the case may be, be paid to or allowed by the Contractor. The reference to 'market price' in this clause shall be construed as including any duty or tax (other than any value added tax which is treated, or is capable of being treated, as input tax (as defined in the Finance Act 1972) by the Contractor) by whomsoever payable under or by virtue of any Act of Parliament on the import, purchase, sale, appropriation or use of the article specified as aforesaid.

Power to agree — Landscape Architect and Contractor
D4 The Landscape Architect and the Contractor may agree any alteration to the methods and procedures for ascertaining the amount of formula adjustment to be made under this clause and the amounts ascertained after the operation of such agreement shall be deemed for all the purposes of this Contract to be the amount of formula adjustment payable to or allowable by the Contractor in respect of the provisions of this Clause. Provided always:

D4·1 that no alteration to the methods and procedures shall be agreed as aforesaid unless it is reasonably expected that the amount of formula adjustment so ascertained will be the same or approximately the same as that ascertained in accordance with Part I or Part II of Sections 2 of the Formula Rules whichever Part is stated to be applicable in the Contract Documents; and

D4·2 that any agreement under this sub-clause shall not have any effect on the determination of any adjustment payable by the Contractor to any sub-contractor.

Position where Monthly Bulletins are delayed, etc.
D5·1 If at any time prior to the issue of the Final Certificate under Clause 4·3 of these Conditions formula adjustment is not possible because of delay in or cessation of, the publication of the Monthly Bulletins, adjustment of the Contract Sum shall be made in each Interim Certificate during such period of delay on a fair and reasonable basis.

D5·2 If publication of the Monthly Bulletins is recommenced at any time prior to the issue of the Final Certificate under Clause 4·3 of these Conditions the provisions of this clause and the Formula Rules shall operate for each Valuation Period as if no delay or cessation as aforesaid had occurred and the adjustment under this clause and the Formula Rules shall be substituted for any adjustment under paragraph D5·1 hereof.

D5·3 During any period of delay or cessation as aforesaid the Contractor and Employer shall operate such parts of this clause and the Formula Rules as will enable the amount of formula adjustment due to be readily calculated upon recommencement of publication of the Monthly Bulletins.

Formula Rules
Rule 3
E1·1 Base Month.................................. 19........
Non-Adjustable Element..............% (not to exceed 10%).

Rules 10 and 30(i)

*Part I/Part II of Section 2 of the Formula Rules is to apply.

---

* *Strike out according to which method of formula adjustment (Part I — Work Category Method or Part II — Work Group Method) has been notified in the Schedules of Quantity issued to tenderers.*

This Supplementary Memorandum is issued by the Joint Council for Landscape Industries comprising:-

Landscape Institute
Horticultural Trades Association
British Association Landscape Industries
National Farmers' Union
Institute of Leisure and Amenity Management

Published for the Joint Council for Landscape Industries by the Landscape Institute
12 Carlton House Terrace London SW1Y 5AH and available from RIBA Publications Limited
66 Portland Place London W1N 4AD
© JCLI April 1985

Printed by Duolith Ltd
Welwyn Garden City, Hertfordshire

Issued October 1985

Practice Note No. 3 (April 1985) JCLI Standard Form of Agreement for Landscape Works

Note: The JCLI Practice Note 3 supersedes No. 1 issued April 1978 and No. 2 on April 1982.

1. **Schedules (1st Recital)** means a list of items giving quantities, as necessary, and descriptions of work required, prepared in accordance with an appropriate method of measurement, which will be priced by tenderers and subsequently form part of the contract. Detailed information on materials and workmanship shall be contained in the Specification.

   Bills of Quantity
   Provision is now made for the option of including in the contract documents Bills prepared in accordance with SMM and the JCLI Rules.

   4th recital
   This provides for the naming of a quantity surveyor; neither the Articles nor the Conditions mention him but the Employer or the Landscape Architect on his behalf may wish to appoint a quantity surveyor in connection with the project, for example, to assist with valuations.

   Article 2
   The reference to VAT is new.

   Article 4: Arbitration
   Follows clause 8 (1978).

   Page 3
   The top part of the page is left blank for the parties to seal the Agreement if so required.

2. **Liquidated and Ascertained Damages: (Clause 2·3)**

   In landscape work it is generally very difficult to define the loss an Employer will suffer when a contract is delayed by the Contractor.

   The method outlined below for assessing the damages to be included in the contract is based on a notional interest on employed capital for the period of delay.

   The value of the project is assessed and interest at 1% over Bank Minimum Lending Rate is charged. This is spread over the contract period which realises a rate per week.

   Example:
   Contract Sum £75,000
   Period 40 weeks
   M.L.R. 12½%
   Interest 13½%

   Liquidated
   and
   Ascertained
   Damages $\dfrac{£75,000 \times 13\cdot5}{52 \times 100} = £194.71$ per week

   The essence of this method is that the damages are both ascertainable and realistic, being based on capital employed and not on some arbitrary assessment. Note: It does not however make any allowance for any additional professional fees which may be incurred as a result of the extended contract period.

3. **Date of Practical Completion: (Clause 2·4)**

   The date of Practical Completion is that date when the Landscape Architect certifies that the Contractor has fulfilled his obligations under the terms of the Contract. This does not preclude partial possession (dealt with under Clause 2·4) but simply determines the commencement of the Defect Liability Period for sections of work.

4. **Defects Liability: (Clause 2·5)**

   Except for plants which are dealt with separately the Contractor is responsible for making good all defects which appear after Practical Completion within a period inserted in the contract. It is recommended that the liability periods for landscape work should differ for hard landscape, grass, shrubs and trees. It is recommended that for hard landscape this period should normally be 6 months. Where paving forms a minor element within a predominantly soft landscape then the period should be as for the associated planting. In all cases the period should begin on the date of Practical Completion.

5. **Plant Failures — at Practical Completion: (Clause 2·7)**

   All plants which have failed prior to Practical Completion or within 6 weeks of the first leafing out in the case of trees and shrubs or grass at the first cut and roll, whichever is the later, are to be replaced by the Contractor entirely at his own expense, unless it arises from theft or malicious damage after Practical Completion. At an appropriate time the Contractor and Landscape Architect should meet to establish the extent of any defects and failures. The Landscape Architect will then prepare a schedule of these defects and send it to the Contractor within 14 days. The Contractor will inform the Landscape Architect when the work has been rectified.

6. **Plant Failures — after Practical Completion: (Clause 2·7(A) or (B))**

   At the time of preparing the tender documents a decision must be made as to whether the Contractor or the Employer is to be responsible for Maintenance of trees, shrubs and grass areas after Practical Completion. Maintenance is defined as those operations carried out by the Contractor or Employer after Practical Completion.

   i. If the Employer is to be responsible for Maintenance following Practical Completion then 2·7(A) is deleted and 2·7(B) is used, the Contractor is then relieved of all further obligations to replace defective plants other than those items listed in the Schedule of Defects referred to in item 5 above.

168

ii. If Maintenance is to be carried out by the Contractor 2·7(B) is deleted and 2·7(A) is used and the Contractor is then responsible for making good all defective plants during the Period, and this maintenance is to be separately scheduled and priced in the Schedules of Quantity. The Landscape Architect must not state for example, 'the Contractor is to allow for all maintenance during the Defects Liability Period', but must specify the operations in the Schedules of Quantity so that the Contractor is fully aware of his commitments and can incorporate the cost of such work in the Contract Sum. This does not include the cost of making good defects at Practical Completion which is deemed to be incorporated in the Contractor's Contract Sum. When the Contractor is responsible for Maintenance the following Defects Liability Periods for plants are recommended:

Grass: 3 months after the first cut and roll.
Shrubs and Trees: 12 months after the first breaking of buds.
Semi mature and ELNS: 2 years after the first breaking of buds.

In all cases the period should begin on the date of Practical Completion.

It is recommended that where varying Defects Liability Periods are required by the Contract, work relating to each Period shall be kept separate under a suitable heading, which can be identified with the particular periods, and only that part of the retention monies proportional to the value of the part of the work certified as being practically complete should be released.

7. P.C. Sums: (Clause 3·7)

Particular attention is drawn to Clause 3·6 where it will be noted that no cash discount is allowable by sub-contractors or suppliers arising out of instructions issued by the Landscape Architect in respect of prime cost sums. As such quotations are accepted nett Contractors are deemed to have included for the lack of cash discount elsewhere in the Contract Sum.

8. Correction of inconsistencies (Clause 4·1)

This does not provide that every correction is to be treated as a variation but only any correction of an inconsistency which results in a change. Where the correction is not a change there is no variation. It may be necessary to determine which of two inconsistent documents is the ruling document or which of two inconsistent statements prevails. For example, if written descriptions appear on a drawing and it is stated in the Contract Documents that any figure in a description shall prevail over any figures otherwise shown on a drawing there would only be a change if it were necessary to correct a figure in a description where the inconsistent figure on the drawing was actually required.

9. Malicious Damage: (Clause 6·5)

The cost of all making good arising from malicious damage or theft after Practical Completion is always the responsibility of the Employer. When the risk of such damage is considered small, if the Landscape Architect wishes such damage or theft prior to Practical Completion to be made good by the Contractor at no extra cost to the Contract as at present, Clause 6·5(A) should be used. The Contractor will then make his own assessment of the likely cost and include for it in his tender and which the Employer then pays whether any damage arises or not.

Of it is preferred to reimburse the Contractor only for the actual cost of such damage which arises prior to Practical Completion then a provisional sum should be included in the tender documents and Clause 6·5(B) used.

10. Supplementary Memorandum (Clause 8·0)

Part A of the Supplement, Tax etc. changes, corresponds with clause 38 of the JCT Standard Form of Building Contract (1980); Part B, VAT, corresponds with the VAT Agreement Supplement to the Standard Form; and Part C, Statutory Tax Deduction Scheme, corresponds with clause 31 of the Standard Form.

11. Temporary Protection:

If temporary protective measures including fencing are required, these must be clearly stated and quantified at tender stage. It is not sufficient to state the 'the Contractor is to allow for the erection of any temporary fencing which may be necessary to protect grass or shrub areas.' Ownership of temporary protection may often with advantage be transferred to the Employer if so stated in the tender documents otherwise it remains the property of the Contractor.

12. Watering

The tender and contract documents should state the frequency and quantity of water required to be provided by the Contractor. In drought conditions when the provision of water is restricted by legislation contractors and sub-contractors should be required to inform the Landscape Architect of the cost of second class water from a sewage works or other approved source and await instructions.

13. Maintenance

When Maintenance is the responsibility of the Contractor in accordance with Clause 2·7A the value of this work is excluded from that included in the penultimate certificate issued in accordance with clause 4·3.

This Practice Note is issued by the
Joint Council for Landscape Industries
comprising:-

Landscape Institute
Horticultural Trades Association
British Association Landscape Industries
National Farmers' Union
Institute of Leisure and Amenity Management

Published for the Joint Council for Landscape Industries
by the Landscape Institute
12 Carlton House Terrace London SW1Y 5AH and
available from RIBA Publications Limited
66 Portland Place London W1N 4AD
© JCLI April 1985

Printed by Duolith Ltd.
Welwyn Garden City, Hertfordshire

Issued October 1985

Practice Note No. 4 (APRIL 1985) JCLI Supplement to the JCT Intermediate Form IFC 84

The JCLI Agreement for Landscape Works was first issued in April 1978 at which time the 1968 JCT Minor Works Form on which it was based had no provision for 2·7 Plant Failures nor 6·5 Malicious Damage, neither did it cover:-

- 2·6 Partial possession
- 3·6 The valuation of variations using tender rates
- 3·8 P.C. Sums and objections to nominations
- 3·9 Direct loss and expense if progress is disturbed
- 4·6 Fluctuations

detailed provisions were therefore incorporated to cover these aspects.

While suitable for the majority of landscape contracts over the six years since it was first published, instances have occurred of Local Authorities expressing reluctance to use the Form on landscape contracts in excess of £75,000.

The JCT has now published an "Intermediate" Form (IFC 84) for use on all contracts both private and public sector local authority, with or without quantities prepared in accordance with the Standard Method of Measurement (SMM6). While it still does not cover Plant Failures and Malicious Damage, the remaining aspects previously omitted are now provided for.

For those larger landscape contracts the detailed provision of the JCT Intermediate Form may be appropriate and the attached landscape supplementary clauses should be incorporated.

This introductory page may be torn off

JCLI Supplement to be read in conjunction with the JCT Intermediate Form (IFC84)

Clause 2·0 Possession and Completion

Add new clause 2·11

Partial Possession by the Employer

2·11 If any at any time before Practical Completion of the Works the Employer with the consent of the Contractor shall take possession of any part or parts of the same (any such part being referred to in this clause 2·11 as 'the relevant part') then notwithstanding anything expressed or implied elsewhere in this Contract:

- for the purpose of clause 2·10 *(Defects liability)* and 4·3 *(Interim payment)* Practical Completion of the relevant part shall be deemed to have occurred and the defects liability period in respect of the relevant part shall be deemed to have commenced on the date on which the Employer shall have taken possession thereof;

- as from the date which the Employer shall have taken possession of the relevant part, the obligation of the Contractor to insure under clause 6·3A, if applicable, shall terminate in respect of the relevant part but not further or otherwise;

- in lieu of any sum to be paid or allowed by the Contractor under clause 2·7 *(Liquidated damages)* in respect of any period during which the Employer shall have taken possession of the relevant part there shall be paid or allowed such sum as bears the same ratio to the sum which would be paid or allowed apart from the provisions of this clause 2·11 as the Contract Sum, less the amount contained therein in respect of the said relevant part, bears to the Contract Sum.

Add new clause 2·12

Failures of Plants (Pre-Practical Completion)

2·2 Any trees, shrubs, grass or other plants, other than those found to be missing or defective as a result of theft or malicious damage and which shall be replaced as set out in clause 6·5 of these conditions, which are found to be defective at practical completion of the works shall be replaced by the Contractor entirely at his own cost unless the Landscape Architect shall otherwise instruct. The Landscape Architect shall certify the dates when in his opinion the Contractor's obligations under this clause have been discharged.

(Post-Practical Completion)

A The maintenance of trees, shrubs, grass and other plants after the date of the said certificate will be carried out by the Contractor for the duration of the periods stated in accordance with the programme and in the manner specified in the Contract Documents. Any grass which is found to be defective within.......... months, any shrubs, ordinary nursery stock trees or other plants found to be defective within .... months and any trees, semi-mature advanced or extra large nursery stock found to be defective within .... months of the date of Practical Completion and are due to materials or workmanship not in accordance with the contract shall be replaced by the Contractor entirely at his own cost unless the Landscape Architect shall otherwise instruct. The Landscape Architect shall certify the dates when in his opinion the Contractor's obligations under this clause have been discharged.

Note:
*Clauses marked * should be completed/deleted as appropriate*

*B The maintenance of the trees, shrubs, grass and other plants after the date of the said certificate will be undertaken by the Employer who will be responsible for the replacement of any trees, shrubs, grass or other plants which are subsequently defective.

Clause 4·0 Payment

Add to clause 4·3

and unless the failures of plants as set out in clause 2·7 are in excess of 10% in which case the amount retained shall be adjusted accordingly.

Clause 6·0 Injury, damage and insurance

Add new clause 6·4

Malicious Damage or Theft (before Practical Completion)

†6·4A All loss or damage arising from any theft or malicious damage prior to practical completion shall be made good by the Contractor at his own expense.

B The Contract sum shall include the provisional sum of £.............. * to be expended as instructed by the Landscape Architect in respect of the cost of all work arising from any theft or malicious damage to the works beyond the control of the Contractor prior to practical completion of the works.

Signed.................... date............
for and on behalf of the Employer

Signed.................... date............
for and on behalf of the Contractor

These Supplementary Clauses are issued by the Joint Council for Landscape Industries comprising:-

Landscape Institute
Horticultural Trades Association
British Association Landscape Industries
National Farmers' Union
Institute of Leisure and Amenity Management

Published for the Joint Council for Landscape Industries by the Landscape Institute
12 Carlton House Terrace, London SW1Y 5AH and available from RIBA Publications Limited
66 Portland Place, London W1N 4AD
© JCLI June 1985

Printed by Duolith Ltd.
Welwyn Garden City, Hertfordshire

Issued October 1985

General conditions, Specification and Schedules of Quantity for the Supply and Delivery of Plants

Fourth Edition — published 1982

Name of Purchaser ....

Tender to be received by .... (date)

ILAM

**HELPS
YOU GROW**

Published by:
The Joint Liaison Committee for Plant Supplies for:
    The Arboricultural Association
    British Association of Landscape Industries
    Horticultural Trades Association
    The Institute of Park & Recreation Administration
    The Landscape Institute
    National Farmers' Union

Forms obtainable from: The Horticultural Trades Association,   19 High Street, Theale, Reading, Berkshire, RG7 5AH.

THIS DOCUMENT MAY BE FREELY REPRODUCED WITHOUT PERMISSION

172

HOW TO PREPARE AND USE THIS FORM

1. SPECIFICATION

When defining the type and size of plant required, ensure that:
(a) The natural habit of the plant is borne in mind e.g.
  i. Some ultimately bushy trees, such as Quercus ilex, are usually only available as small plants.
  ii. In general, conifers are not available as standard trees, with only a few specific exceptions such as Ginkgo biloba.
(b) Terms used are as defined under Specification in the General Conditions of this form.
(c) Overall heights are stated for all upright-growing shrubs, conifers, climbers. Diameters are stated for all spreading shrubs and ground cover plants.
(d) Sizes of trees are stated as set out in the table below. Clear stem heights are stated if required in excess of 1.8m.
(e) Container-grown plants are marked by the abbreviations 'CG' (unless so marked it will be assumed that plants are either bare-root or balled). The required volume of the container is stated. Plants specified as having been container grown shall have root systems sufficiently established in the container to be conducive to successful transplanting.
(f) It is stressed that all root systems must be adequate in relation to the size of the plant and conducive to successful transplantation. Worked trees are to be bottom worked unless declared otherwise.

2. QUANTITIES

Quantities of each variety should be totalled so the variety is entered once only in the Schedules of Quantity. It is recommended that shrubs and transplants are rounded up to units of 10 instead of odd figures, e.g. 187 up to 190. Preferably this should apply also to trees.

3. PACKAGING

Any additional requirements to the specification in the plant handling code below should be clearly stated. It must be recognised that these will be charged for as extras at cost.

4. TYPING OF SCHEDULES OF QUANTITIES

Type the plant name and form or size high up in the appropriate boxes so as to allow any substitutes to be named clearly, should they be permitted.

5. NUMBER OF COPIES

It is essential that two copies be sent to each Supplier requested to quote so one copy may be retained on their file. The reply envelope should show the closing date clearly.

6. TIME ALLOWED FOR TENDERING

It is essential to allow Suppliers a minimum of two clear working weeks in which to tender, and a period of three weeks is recommended.

7. ORDERING

It is strongly recommended that orders are placed as soon as possible after the closing date so as to ensure supply, as all offers are made subject to stock remaining unsold on receipt of order.

8. INSPECTION

Experience has shown that the best way of relating prices tendered by several Suppliers to the quality of the stock offered is by inspection — this is strongly recommended, and should be strictly by appointment.

DIMENSIONS OF TREES

Relevant British Standard	Designation	Circumference of stem measured 1.0m from ground level	Height from ground level	Clear stem height from ground level to lowest branch
BS 3936 Part 1	Younger Nursery Stock Seedlings (1+0)) (2+0)) Undercut (1u1)) Seedling (1u2))	not specified	max 0.90m	not specified
	Transplant (1+1) (1+2)	not specified	max 1.20m	not specified
	Whip	not specified	1.20–1.50m 1.50–1.80m 1.80–2.10m 2.10–2.50m	not specified
BS 3936 Part 1	Standard Nursery Stock Standard/feathered/ weeping			
	short	not specified	not specified	1.00–1.20m
	half	not specified	1.80–2.10m	1.20–1.50m
	....	4 – 6cm	2.10–2.50m	1.50–1.80m
	Light	6 – 8 cm	2.50–2.75m	1.50–1.80m
	Standard	8 – 10cm	2.75–3.00m	1.80m min.
	Tall	8 – 10cm	3.00–3.60m	1.80m min.
	Selected	10 – 12cm	3.00–3.60m	1.80m min.
	Note: Feathered trees — circumference and clear stem heights do not apply. Weeping trees — minimum heights do not apply.			
BS 5236	Advanced Nursery Stock Heavy	12 – 14cm	3.60–4.25m	1.80m min.
	Extra Heavy	14 – 16cm	4.25–6.00m	1.80m min.
	....	16 – 18cm	....	1.80m min.
	....	18 – 20cm	....	1.80m min.
BS4043	Semi Mature	20 – 75cm	6.00–15.00m	not specified

STANDARD FORM OF TENDER FOR THE SUPPLY AND DELIVERY OF PLANTS

From (Name of Supplier) _____

To (Name of Purchaser) _____ Telephone: _____

_____ Date: _____

Address _____ Ref. No. _____

_____

Project _____

Delivery to the site of _____ which will/willnot be continuously manned.*

Delivery date: Autumn 198...../Spring 198....... _____ (date and time or as specified)*

THIS TENDER IS TO BE RETURNED BY NOT LATER THAN _____ (date and time)

Subject to the Plants being unsold on receipt of order, we undertake to supply the plants shown on the attached Schedules numbered 1 to .... in accordance with the General Conditions for the sum of £ _____

_____ pounds _____ pence (amount in words)

exclusive of any Value Added Tax due in accordance with the Finance Act 1972.

This Tender is open for acceptance within 8 weeks from the date shown below, or (in the case of bare root plants) until 31st January, whichever is the sooner.

These prices are fixed for delivery during the current bare root planting season or on such other dates as are specified.

The purchaser does not bind himself to accept the lowest or any offer. If the plants are to be supplied through a Contractor whose identity is not known to us at the time of tender we reserve the right to withdraw this tender within 14 days of the name of the Contractor being made known to us.

Date _____ Signed ....

For and on behalf of the Supplier

Tel: _____

Ref. No.: _____

SUMMARY OF TENDER

Schedule No.	£	p	Schedule No.	£	p	Schedule No.	£	p
			B/f:			B/f:		
						Delivery Charge		
C/f:			C/f:			Total		

* complete or delete as appropriate

174

GENERAL CONDITIONS

1. GENERAL SPECIFICATION: All stock must comply in all respects with the current relevant editions of British Standards, except as trees in BS 3936 Part 1 are amended and developed by the definitions above agreed between the subscribing organisations to this form.

2. COUNTRY WHERE GROWN: The country where grown is to be stated in the Schedules. Plants grown in Britain for one growing season or longer shall be considered British grown.

3. INSPECTION: The purchaser reservces the right to inspect the stock by appointment.

4. FAIR WAGES: Suppliers are to observe Fair Wages Clauses as applicable to the Nursery Trade for at least three months preceding their offer, in accordance with The Fair Wages resolution passed by the House of Commons in October, 1946.

5. PARTIAL ORDERS: The purchaser reserves the right to accept offers in whole or in part. It is accepted that the Supplier will re-negotiate rates where (a) the quantity of a variety ordered differs significantly from the quantity quoted. (b) the value of the order placed differs significantly from the value of the original offer.

6. ORDER: No plants are to be supplied except on receipt of a duly signed official order.

7. SUBSTITUTES: Where stocks have been sold on receipt of order substitutes may only be made by mutual agreement.

8. DELIVERY:
   (a) Delivery is to be by the date specified, subject to adverse weather or other factors beyond the Supplier's control. The Supplier is to advise in advance of the week of delivery and for sites not continuously manned to give 48 hours notice of the date and time of delivery.
   (b) Delivery is to be during normal working hours and to the one location specified except where otherwise stated.
   (c) Plants must be labelled and protected in accordance with the JLCPS Code of Practice for Plant Handling, throughout which the word 'should' is to be read as 'shall'.

9. COMPLAINTS: Complaints regarding quantity must be made in writing within 7 days of receipt of goods, and complaints regarding quality within 14 days of receipt of goods. The purchaser has the right to return (at the Suppliers expense) any plants supplied below specification.

10. PAYMENT: Invoices are due for monthly settlement. Invoices may be rendered for each consignment. Prices quoted are strictly nett and are inclusive of delivery. Value added tax will be charged at the rates ruling at the time of delivery.

11. ARBITRATION: In the event of a dispute on an order based on these General Conditions, either party may contact one of the subscribing bodies, named on the front cover of this form, who will ask the President of the Institute of Arbitrators to appoint an Arbitrator.

12. CANCELLATION: On orders received before 1st January, cancellation or postponement of delivery of plants after 31st March until the following planting season, either by the purchaser or by the Supplier, shall be subject to a charge of 50% of the value of each such cancelled or postponed item.

13. SPECIAL CONDITIONS: Any special conditions or requirements should be clearly stated. It must be recognised that these may incur an additional cost.

CODE OF PRACTICE FOR PLANT HANDLING

PREPARED AND PUBLISHED BY THE JOINT LIAISON COMMITTEE ON PLANT SUPPLIES

1.0 GENERAL NOTE: During the period from lifting until receipt by the Purchaser, the Supplier is responsible and from receipt until planting the Purchaser is responsible for ensuring that plants retain moist fibrous root (according to species), and that by careful treatment the plants are protected from the effects of drying-out, heating up, freezing, waterlogging or physical damage.

2.0 LIFTING SEASON

2.1 Bare-rooted or Ball-rooted

2.1.1 DECIDUOUS – lift only when the plants exhibit dormant characteristics, generally from October to March – later where local conditions or season permit. Avoid lifting during severe ground frost.

2.1.2 EVERGREEN – lift from October to May, except during severe ground frost or drought. Bare-rooted plants should be not more than three years from propagation.

2.2 Container-grown plants

2.2.1 DECIDUOUS OR EVERGREEN – move at any season, provided the root system is well-established in the container and the plants are fully hardened-off.

3.0 BUNDLING

3.1 General
Bundles should consist of graded plants with all shoots facing in the same direction. Foliage should be as surface-dry as possible at the time of bundling to reduce the incidence of heating-up. Bundles should be tied securely with string, twine, plastic strip or other supple material which will not by its nature or tension cause damage to the plants.

3.2 Container-grown or ball-rooted plants should not be bundled.

3.3 Plants up to approximately 2.5m tall
Each consignment should be tied in bundles of equal numbers. The maximum number of plants in each bundle will depend on the size of the plant, the most important factor being that bundles should be of a mangeable size.

3.4 **Trees in excess of 2.5m tall**
The recommended maximum quantity in each bundle related to the girth is as below, but this should be reduced where larger heads would be subject to damage. Laterals should be securely tied in if it appears that they would otherwise be damaged during transit.

Up to 4 — 6cm. girth, 15 per bundle   6 — 8cm. girth, 10 per bundle
8 — 10 cm. girth, 5 per bundle   10 — 12 cm. girth, 3 per bundle

3.5 Trees in excess of 10 — 12 cm. girth should not normally be bundled.

4.0 PACKAGING

4.1 **Trees up to 45cm. tall (excluding coniferous foresty trees)** — should be entirely enclosed in plastic film bags (250 gauge minimum), securely tied at the top. Plants should not be packed too tightly and should be loosely bundled within the bag. Foliage should be as surface-dry as possible, with all shoots facing in the same direction, so that roots and shoots are not in contact. Thorny or very bushy plants need only have their roots enclosed in the bag, which should be securely tied around the stems.

4.2 **Bare-rooted trees up to 14cm. girth and Shrubs** — will not normally receive individual packaging.

4.3 **Container-grown plants** — will not normally receive additional packaging.

4.4 **Ball-rooted plants**
Root-balls should be supported to prevent collapse, and protected against drying-out by wrapping firmly with hessian, plastic film, or other recommended materials. Packaging should be firmly tied over the top of the root-ball.

4.5 **Trees in excess of 14cm. girth**
These will be supplied without soil adhering to the roots unless otherwise specified, but with roots packed with moist straw, or other suitable material, and enclosed in hessian or plastic film (500 gauge minimum), securely tied to the stem.

5.0 LABELLING

Plants must be adequately and accurately labelled by the Supplier. Each individual specimen tree, bundle, bag, or lot of one species of plants, shall bear a securely attached durable primary label. the PLANT NAME, GRADE and QUANTITY in the bundle or bag, and the TOTAL QUANTITY in the consignment should be clearly displayed on the label, together with the SUPPLIER'S NAME. A reasonable proportion of a large consignment of distinct plants shall bear a secondary label easily related to the primary labels.

6.0 TEMPORARY STORAGE

6.1 **General**
The supplier should limit the period between lifting and despatch, and the Purchaser should limit the period between receipt and planting.

6.2 **Bare-rooted plants**
Plants may be stored briefly with a covering of damp sacking, straw or other suitable material, to keep the roots moist. Where delays of more than a few days occur, plants should be heeled-in moist friable soil, placed in an indirect or humidified cold store, or supported upright on a well-drained site and the roots immersed in a deep layer of moist straw, hay, sand, peat, pulverised bark, wood shavings, or other suitable material. The material should be firmed to exclude air (particularly on the inside of bundles) and watered periodically as the condition of the material requires. Protection should be given against damage by small mammals.

6.3 **Container-grown plants** —
Containers should be maintained upright and watered as required.

6.4 **Ball-rooted plants**
Permeable wrappings should be kept moist by watering and polythene wrappings protected from direct sunlight. For longer period of storage, root-balls with permeable wrappings should be placed on a well-drained surface and covered with one of the materials listed in 6.2 above.

6.5 **Plants in polythene bags**
The bags should be protected from direct sunlight at all times. Where delays of more than a few days occur, the bags should be stored upright, **NOT STACKED**, in a cool shady position, or shed, or placed in a cold store.

7.0 TRANSPORT

7.1 **Open Lorries**
Bare-roots should be lightly dampened with water if they become dry during the loading operation. All materials should be stacked in such a way that breakage or crushing by the weight of plants above, or the securing ropes, will not occur. The consignment should be completely sheeted. Where more than one delivery destination is involved, additional sheeting should be used to limit the period of exposure of the plants. Plants in polythene bags should be sheeted so that they are shaded from direct sunlight.

7.2 **Closed Lorries or Containers**
Foliage should be as surface-dry as possible and contact between root and foliage minimised. All materials should be loaded in such a way that breakage or crushing by the weight of plants above is avoided during loading, transit and unloading.

7.3 **Post or Rail**
Consignments should be in manageable units, securely crated or packaged to withstand damage during a possibly prolonged journey.

8.0 RECEIPT BY THE PURCHASER
The Purchaser is responsible for providing sufficient staff and facilities for unloding the consignment without delay and for all further steps to minimise damage, as specified.

9.0 ADDITIONAL PACKAGING
In addition to the above basic specification, the **Purchaser may specify packaging variations or other special treatment at the time of quoting** which will be SUBJECT TO ADDITIONAL COST.

176

SCHEDULES OF QUANTITY

To (Name of Purchaser) ....

Ref No. ....   Schedule No. ....

Item No	Plant Name	Country where grown	Form and/or size and/or volume	Quantity	Rate £	Total £
1						
2						
3						
4						
5						
6						
7						
8						
9						
10						
11						
12						
13						
14						
15						

Name of Supplier:

Page total carried forward
to summary sheet ....

....

£...................

Should substitutions be permitted Schedules should be typed in the upper space to allow any alternative to be inserted by the supplier.

JCT

JCT Standard Form of Tender by Nominated Supplier

Tender TNS/1

For use in connection with the Standard Form of Building Contract (SFBC) issued by the Joint Contracts Tribunal, 1980 edition, current revision

Job Title:
(name and brief location of Works)

[a] To be completed by or on behalf of the Architect/Supervising Officer.

Employer: [a]

Main Contractor: [a]
(if known)

Tender for: [a]
(abbreviated description)

Name of Tenderer:

To be returned to: [a]

[b] To be completed by the supplier; see also Schedule 1, item 7.

Lump sum price: [b] £ _____

_____ *(words)*

and/or Schedule of rates (attached)

1   We confirm that we will be under a contract with the Main Contractor:

·1   to supply the materials or goods described or referred to in **Schedule 1** for the price and/or at the rate set out above; and

·2   in accordance with the other terms set out in that Schedule, as a Nominated Supplier in accordance with the terms of SFBC clause 36·3 to ·5 (as set out in **Schedule 2**) and our conditions of sale in so far as they do not conflict with the terms of SFBC clause 36·3 to ·5 [c]

[c] By SFBC clause 36·4·9 none of the provisions in the contract of sale can override, modify or affect in any way the provisions incorporated from SFBC clause 36·4 in that contract of sale. Nominated Suppliers should therefore take steps to ensure that their sale conditions do not incorporate any provisions which purport to override, modify or affect in any way the provisions incorporated from SFBC clause 36·4.

provided:

·3   the Architect/Supervising Officer has issued the relevant nomination instruction (a copy of which has been sent to us by the Architect/Supervising Officer); and

·4   agreement on delivery between us and the Main Contractor has been reached as recorded in **Schedule 1** Part 6 (see SFBC clause 36·4·3); and

·5   we have thereafter received an order from the Main Contractor accepting this tender.

2   We agree that this Tender shall be open for acceptance by an order from the Main Contractor within _____ [d] of the date of this Tender. Provided that where the Main Contractor has not been named above we reserve the right to withdraw this Tender within 14 days of having been notified, by or on behalf of the Employer named above, of the name of the Main Contractor.

[d] May be completed by or on behalf of the Architect/Supervising Officer; if not so completed, to be completed by the supplier.

[e] To be struck out by or on behalf of the Architect/Supervising Officer if no Warranty Agreement is required.

3 [e]   Subject to our right to withdraw this Tender as set out in paragraph 2 we hereby declare that we accept the Warranty Agreement in the terms set out in **Schedule 3** hereto on condition that no provision in that Warranty Agreement shall take effect unless and until

a copy to us of the instruction nominating us,
the order of the Main Contractor accepting this Tender, and
a copy of the Warranty Agreement signed by the Employer

have been received by us.

For and on behalf of

Address

Signature   Date

© 1980 RIBA Publications Ltd

Schedule 1

1. Description, quantity and quality of materials or goods:

1A

1B

1C

SPECIMEN

Note: 1A to be completed by or on behalf of the Architect/Supervising Officer setting out his requirements. If the supplier is unable to comply with 1A he is to state in 1B what modifications he proposes, and the Architect/Supervising Officer is to state in 1C if such modifications are acceptable.

2. Access to Works:

2A

2B

*Note: 2A to be completed by or on behalf of the Architect/Supervising Officer. The supplier in 2B **either** confirms that the access in 2A is acceptable **or** states what modifications etc. to the access he requires **or** if 2A has not been completed, completes 2B.*

3. Provisions, if any, for returnable packings:

4. Completion Date of Main Contract (or anticipated Completion Date if Main Contract not let):

Note: To be completed by or on behalf of the Architect/Supervising Officer.

5. Defects Liability Period of the Main Contract   months.

Note: To be completed by or on behalf of the Architect/Supervising Officer.

179

6A Anticipated commencement and completion dates for the nominated supply after any necessary approval of drawings (subject to SFBC clause 36·4·3, which provides that delivery shall be commenced, carried out and completed in accordance with any delivery programme agreed between the Contractor and supplier or in the absence of such programme in accordance with the reasonable directions of the Contractor):

6B ·1   Supplier's proposed delivery programme to comply with 6A:

SPECIMEN

·2   If 6B·1 not completed, delivery programme shall be to the reasonable directions of the Contractor.

6C Delivery programme as agreed between the supplier and the Contractor, if different from 6B:

Note: 6A to be completed by or on behalf of the Architect/Supervising Officer. The supplier to complete 6B·1 to take account of 6A; but the completion of 6B·1 is subject to the terms of 6C which may need to be used when the Contractor and supplier are settling item 6.

7.   Provisions, if any, for fluctuations in price or rates:

7A

7B

7C

Note: 7A to be completed by or on behalf of the Architect/Supervising Officer. If the supplier is unable to comply with 7A he is to state in 7B what modifications to the provisions in 7A he requires, and the Architect/Supervising Officer is to state in 7C if such modifications are acceptable.

8.   SFBC clause 25 (extensions of time) applies to the Main Contract without modification except as stated below:

The liquidated and ascertained damages (SFBC clause 2·4·2 and Appendix entry) under the Main Contract are at the rate of £_____ per _____ .

Note: To be completed by or on behalf of the Architect/Supervising Officer.

9.   Contract of sale with Contractor to be under hand/under seal.

Note: Alternative not to be used to be deleted by the supplier subject to agreement on the method of execution of the sale contract with the Main Contractor.

180

Schedule 2

JCT Standard Form of Building Contract

Clause 36·3 to ·8 provides as follows:

Ascertainment of costs to be set against prime cost sum

36·3 ·1 For the purposes of clause 30·6·2·8 the amounts "properly chargeable to the Employer in accordance with the nomination instruction of the Architect/Supervising Officer" shall include the total amount paid or payable in respect of the materials or goods less any discount other than the discount referred to in clause 36·4·4·, properly so chargeable to the Employer and shall include where applicable:

·1·1 any tax (other than any value added tax which is treated, or is capable of being treated, as input tax (as referred to in the Finance Act 1972) by the Contractor) or duty not otherwise recoverable under this Contract by whomsoever payable which is payable under or by virtue of any Act of Parliament on the import, purchase, sale, appropriation, processing, alteration, adapting for sale or use of the materials or goods to be supplied; and

·1·2 the net cost of appropriate packing carriage and delivery after allowing for any credit for return of any packing to the supplier; and

·1·3 the amount of any price adjustment properly paid or payable to, or allowed or allowable by the supplier less any discount other than a cash discount for payment in full within 30 days of the end of the month during which delivery is made.

·2 Where in the opinion of the Architect/Supervising Officer the Contractor properly incurs expense, which would not be reimbursed under clause 36·3·1 or otherwise under this Contract, in obtaining the materials or goods from the Nominated Supplier such expense shall be added to the Contract Sum.

Sale contract provisions – Architect's/Supervising Officer's right to nominate supplier

36·4 Save where the Architect/Supervising Officer and the Contractor shall otherwise agree, the Architect/Supervising Officer shall only nominate as a supplier a person who will enter into a contract of sale with the Contractor which provides, inter alia:

·1 that the materials or goods to be supplied shall be of the quality and standard specified provided that where and to the extent that approval of the quality of materials or of the standards of workmanship is a matter for the opinion of the Architect/Supervising Officer, such quality and standards shall be to the reasonable satisfaction of the Architect/Supervising Officer;

·2 that the Nominated Supplier shall make good by replacement or otherwise any defects in the materials or goods supplied which appear up to and including the last day of the Defects Liability Period under this Contract and shall bear any expenses reasonably incurred by the Contractor as a direct consequence of such defects provided that:

·2·1 where the materials or goods have been used or fixed such defects are not such that reasonable examination by the Contractor ought to have revealed them before using or fixing;

·2·2 such defects are due solely to defective workmanship or material in the materials or goods supplied and shall not have been caused by improper storage by the Contractor or by misuse or by any act or neglect of either the Contractor, the Architect/Supervising Officer or the Employer or by any person or persons for whom they may be responsible or by any other person for whom the Nominated Supplier is not responsible;

·3 that delivery of the materials or goods supplied shall be commenced, carried out and completed in accordance with any delivery programme agreed between the Contractor and the Nominated Supplier or in the absence of such programme in accordance with the reasonable directions of the Contractor;

·4 that the Nominated Supplier shall allow the Contractor a discount for cash of 5 per cent on all payments if the Contractor makes payment in full within 30 days of the end of the month during which delivery is made;

·5 that the Nominated Supplier shall not be obliged to make any delivery of materials or goods (except any which may have been paid for in full less only any discount for cash) after the determination (for any reason) of the Contractor's employment under this Contract;

·6 that full discharge by the Contractor in respect of payments for materials or goods supplied by the Nominated Supplier shall be effected within 30 days of the end of the month during which delivery is made less only a discount for cash of 5 per cent if so paid;

·7 that the ownership of materials or goods shall pass to the Contractor upon delivery by the Nominated Supplier to or to the order of the Contractor, whether or not payment has been made in full;

·8 that if any dispute or difference between the Contractor and Nominated Supplier raises issues which are substantially the same as or connected with issues raised in a related dispute between the Employer and the Contractor under this Contract then, where *articles 5·1·4 and 5·1·5 apply, such dispute or difference shall be referred to the Arbitrator appointed or to be appointed pursuant to article 5 who shall have power to make such directions and all necessary awards in the same way as if the procedure of the High Court as to joining one or more defendants or joining co-defendants or third parties was available to the parties and to him and in any case the award of such Arbitrator shall be final and binding on the parties:

·9 that no provision in the contract of sale shall override modify or affect in any way whatsoever the provisions in the contract of sale which are included therein to give effect to clauses 36·4·1 to 36·4·9 inclusive.

36·5 ·1 Subject to clauses 36·5·2 and 36·5·3, where the said contract of sale between the Contractor and the Nominated Supplier in any way restricts, limits or excludes the liability of the Nominated Supplier to the Contractor in respect of materials or goods supplied or to be supplied, and the Architect/Supervising Officer has specifically approved in writing the said restrictions, limitations or exclusions, the liability of the Contractor to the Employer in respect of the said materials or goods shall be restricted, limited or excluded to the same extent.

·2 The Contractor shall not be obliged to enter into a contract with the Nominated Supplier until the Architect/Supervising Officer has specifically approved in writing the said restrictions, limitations or exclusions.

·3 Nothing in clause 36·5 shall be construed as enabling the Architect/Supervising Officer to nominate a supplier otherwise than in accordance with the provisions stated in clause 36·4.

*The Architect/Supervising Officer should state whether in the Appendix to the SFBC the words "Articles 5·1·4 and 5·1·5" have been struck out; if so then clause 36·4·8 will not apply to the Nominated Supplier.

Appendix G   NJCC Code of Procedure for Single-stage Selective Tendering

Note: The Code applies in the whole of the United Kingdom, but where Scottish practice differs, suitable recommendations are printed in *italics*.

---

1 Foreword

1.1 This Code has been prepared for all who commission building work, whether they be private clients or public authorities, and envisages the use of traditional single stage tendering by a selected list of tenderers. It is the prerogative of the employer to decide the method of tendering to be adopted, but the National Joint Consultative Committee for Building and the Department of the Environment believe that single stage selective tendering will be found the most appropriate method of obtaining tenders for the majority of building contracts. On contracts where it is desired to secure the early involvement of the contractor before the development of the design is completed two stage tendering procedures may be adopted. These procedures will be detailed in a companion NJCC Code of Procedure for Two Stage Tendering. Nothing in this Code should be taken to suggest that the employer is obliged to accept the lowest or any tender, although if the procedure advocated in the Code is followed, the successful tenderer will normally be the one offering the lowest price.

1.2 Consequent upon entry into the European Economic Community tenders for public sector construction contracts above a specified value must be invited and contracts awarded in accordance with the EEC Directive 71/305. In these instances the provisions of this Code will be qualified by the supplementary tendering procedures specified in the Directive.

1.3 Guidance on the operation of the procedures laid down in the Directive is given in DoE Circular 59/73, obtainable from Her Majesty's Stationery Office.

* 1.3 *In Scotland guidance on the operation of the procedures laid down in the EEC Directive is given in SDD Circular 45/73 dated 11th May, 1973, obtainable from the Scottish Development Department.*

1.4 This Code is complementary to the other NJCC publications, The Client's Guide, Tendering Procedure for Industrialized Building Projects and Management of Building Contracts. Throughout the Code the word 'architect' is used to mean architect or supervising officer and the word 'employer' to mean building owner or employing body in the sense that the terms are used in the standard forms of building contract.

2 Introduction

2.1 The general principles of the Code are fully supported by the Department of the Environment and take into account the relevant recommendations of the National Economic Development Office (NEDO) report 'The Public Client and the Construction Industries (1975)', the report 'The Placing and Management of Contracts for Building and Civil Engineering Work' (The Banwell Report), and of the 'Action on the Banwell Report'.

* Applicable in Scotland only.

2.2 In order that its detailed recommendations may be most widely applicable, this Code assumes, in the contract which will follow tendering, the use of standard forms of building contract. This assumption in no way precludes the use of the Code where other forms of contract are employed, though certain details may require some modification.

2.3 The contractor's tender is the price for which he offers to carry out and complete, in accordance with the conditions of the contract, the work shown on the drawings and described in the bill(s) of quantities and/or specifications.

2.4 Good tendering procedure demands that the contractor's tendered price should not be altered without justification. Difficulties have arisen when an examination of the priced bill(s) revealed errors or a discrepancy between these prices and the tender figure. The Code lays down, in Section 6, alternative methods of dealing with this situation before the contractor's offer is accepted. The first alternative does not permit the correction of errors in priced bill(s) of quantities, the second does.

The choice must be made before contractors are invited to tender.

2.5 It should be a condition of tender that obvious errors in pricing or significant errors in arithmetic discovered before the acceptance of the contractor's tender should be dealt with in accordance with one of the alternatives in Section 6 of this Code.

3 The List of Tenderers

3.1 Once it has been decided that a contractor is to be selected by competitive tender a short list of suitable tenderers should be drawn up either from the employer's approved list of contractors or from an *ad hoc* list of contractor's of established skill, integrity, responsibility and proven competence for work of the character and size contemplated. The following scale should be taken as a guide in determining the number of tenders to be invited:

Size of contract	Maximum number of tenderers
Up to £50,000	5
£50,000 to £250,000	6
£250,000 to £1 million	8
£1 million +	6

It should be appreciated that because of the cost of preparing tenders the larger the tender lists become the greater will be the cost of abortive tendering, and this must be reflected in building prices. Regard should also be paid to contracts such as specialist engineering contracts involving relatively high tendering costs and it is recommended that for such contracts the maximum number of tenderers for contract values above £250,000 should be reduced to six and four respectively. When the list has been settled, one or two further names should be appended in order that they may replace any firms on the list that do not accept the preliminary invitation.

3.2 When selecting the short list the following are among the points which should be considered:

3.2.1 the firm's financial standing and record;

3.2.2 whether the firm has had recent experience of building at the required rate of completion over a comparable contract period;

3.2.3 the firm's general experience and reputation in the area in question;

3.2.4 whether the management structure of the firm is adequate for the type of contract envisaged; and

3.2.5 whether the firm will have adequate capacity at the relevant time.

3.3 Approved lists should be reviewed periodically to exclude firms whose performance has been unsatisfactory, and to allow the introduction of suitable additional firms.

3.4 The object of selection is to make a list of firms, any on of which could be entrusted with the job. If this is achieved, then the final choice of contractor will be simple—the firm offering the lowest tender. Only the most exceptional cases justify departure from this general recommendation.

4 Tendering procedure

4.1 Preliminary Enquiry
4.1.1 In order that contractors may be able to decide whether they will tender, and to anticipate demands on their tendering staff, each firm should be sent, and should reply promptly to, a preliminary invitation to tender as illustrated in Appendix A – 'Preliminary Enquiry for Invitation to Tender'.

It is essential that all the details listed in sub-paragraphs (a) to (u) Appendix A are stated in the preliminary enquiry. The omission of relevant information may seriously impede contractors in deciding whether or not to tender.

4.1.2 It is suggested that an appropriate period of time between the preliminary enquiry and the despatch of tender documents is 4 to 6 weeks, although in some instances a period of 3 months would not be unreasonable. In cases beyond 3 months the preliminary invitation should be confirmed a month before tenders are invited.

4.1.3 Once a contractor has signified initial agreement to tender it is in the best interests of all parties that such acceptance should be honoured. If in exceptional circumstances a contractor has to withdraw his acceptance he should give notice of this intention before the issue of tender documents. If for any reason this is not possible, notice should be given not later than two working days after receipt of the tender documents.

4.1.4 After the latest date for the acceptance of the preliminary invitation the final short list of tenders will be selected, and firms which notified their willingness to tender, but are not included in the tender list should be promptly informed.

4.2 The Tender Documents
4.2.1 On the day stated in the preliminary invitation all tender documents should be despatched to the tenderers. See Appendix B for suggested 'Formal Invitation to Tender' and Appendix C for suggested 'Form of Tender'.

4.2.2 The conditions of tendering should be absolutely clear so that all tenders are submitted on the same basis. The contract period should be specified in the tender documents and tenderers should be required to make offers based on the same period of completion in order to limit competition to price only. Tenders for alternative periods of completion should only be admitted by invitation at the time of receipt by tenderer of the tender documents and in the event of alternative tenders being sanctioned they must all be submitted at the same time.

4.2.3 The NJCC strongly recommends the use of the standard forms of building contract in unamended form.

Although it is recognised that the terms of the standard forms are not mandatory and that the employer and his professional advisers may alter them at their discretion, the NJCC believes that alterations to the standard forms impede the efforts being made towards achieving greater standardisation of building procedures. The NJCC is firmly of the opinion that if alterations to the standard forms have to be made it is essential in the interests of good practice and of economic building that they be kept to an absolute minimum. They should not be undertaken without serious prior consideration and should then be drafted by a person competent to ensure that all consequential alterations to other clauses are made.

The tenderer's attention should be specifically drawn in the Preliminary Invitation to Tender (see Appendix A) to any alterations to be made to the standard form of contract and, where appropriate, reasons should be given, so that the implications of such amendments may be considered by the tenderers prior to acceptance of the invitation to tender, and so minimise the risk of subsequent queries at tender stage which may result in an extension of the tender period (see clause 4.4).

4.3 Time for Tendering
4.3.1 The time allowed for the preparation of tenders should be determined in relation to the size and complexity of the job. A minimum of four working weeks should normally be allowed; major projects, smaller works without quantities or other special circumstances may require a longer period. The tender period must be sufficient to enable the tenderer to obtain competitive quotations for the supply of materials and for the execution of works to be sub-let. The latest time for submission should be specified as an hour of a day and should be chosen to allow as short a time as possible to elapse before opening the tenders. Tenders received after time should be promptly returned unopened to the sender and should not be admitted to the competition.

4.3.2 If bills of quantities are issued to tenderers in sections, it is important that the time for tendering should be calculated from the date of issue of the last section.

4.4 Qualified Tenders

4.4.1 For fair competitive tendering it is essential that the tenders submitted by each tenderer be based on identical tender documents and that the tenderers should not attempt to vary that basis by qualifying their tenders (see clause 4.2.2).

4.4.2 If a tenderer considers that any of the tender documents are deficient in any respect and require clarification, or contain unacceptable alterations to the standard form of building contract not previously set out in the Preliminary Invitation to Tender (see Appendix A) he should inform the issuing authority or the architect (with a copy to the quantity surveyor) as soon as possible and preferably not less than seven days before the tenders are due. If it is decided to amend the documents the issuing authority or architect should inform all tenderers and extend the time for tendering if necessary.

4.4.3 A tenderer who otherwise submits a qualified tender should be given the opportunity to withdraw the qualifications without amendment to his tender; if he fails to do so his whole tender should be rejected if it is considered that such qualifications afford the tenderer an unfair advantage over other tenderers.

4.5 Withdrawal of Tender before Acceptance
4.5.1 Under English law a tender may be withdrawn at any time before its acceptance.

* 4.5.1 *Under Scots law, if the provision for the tender to be withdrawn at any time·before its acceptance is to be available, the words 'unless previously withdrawn' should be inserted in the tender after the words 'this tender remains open for consideration . . .' (Note: this clause is not, however, contained in tenders issued in Scotland by the Department of the Environment) (See Appendix C for suggested 'Form of Tender').*

5 Assessing Tenders and Notifying Results

5.1 Tenders should be opened as soon as possible after the time for receipt of tenders.

5.2 The lowest tenderer should be asked to submit his priced bill(s) of quantities as soon as possible and in any case within four working days.

* 5.2 *The priced bill(s) of quantities, contained in a separate envelope, endorsed with the tenderer's name, should be submitted at the same time as the tender.*

5.3 It is important that all but the three lowest tenderers should be informed immediately that their tenders have been unsuccessful, as this information is critical in relation to a contractor's strategic tender planning. In order to serve the employer's interests in the event of the lowest tenderer withdrawing his offer, the second and third lowest tenderers should be informed that their tenders were not the most favourable received but that they will be approached again if it is

decided to give further consideration to their offers. They should subsequently be notified at once when a decision to accept a tender has been taken.

* 5.3 *The envelope containing the bill(s) of the lowest tenderer should be opened and the bill(s) examined. Alternatively the three lowest tenderers should be advised that their offers are under consideration and the envelopes containing the bill(s) of the three lowest tenderers should be opened and the bill(s) examined. Tenderers whose offers are being rejected should be informed immediately or as early as possible.*

5.4 Once the contract has been let every tenderer should be promptly supplied with a list of tender prices.

* 5.4 *Once the contract has been let every tenderer should be supplied with a list of the firms who tendered (in alphabetical order) and list of the tender prices (in ascending order of value).*

6 Examination and Adjustment of the Priced Bill(s)

6.1 The examination of the priced bill(s) of quantities supporting the tender under consideration should be made by the quantity surveyor who should treat the document as confidential; on no account should any details of the tenderer's pricing be disclosed to any person, other than the architect or other appropriate consultant, except with the expressed permission of the tenderer.

6.2 The object of examining priced bills is to detect errors in computation of the tender. If the quantity surveyor finds such errors, he should report them to the architect who, in conjunction with the employer, will determine the action to be taken under whichever is appropriate of the alternatives set out below and referred to in the Formal Invitation to Tender and the Form of Tender. (See Appendices B & C.)

6.3 Alternative 1
6.3.1 The tenderer should be given details of such errors and afforded an opportunity of confirming or withdrawing his offer. If the tenderer withdraws, the priced bill(s) of the second lowest should be examined, and if necessary this tenderer be given a similar opportunity.

6.3.2. An endorsement should be added to the priced bill(s) indicating that all rates or prices (excluding preliminary items, contingencies, prime cost and provisional sums) inserted therein by the tenderer are to be considered as reduced or increased in the same proportion as the corrected total of priced items exceeds or falls short of such items. This endorsement should be signed by both parties to the contract.

6.4 Alternative 2
6.4.1 The tenderer should be given an opportunity of confirming his offer or of amending it to correct genuine errors. Should he elect to amend his offer and the revised tender is no longer the lowest, the offer of the firm now lowest in the competition should be examined.

6.4.2 If the tenderer elects not to amend his offer, an endorsement will be required as in 6.3.2. If the tenderer does

* Applicable in Scotland only.

184

amend his tender figure, and possibly certain of the rates in his
bill(s), he should either be allowed access to his original tender
to insert the correct details and to initial them or be required
to confirm all the alterations in a letter. If in the latter case his
revised tender is eventually accepted, the letter should be
conjoined with the acceptance and the amended tender figure
and the rates in it substituted for those in the original tender.

* 6.4 Alternative 2
   6.4.1 *The lowest tenderer or each of the three lowest tenderers*
   should be given an opportunity of confirming his offer or
   amending it to correct genuine error.

6.5 When a tender is found to be free of error, or the tenderer is
prepared to stand by his tender in spite of an error, or a tender
on amendment is still the lowest, this should be recommended
to the employer for acceptance.

7 Negotiated Reduction of Tender

7.1 Should the tender under consideration exceed the employer's
budget the recommended procedure is for a price to be
negotiated with this tenderer. The basis of negotiations and any
agreements made should be fully documented.

7.2 Only when these negotiations fail should negotiations proceed
with the next lowest tenderer. If these negotiations also fail,
similar action may be taken with the third lowest tenderer.

7.3 If all these negotiations fail, new tenders may be called for.

8 Post Tender Period

Although the period between the appointment of a contractor
and the commencement of work on site does not strictly fall
within the scope of tendering procedure, action taken within
this period is so critical to the successful outcome of any
project as to justify comment in this Code. The NJCC
recommends that a due period be allowed for thorough project
planning and for the contractor to organise his resources.
Undue haste to make a physical start on site may result in
extensive and costly variations which can lead to prolongation
and not reduction of the total construction period. Regard also
should be had, however, to the fact that unnecessary delay in
achieving a start on site may involve the employer in extra costs
whether or not the contract is based on variation of price
conditions. These points should be borne in mind when
determining the anticipated date for possession of the site.
(See Appendix A.)

* Applicable in Scotland only.

Index

Acclimatization, indoor plants, 121
Advanced nursery stock
  graphic symbols for, 6, 10
  protection in transit of, 93, 94
  standard for, 21 85, 145
Aftercare procedures, 97–8
Agricultural Chemical Approval
    Scheme (ACAS), 19, 20, 127
Approvals, 109
Arbitration clauses
  JCLI Standard Form 44, 52, 162
  plant supplies tendering, 86, 180
Arbitration procedures, 44–5
  advantages of, 45
  example letter to start, 45
Arboricultural Association (AA), ix, 78,
    163, 167, 169, 171
Arbrex 805 fungicidal sealant, 127, 130
Architect, use of title, 43, 99
Articles of Agreement, definition, 1
Artists and tradesmen clause, 61–2
Assembly details, 8, 10–11
Assignment, preluded in JCLI Standard
    Form, 48, 159

Ball-rooted plants: see Root-balled
    plants
Banwell Report, 65, 182
Bare-root plants
  handling of, 90, 91, 92–3, 94, 96, 176

protection in transit of, 92–3, 94, 176
temporary storage, precautions, 91,
    96, 176
Bedding plants, British Standard for,
    21, 142
Bibliography, 137
Bills of Quantities, 31
  in SMM6, 35
Brick paving, graphic symbol for, 9
British Association of Landscape
    Industries (BALI)
  indoor plant maintenance contract,
    126, 127
  as member of JCLI, ix, 78, 163, 167,
    169, 171
  Method of Measurement, 31
British Container Growers Group
  members listed, 80
  plant list and specification of
    standards, 73, 80—2
British Standards
  BS 589: softwoods nomenclature, 21,
    147
  BS 881: hardwoods nomenclature, 21,
    147
  BS 1192: drawing practice, 21, 148
    graphic symbols, 2, 4, 5, 6
    information checklist, 7, 8
    objectives of, 3
  BS 1831: pesticide names, 21, 147–8

Askham Bryan College
of Agriculture and Horticulture
LIBRARY BOOK